LYDIA FRIEND

The Diaries of a Teenage Pilgrim The Early Journey

Book 1

First published by Lydia Friend 2026

Copyright © 2026 by Lydia Friend

All rights reserved. No part of this publication may be reproduced, stored, or transmitted in any form or by any means, electronic, mechanical, photocopying, recording, scanning, or otherwise without written permission from the publisher. It is illegal to copy this book, post it to a website, or distribute it by any other means without permission.

The author asserts the moral right to be identified as the author of this work. This is a work of memoir. It reflects the author's present recollections of experiences over time, drawing primarily from personal journal entries written during her teenage years. Some names and identifying details have been changed to protect the privacy of individuals. While most scenes are based directly on diary entries written at the time, some events have been compressed, reordered, or recreated according to the author's memory to serve the narrative flow. Dialogue has been reconstructed to the best of the author's ability. While every effort has been made to ensure accuracy, memory is subjective, and some details may differ from others' recollections of the same events. The author designed the cover. First published August 2025. This revised and expanded edition includes "On Pilgrimage and the Divine Romance," a new essay exploring the author's journey through the frameworks of Pilgrimage Anthropology and Biblical Theology.

Second edition

ISBN (paperback): 979-8-9930361-4-4
ISBN (hardcover): 979-8-9930361-2-0

This book was professionally typeset on Reedsy.
Find out more at reedsy.com

*To my family circle of love—
Where each relationship is unique,
But the love flows as one stream.
To my friends and readers who joined in my adventure,
May you know the security
Of the Fortress of Hope in this dark age,
May you know the joy
Of Your Beloved singing over you,
And calling you up higher.*

Come, friend, cross the threshold here,
Where diary pages whisper near
Of pilgrimage through passing years.

The Good Shepherd walks beside
And calls His Lovely to abide.
From Wisconsin woods to Galilee's shore,
A young heart holds the golden thread
That weaves the path her soul has led.

Here, the Beloved Bridegroom sings
Over the broken, beautiful things.
Each Stranger Lovely in His sight,
Finding home in Love's delight.
Enter now, the story waits.

Lydia Friend

Contents

Preface	iii
Acknowledgments	iv
Introduction	v
1 Leaving the Little House in the Big Woods	1
2 Journey to the Holy Land	14
3 My First Year Back	23
4 From Thanksgiving to Uncertainty	36
5 Between Jerusalem and the Mountains of the North	47
6 Gates of the North	60
7 Between Fire and Ice	75
8 The True Champion	91
9 Between Thunder and Ice	98
10 Wind	103
11 Flood	110
12 Return & Revival	122
13 When Darkness Births Light	135
14 The Weight of Distance	147
15 Home for the Holidays	151
16 Between Two Worlds	156
17 The Architecture of Displacement	163
18 Spiritual Warfare and Growing Faith	166
19 Wrestling	186
20 Finding My Place in the Rain	205
21 Called Aside	213
22 Stranger Lovely	222
23 The Last Days of School	235

24	Resistance	244
25	The Accident	248
26	The Valley of Shadows	257
27	When Heaven Mobilizes	264
28	The Journey of Recovery	274
29	The Flight Home	283
30	Postscript	294
31	On Pilgrimage and the Divine Romance	296
32	Dear Reader	308
About the Author		309
Also by Lydia Friend		310

Preface

"And they overcame him by the blood of the Lamb and by the word of their testimony, and they did not love their lives to the death." — **Revelation 12:11**

This is a mixture of memoir and diary entries from my teenage years, when the world felt both impossibly large and intimately small. These pages hold fragments of those formative years: thoughts, prayers, and poetry scribbled in the margins of a life lived between cultures. Many names have been changed to preserve privacy, but these are the moments that shaped my understanding of God's faithfulness through ordinary teenage chaos—car accidents and loneliness, international travel, and the daily work of learning to trust Him. I overcome darkness not through perfection, but through honest witness to His faithfulness in our imperfect lives. May my story remind you that God can use ordinary teenagers when they're willing to step outside their comfort zones. Your own story matters more than you know.

In His love,
Lydia Friend

Acknowledgments

Special thanks to Heidi Malikowski for her meticulous editing and editorial vision. Her thoughtful suggestions strengthened the narrative flow, clarified complex passages, and helped me discover the heart of what I was trying to say. Heidi, thank you for your invaluable contribution to this project and for giving me the encouragement I needed to bring it to completion.

I am grateful to I am also deeply grateful to Twila Stone and Kay Moja for their insightful suggestions that helped me polish and refine the manuscript. Your time, expertise, and influence on this project mean more than I can express.

Introduction

"And they overcame him by the blood of the Lamb and by the word of their testimony, and they did not love their lives to the death." — **Revelation 12:11**

This is a mixture of memoir and diary entries from my teenage years, when the world felt both impossibly large and intimately small. These pages hold fragments of those formative years: thoughts, prayers, and poetry scribbled in the margins of a life lived between cultures. Many names have been changed to preserve privacy, but these are the moments that shaped my understanding of God's faithfulness through ordinary teenage chaos—car accidents and loneliness, international travel, and the daily work of learning to trust Him. I overcome darkness not through perfection, but through honest witness to His faithfulness in our imperfect lives. May my story remind you that God can use ordinary teenagers when they're willing to step outside their comfort zones. Your own story matters more than you know.

In His love,
Lydia Friend

1

Leaving the Little House in the Big Woods

◆ ◇ ◆

Spooner

The year was 1994, and our little parsonage sat nestled among the towering pines and maples in the small Wisconsin town of Spooner. In these Wisconsin woods, deer and black bears wandered through, though we weren't always fast enough to see them. I loved the way the morning light filtered through the canopy of leaves, casting dancing shadows on our kitchen table where Mom served breakfast and Dad read his morning devotions.

Our lovely yellow kitchen was filled with sunshine and cabinet space. It was the heart of our home, where the smell of oatmeal, pancakes with Wisconsin maple syrup, and scrambled eggs with Wisconsin cheese would fill the air most mornings. Sometimes Mom would make her Texas-style eggs and rice with onions and spices—a reminder of her childhood.

The wooden floors throughout the house creaked pleasantly as we moved from room to room, from the basement up to the attic, each footstep announcing our presence in this old Victorian parsonage that had become our sanctuary.

The afternoon light would also stream through the beautiful old wooden windows, illuminating the heirloom china cabinet in our dining room, where we'd gather around the table for homeschool lessons and Bible studies, carefully stenciling patterns along the borders of walls we'd painted together.

I was 13 years old, going on 14, wearing cute glasses that were stylish at the time but still made me feel a little like a nerd. Life as a pastor's kid wasn't predictable, especially when your dad was a spirit-filled pastor, but it was home, and we had a rhythm to it, and it was beautiful. Wisconsin winters could drop to thirty below zero, and we were used to those bitterly cold temperatures that made the house creak and settle around us.

I was born in Israel in 1980 while my parents were working at a Christian radio station in South Lebanon, and we had lived just across the border in a little town called Metulla. We'd left Israel when I was almost three years old, and my brother was a baby. The first year we were back in Missouri, Dad completed his master's in teaching at a seminary program. We spent time in Texas County, Missouri, before Dad joined the military and was stationed in San Diego and Monterey, California. Then we moved on to the deserts of Texas, Georgia, and Milwaukee, Wisconsin. But these last four years in Spooner had been the golden years! Dad was finally home, not deployed, serving as our pastor, where I could see him every day. I thought this was the best home we'd ever had.

For several years, I'd heard my parents go on and on about how much they missed Israel, the country of my birth. Israel existed in my life only through their stories, their wistful conversations about places and people I couldn't picture, their occasional Hebrew and Arabic phrases that sounded exotic and foreign in our American home.

The Family Meeting

That particular morning started like any other. Dad had been away on one of his trips, something church-related, I'd assumed; since pastors sometimes traveled for conferences or meetings. He had gone to Israel, and now we were happy to see he had returned. Life resumed its sense of normalcy until a couple of days later, when he called us together.

Mom bustled around the kitchen, humming softly as she prepared his coffee just the way he liked it, strong and black. Tom and I were probably arguing over something trivial, the way siblings do when life feels predictable and safe. At eleven and a half, he was quieter than I, more likely to play with the younger kids at church than analyze every adult conversation the way I did. Where I overthought everything to a fault, Tom just went with the flow—a trait that would serve him differently than what I experienced in the changes to come.

Everything was about to change.

"Family meeting," Dad announced, with that look on his face—the one that meant something big was coming.

We gathered in our living room, with its cream-colored carpet. I settled into my favorite spot on the dark brown sofa, Snowflake snuggled on my lap, her soft white fur against my hands as she purred contentedly. Through the large window, I could see our yard, with its pine and willow trees. The sweet lilac scent, mixed with our orange Easy Love lilies, drifted in through the open window. Dad had souvenirs from his Israel trip spread out on the coffee table—small treasures that hinted at the adventure he was about to describe.

His hair had turned silver from his experiences working at an Arab Christian radio station during the intense conflict in South Lebanon in the years before and after "Operation Peace for Galilee." I was only a toddler then, but those experiences had crowned him with silver while he was still in his twenties.

He started telling us about his trip to Israel with a group of Wisconsin Assembly of God pastors. His voice grew more animated as he described their Joshua and Caleb Mission—going to see what doors might be open for ministry in the Holy Land. Joel Pavia, the Wisconsin Superintendent, had given him the go-ahead: if the Assemblies wouldn't officially send him, he should go anyway.

Dad's face lit up in that way it did when he talked about God opening doors, "I met Chuck Kopp at the Baptist House in Jerusalem. He offered us a visa if we'd come." I could see Mom's face already beginning to glow—she knew what was coming next. Her dark brown hair, almost black and curly to her shoulders, framed her face as she looked up at Dad. She was shorter than both Dad and me, but she was still the one who got things done.

"When I got home, your mom and I spent time in prayer about this opportunity over the next day or two," Dad continued. "We don't have full support raised yet, but we have savings that could last us about a year. I'm setting up a non-profit organization—Living Stones Ministry—so we can start receiving donations. After praying together, we both feel this is God's timing."

Then came the words that hit our quiet Wisconsin life like a thunderbolt: "We're going to Israel. We need to leave in about forty days."

Forty days. I felt the number hit me like a physical blow. I knew Dad had been accepted into a doctoral program in Saint Paul, Minnesota, so this move would mean he must be giving it up for the opportunity. This wasn't a maybe or a someday. This was happening now.

The weight of his words settled over me as I tried to process what this meant—going to Israel. Those words felt strange. How do you go back to a place you don't remember? I was born in Israel, yes, and had spent the first two and a half years of my life there, but that was ancient history to me—I'd left when I was just a toddler. Now, at thirteen and a half, we were going "home" to a place that felt as foreign as any fairy tale.

"Israel?" I managed to say, my voice smaller than I intended.

"The Holy Land," Dad said, his eyes lighting up as he talked about his adventures in Israel and Lebanon, about Scripture coming alive, about returning to the land they both loved. "We're going home."

It didn't feel like going home to me. I loved our little town—the rollerskating rink, the ice skating rink, and biking freely through town in the early '90s. The public library blocks away, the small country church that felt like a part of me, where I'd learned to read by following the lyrics on the overhead projector during congregational singing, and where I'd played tag outside in the frozen snow. I would run around that church with boys and girls, laughing in such good times.

Just the year before, Mom and I had fought to save our community center from being converted into a casino. For months, we'd gone door-to-door alerting neighbors, made anti-casino signs, and stood outside town hall windows protesting. I'll never forget the town hall confrontation, in which the mayor was upset for us spoiling his plans. He had hoped to turn our community center into an Indian reservation, where local law enforcement couldn't enter. We learned about the mafia connections with places like the Turtle Lake Casino, where people were being threatened.

Mom had taken it on herself to lead this grassroots campaign, and the community rallied behind her. Our demonstration even made it onto state TV news, and we successfully prevented it from happening.

Our family wasn't just fighting civic battles. Dad had been waging spiritual warfare, too. He'd put an ad in the local paper offering help to anyone having trouble with ghosts and witches, actually. They called our number for help because they were unable to control the spirits in their home. When Dad prayed for them, they gave their hearts to Jesus, and they were set free.

During his season of fasting and praying for the town, a Halloween snowstorm hit—unusual timing that felt like more than a coincidence. Around that same time, Uncle David, Aunt Sherry, and my cousins Jimmy, Amy, and Katie had moved up from Texas. They stayed with us for a few months until they found their own place. Uncle David would eventually pastor at Round Lake on the Indian reservation. Going door-to-door, speaking up boldly, standing against both corruption and spiritual darkness—it was training in fearlessness. Now, right after these victories that had shaped me, we were leaving it all behind.

I felt their excitement wash over me until I felt it too - this electric possibility of adventure. But then fear crept in alongside the excitement. What about Snowflake? What about everything we'd built here? I looked around at the walls we'd painted together, at the floors that reflected our family's care and attention. Tom sat quietly through all of this, not creating any drama, just accepting what the adults had decided, the way he always did at that age. I, however, had one non-negotiable demand.

"I'll go on one condition," I announced, holding Snowflake, my beautiful white cat. She had been a gift earlier that year, her fur soft against my cheek as she purred, oblivious to the chaos around her. Dad looked up, one eyebrow raised.

"Snowflake comes with us," I said firmly. "If she can't come, I'm not going."

I expected him to argue, to explain about quarantine laws and international travel complications. Instead, he nodded. "Okay," he said simply. "I'll make it happen." And he did. Somehow, in the midst of what followed, Dad managed to arrange for my cat to fly across the ocean—forms, phone calls, veterinary visits, and fees I couldn't even imagine.

The Great Packing

What followed was a whirlwind that I still remember as a blur of cardboard boxes and impossible decisions. We could only take what fit in a small U-Haul trailer attached to our car. Everything else had to go.

Dad's book collection had filled our home. Those books were Dad's pride and joy: theology texts and commentaries from seminary, linguistic studies in several languages from his time with Bible translators, history volumes from around the world, and archaeological studies about the Middle East. They'd made our little parsonage feel like a library, like we were living inside Dad's brilliant mind. I watched as Dad started giving them away, feeling amazed and a little horrified. Lines of people came to take stacks from his rare collection. Dad seemed almost relieved as the shelves emptied, as if each donated volume was one less thing tying us to this place; he was suddenly eager to leave.

Even Grandma Rose, my mother's mother and my only surviving grandparent, came by to help us pack and take a few items we couldn't bring with us. Uncle David and Aunt Sherry came by to help us pack as well. Uncle David had offered to drive with us to Milwaukee and Chicago and help Grandma Rose drive our two cars back to Spooner after we left for the airport. My good friends Mary and Sabrina came to say goodbye and visit me before I left. It was hard to say goodbye to friends.

The days blurred together. Our house, once cozy and full, began to feel hollow as our belongings disappeared. The rooms echoed differently. Even our voices sounded strange in the increasingly empty spaces. Mom carried her sewing machine from room to room, unable to decide where to pack it. That sewing machine had made all my homemade dresses—dresses that made me feel like Laura Ingalls Wilder. We had cousins who were her closest living relatives. Tom got to wear simple t-shirts, jeans, and flannel shirts.

Mom's digital keyboard was also to come. She filled our home with music when she practiced. I loved to accompany her, singing along as she played, both at home and church. Music was one of our favorite ways to spend time together.

Dad's toolbox was to come as a carry-on as well. "A man needs his tools," he muttered, though I suspected he was just as attached to those familiar implements as Mom was to her sewing machine. As for me, I had Snowflake and whatever clothes would fit in my suitcase. Tom's harp somehow made the cut too. I watched them figure out how to transport this delicate instrument across the ocean to our new life.

I would miss our little house in the big woods—the way the light came through the trees in the morning, how deer jumped across the road, and the neighbors who waved when we drove through town. I remember the smell of Mom's meatloaf and mashed potatoes, her fried chicken schnitzel, the taste of corn on the cob from Wisconsin fields, and apple pie. I remember the creaking of our wooden floors as we moved through our daily routines, the one bathroom we all shared, and the warmth of our cheery kitchen, where Mom would hum while cooking. I remember taking pictures with my cousins Amy and Katie before we left, and going on walks together around our neighborhood.

LEAVING THE LITTLE HOUSE IN THE BIG WOODS

One Last Ride

"Want to go for a bike ride?" I asked Tom one afternoon, when we took a break from packing. I needed to see our town one more time before everything changed forever. He looked up from his Legos spread across the living room floor and nodded, going to get his bike.

We pedaled slowly through Spooner, taking the route we'd ridden dozens of times before, but this time every turn felt significant. First, we headed to the hospital parking lot, where I'd learned to skate backwards going down the hill. The sloped pavement didn't look as steep now as it had when I was learning. I could still remember the thrill of finally mastering the challenge of skating backwards down that slope.

"Remember when I could finally do it?" I asked Tom. He smiled and nodded, pedaling steadily beside me in his quiet way. Our route then wound through the forest near the hospital, our favorite place to explore. The pine trees towered above us, and I wondered if Israel would have any forests like this. From there, we rode to the fish hatcheries, where Mom would take us fishing at the lake.

One important stop was the community center—the building Mom and I had fought to save from becoming a casino. I stared at it, remembering the protest signs we'd made; the doors we'd knocked on.

"We helped save this place," I said to Tom.

He looked at the building and then at me, understanding in his own way what it meant to be leaving after such a victory. At the library, I went inside one last time to say goodbye to the librarian who'd helped me find so many books over the years. She hugged me tightly.

Finally, we pedaled to Main Street and the candy store that'd been our destination for so many bike rides. The bells jingled as we pushed open the door, and the familiar smell of chocolate and penny candy filled the air.

"Pick whatever you want," I told Tom, though we both knew our usual routine. He chose a chocolate bar; I picked some gummy bears. We pedaled the few blocks to our home, where we would sit and savor our treats, with the familiar small-town life of Spooner surrounding us. We were hopeful that this moment wouldn't be forgotten, nor the simple joys of brother-sister adventures. Soon, this would all be a memory.

The ride home was quiet, as both of us were lost in our thoughts. The late afternoon sun filtered through the trees. Tom didn't say much, but I knew he felt it too—this sense of ending, of saying goodbye. Back in our driveway, we put our bikes away in the garage, aware this would probably be the last time we'd ride them through these streets together.

The Last Sunday In Spooner

The familiar maroon seats of the Christian Life Assembly Church felt comforting that Sunday morning, like everything was already fading into a memory even as it happened. I smoothed my dress—the good one Mom insisted I wear for our last service—and tried not to think about how this would be the final time I'd be here with my friends and family.

For those cherished hours, I almost forgot we were leaving. Almost. The service itself felt electric in that way small churches do when something special is happening. Dad preached a powerful sermon. I could feel the whole congregation's attention on us, a bittersweet mixture of excitement for our adventure and sadness at our leaving.

It was after the service that I felt the full weight of how differently we were all experiencing this goodbye. The church women surrounded Mom. I watched with growing embarrassment as she practically glowed with excitement. Mrs. Johnson hugged her with tears in her eyes, murmuring about how much they'd miss us. Mom hugged her back, crying too, but her whole face was radiant. Her words tumbled out, her hands gesturing energetically. She described Jerusalem, the Holy Land, as a place where Scripture came alive. She'd wipe away a tear and then bounce a little as she talked about her memories of Israel, about finally going home.

"Oh, I know we'll miss you all so much," she'd say, her voice trembling with emotion, "but I just can't help being excited about—" Then she'd launch into another story about Israel, her eyes shining.

I was embarrassed. Couldn't she see that her excitement was making their sadness feel unimportant? I thought she should just contain her joy until after we left Spooner—then she could be as happy as she wanted. It seemed so simple to me: read the room, match the mood, wait your turn to be joyful.

Now, I understand how impossible it is to schedule emotions. How someone can simultaneously grieve leaving people they love and feel overwhelming joy about returning to a place that calls to their heart. At thirteen, I had no idea that feelings could be that complicated.

I watched people's confused expressions as they lovingly grieved her departure, while Mom was both heartbroken and overjoyed. They had patted her shoulder sympathetically while she beamed about returning to the Land of Milk and Honey. She was too happy to grieve properly with them, and I wanted to disappear into the church carpet.

It was Rachel who made everything real. She appeared at my elbow as we were gathering our things, her blonde hair crowning her face. "I made this for you," she said, her voice barely above a whisper. She thrust a handmade card toward me, decorated with stickers and written in her delicate cursive. I opened it carefully. Inside, Rachel had written: *You are my best friend. You were always nice to me when others weren't. I will never forget you.* My throat tightened. Rachel and her siblings were homeschoolers like me, and we'd done fun things together—played outside in the winter snow; run around the little Spooner Church playing tag.

"Rachel…" I began, "I'm going to miss you so much," and then she hugged me tight.

"We'd like you to join us for a farewell dinner," Mrs. Peterson announced, gesturing toward the fellowship hall. "Please sit at our head table." There we were—Mom, Dad, Tom, and I—being escorted to seats at the front of the room. As the entire congregation filed past to fill their plates, they then sat facing us.

It felt overwhelming. Every bite of casserole felt enormous, and every sip of punch seemed to echo through the room. People kept catching my eye and smiling, waving, and mouthing, "We'll miss you." Tom had wandered off to play with the other kids, as he always did, leaving me to navigate all the intense emotions swirling around us. The reality was hitting me in waves: we leave for the big cities on Friday morning. We leave on the airplane on Monday. Four days. Four days until everything I knew would be an ocean away.

After the potluck dinner, which was filled with numerous delicious home-baked foods, the women of the church, led by Kathy, presented us with parting gifts. The congregation had pooled together to buy me two journals—beautiful ones that smelled like possibility and adventure. Kathy explained that they wanted me to document my journey and to remember this little church in Wisconsin, even when I was walking the streets of Jerusalem.

Then came the quilt. Each family had contributed a square, and somehow they had managed to make it all work together. Each piece told a story, held a memory. "Every family in our church family is represented here," the ladies explained, their voices filled with emotion. Kathy handed me a large card that'd been passed around the congregation. "Dear Michael, Ruth, Lydia, and Tom Friend," she read aloud from the front, "this quilt represents the love and prayers of your church family. We will miss your faithful service here in Spooner and pray God's richest blessings on your ministry in the Holy Land; with love from all of us." The card was covered with signatures and personal messages from everyone in the church.

Walking to the car that night, my arms full of journals and small farewell gifts, I turned back to look at the little brick church one more time. The windows glowed with golden warmth in the darkness, and I could still hear voices and laughter. This was where I spent a lot of time helping Dad clean the church and singing with Mom before and after services. I felt so free here, like it belonged to me. This was what I would most miss: the church and the freedom I felt there, how I'd learned to read by following the songs on the overhead projector, how I would sing on the microphone when no one was there, and how I had started singing solos and helping Mom lead worship.

I was excited to be going on this journey. I was also afraid. Would I see my friends again? Would they forget me? Would I ever come back to my house in the big woods? Most of all, I hoped that someday, somehow, I would find my way back to this feeling—this sense of being completely, unconditionally loved by a community that had watched me grow up. The car doors slammed, and we drove away into the Wisconsin night, carrying our memories and our fears toward whatever waited beyond the ocean.

✦ ◊ ✦

2

Journey to the Holy Land

✦ ◇ ✦

The Last Days

Friday morning came too soon and too slow all at once. I stood in our empty parsonage one final time, the echo of my footsteps strange in rooms that had once been filled with Dad's books and our family's laughter.

This was it—I was leaving Spooner. Our small silver Toyota Starlet was packed with a U-Haul trailer hitched behind it. Snowflake, securely crated inside, was already panting with stress, her green eyes wide as we pulled away. "It's okay, girl," I whispered through the carrier's mesh. "I'm with you." Dad and Uncle David drove in one car while Mom, Grandma, Tom, and I rode in the other.

Seeing Milwaukee again stirred something unexpected in me. This was where we'd lived before Spooner, where some of my earlier childhood memories were rooted. We drove by one of our old apartments, where I remembered playing outside on the lawn with a little stuffed bunny that had been a gift from my Uncle Bill. The toy looked so real that my brother and I would hide behind the bushes and watch drivers go by, who would point at the rabbit, thinking it was real. We'd laugh from behind the bushes at how we'd tricked them—such sweet memories from when I was 8 years old.

"We're going to Pam's," Mom announced, and I could hear the relief in her voice. Pam was Mom's good friend. Dad and Uncle David weren't at Pam and Bob's house yet, so we sat in their warm living room and waited. Since we came in two silver Toyota Starlets, Uncle David would be helping drive the vehicles home after going to the airport. Pam fussed over us, bringing drinks and asking gentle questions about our journey. The room Pam gave me was perfect—quiet and cozy, with everything arranged just so.

Sunday morning, we attended the church where I'd once gone to school. Welcoming faces greeted us with the type of warmth that made leaving even harder. When the pastor asked Dad and Mom to share, I watched from the congregation as they stood at the front and told our story. Their voices were strong, but emotional as they talked about returning to the Holy Land.

That evening, we went to a different church—West Layton Church, a place thick with my personal history. I walked into the sanctuary, scanning faces, looking for my best friend. I didn't see her, but I did see one familiar face: the boy I'd known when I was eight or nine. Seeing him there somehow grounded me in my past. Here was proof that I'd existed in this place and had been part of this community. This was the church where I'd stood before everyone to profess my belief in Jesus and was baptized in water.

One strong memory from the same time period was that of having an argument with my brother, and my dad taking me aside in our living room to pray and repent for my wrongdoing. I cried and cried and repented sincerely. All at once, I started speaking in another language, one that my father recognized as Arabic. I said in Arabic, "Jesus, I want to be in You." I was so overcome with joy at my first few words in tongues that I ran around the house dancing. My mother's friend showed up, and I remember running outside, dancing, and telling her my exciting news. Those were happy memories rooted in Milwaukee.

The people at West Layton Church were incredibly kind. They placed their hands on our shoulders and prayed for us, took up an offering to help with our journey, and made us feel like we were embarking on something sacred. Then they sang—Hebrew songs that somehow bridged where we were going with where we'd been—melodies of hope.

Back at Pam and Bob's that night, I lay in my borrowed bed, trying to sleep but unable to quiet my racing mind. Tomorrow, I'd be in an airplane, flying across an ocean toward a country I was born in but couldn't remember. Tomorrow, everything familiar would disappear below the clouds.

I got up early the next morning. As we drove toward the airport, the sky opened up with the typical Midwest storm. I pressed my face to the glass, watching the rain. Little did I know, as I watched those drops race down the window, that I wouldn't see rain like that for months to come. It seldom rains in Israel in the summer. This storm was Wisconsin's farewell gift, a last taste of warm rain. The adventure was unfolding, but first, I had to say goodbye to the rain.

Crisis at the Gate

The hail hammered our car as we pulled into the Milwaukee airport parking lot. Each frozen pellet struck the windshield like tiny fists trying to keep us from leaving. Through the storm, the terminal building looked both welcoming and ominous—our gateway to everything unknown.

"This is it." Dad's voice was nearly drowned out by the drumming of ice on metal. I felt something electric shoot through my chest—equal parts terror and excitement crackling like lightning. As soon as we stopped, I was out of the car and running, my feet splashing through puddles as I helped grab suitcases and bags.

"Slow down!" Mom called, but I couldn't slow down. I was frantic, checking and rechecking that we had everything. That Snowflake's carrier was secure, and every piece of luggage.

Our footsteps echoed on the polished floor as we made our way to the ticket counter, wheeling our life's possessions behind us in suitcases and carriers. The woman behind the counter looked at our documents, frowned, looked again, then glanced up at us with an expression I'll never forget.

"I'm sorry," she said, "but you can't go to Israel." The words almost knocked me off my feet. *You can't go to Israel.* I felt tears spring to my eyes immediately, my thirteen-year-old world tilting dangerously. *Why couldn't we go? After everything—after giving away Dad's books, after leaving Spooner forever, after saying all those goodbyes—why couldn't we go?*

"It's okay," Mom said quickly, reaching for my hand, but her voice was tight with worry. The ticket agent made phone calls, consulted with supervisors, and shuffled through papers while we waited in agonizing limbo. Then someone mentioned calling the Israeli embassy, and suddenly there was hope again.

While we waited for answers, Dad gathered us together. "We need to pray," he said simply. Right there in the middle of the busy airport, we formed a small circle and bowed our heads. The wait seemed to stretch on forever. Gate announcements echoed around us. Other families moved through the terminal with easy confidence, while we sat in our bubble of uncertainty. Eventually, a man approached Dad with news.

"Well," he said, "you can go. But they might refuse you when you get there."

He paused, letting that sink in. "If that happens, you'll have to catch the next plane back, and you can't sue us for the trouble."

Relief flooded through me so suddenly that I felt dizzy. We could go. Whatever might happen on the other end, at least we could go. The next hour was a whirlwind of activity. Snowflake disappeared into the cargo area, her carrier looking so small as it moved away on the conveyor belt. The electric keyboard followed, along with all our suitcases containing our compressed life.

Then we were hurrying toward the gate, and suddenly we were at that awful moment I'd been dreading: goodbye. Six minutes. That's all they gave us to say goodbye to Grandma and Uncle David, the last family members we'd see for who knew how long.

On the plane, Tom got the window seat. I sat in the middle with Mom on my other side. We carefully placed my brother's harp in the overhead compartment along with our carry-on bags, making sure everything was secure.

Outside, the weather was worsening, not improving. As we lifted off, the plane was immediately caught in the storm's fury. We rocked back and forth violently, climbing and dropping with sickening lurches that made my stomach revolt. The turbulence was unlike anything I'd ever experienced—it felt like the sky itself was trying to shake us back down to earth. I felt sick during the flight from all the stress. Through my misery, I could hear other passengers gasping and praying as the plane continued its wild dance through the storm.

What I didn't know—what none of us knew as we fought through that turbulent takeoff—was that Grandma was fighting her own battle with the storm down below. We would find out later what happened after we had left. Grandma, driving through that same terrible weather of sleet and rain, had to stop quickly at a toll booth. The semi-truck behind her couldn't stop in time on the slick road and smashed right into her car.

Thank God, Dad had given her extra money "in case something happens"—money that was supposed to be for a nice hotel or an emergency meal. Poor Grandma! While we were being tossed around in the sky above, she was dealing with her own crisis on the ground below—both of us experiencing different storms that seemed determined to mark our departure with chaos.

However, there was something else we discovered about this day, something that made all the crisis and confusion feel like part of a larger plan. We were leaving for Israel on Passover—one of the year's biggest Jewish holidays. Mom had prayed that we'd return to Israel at the right time. Our departure coincided with the same day we'd left Israel many years ago. Here we were, flying toward the Holy Land on the very day that commemorated the Israelites' exodus from a foreign land.

Mom had wanted to wait until July to leave, but the tickets would've cost hundreds of dollars more. Instead, we were flying in April, on Passover, after about a month of frantic preparation. We were going home to a place I'd forgotten, on the day that celebrated going home.

Atlanta

As our plane descended toward one of the world's largest airports, the passengers rushed to disembark. "Stay put," Mom said firmly, her hand on my arm. "Let them go first."

I fretted as I felt crucial minutes ticking away. We were already two hours late due to the storm and turbulence we'd experienced back in Wisconsin.

Two hours that we didn't have. When we gathered our things and made it off the plane, the reality of our situation hit us like a wall. We had forty minutes to get to the other side of this massive airport—forty minutes to catch our connecting flight to Paris, which would then take us to Israel. Forty minutes, and we were drowning in baggage. We shuffled and struggled through the Atlanta airport. Our family of four was trying to move as one person but failing miserably.

"We need to ask someone," Dad said, stopping a man in an airline uniform. *Wrong person. Completely wrong person. He sent us in the entirely wrong direction!* By the time we realized our mistake, we'd lost valuable minutes backtracking through the maze of terminals. My thick Wisconsin coat was sticking to my skin in the Atlanta heat, and I could feel sweat running down my back as we hurried along moving walkways and around corners.

Finally, we reached a baggage checkpoint where harried-looking security guards were scanning bags and waving people through. "How much farther to Delta 4?" Mom asked breathlessly.

"About a quarter mile," one of them replied without looking up. *A quarter mile. With all our stuff. In less than thirty minutes now.* That's when I heard it—the voice that made my blood freeze, "Last call for Delta…"

I didn't think. I just acted. I grabbed the harp—Tom's beautiful, delicate harp that had made the cut when everything else was left behind—and swung it onto my back. Behind me, I heard the beeping of security alarms as Dad's toolbox went through the scanner, and I saw his hands go up over his head as guards stopped him for additional screening.

"I'm going ahead!" I called back to Mom, who was already urgently asking the security guards, to call Delta, to ask them to wait; to somehow hold that plane for a desperate family trying to get home. I didn't wait for an answer. I took off running.

The Atlanta airport stretched endlessly before me, a labyrinth of gates and shops and restaurants, all blurring together as I ran. The harp bounced on my back with each step, its weight awkward but not unbearable.

My feet pounded against the polished floor. Gate numbers flashed by: *A12, A14, A16...* I was looking for Delta 4, and it felt like I was running toward the end of the world. I looked back once and saw Dad running behind me, his longer strides starting to catch up. Behind him, I could see Mom and Tom with all our remaining belongings piled into a wheelchair that my brother was pushing as fast as his eleven-year-old arms could manage.

I saw the sign: *Delta 4.* I slowed down, gasping for breath, my heart hammering so hard I could hear it over the airport noise. That's when I heard the gate agents talking, and one word jumped out at me like a lifeline: "Snowflake." They were talking about my cat.

"How is she?" I asked, trying to catch my breath.

"Oh, she's fine," one of them said with a smile. "She's been a good traveler."

Dad arrived just as they were finishing their reassurances about Snowflake, and moments later, Mom and Tom appeared with a wheelchair full of belongings.

We made it. We boarded the plane to Paris with minutes to spare, collapsing into our seats with the exhausted relief of people who'd just narrowly avoided catastrophe. The flight to Paris was long and surreal. When we arrived in Paris and boarded our next airplane, Dad's toolbox, which he had brought as a carry-on, was taken by security. Years later, we still find it amusing how we managed to carry a full box of tools as a carry-on all the way to Paris without any issues. It even had sharp objects. A great deal has changed since 1994.

I spent hours staring over my brother's shoulder out the window, watching the world change below us. We saw the Alps, snow-covered peaks that looked like something from a fairy tale. The Mediterranean Sea sparkled blue-green below us, connecting continents and carrying us toward our destination. I pressed my face to the window in awe when we began circling Tel Aviv. Somewhere down there was the place where I was born. It was the country my parents had been dreaming about for years, the Holy Land that had beckoned to our family across an ocean.

The landing was smooth—a gift after all the turbulence we'd endured. Mom immediately ran to check on Snowflake, who'd survived her international journey in the cargo hold. The cat was stressed but alive, and seeing her again felt like a small miracle.

Getting our passports stamped was surprisingly straightforward. The officials were efficient and friendly, stamping our documents with casual authority. Then came customs. We were traveling with so much luggage, but the official examining Mom's keyboard and sewing machine waved us through without the enormous fee we'd been dreading. That's when I noticed everyone staring—not at us exactly, but at something we were carrying. It took me a moment to realize what had captured their attention: Snowflake. A white cat in a carrier had arrived in the Holy Land on Passover with an American family who looked like they'd been through a storm.

Chuck Kopp stood there in the crowd, waiting for us. More than just the head of the Baptist House, he was a pillar of faith in the Holy Land, a shepherd of shepherds. He was a man who had opened doors for countless families like ours, the one whose invitation had called us across an ocean, now welcoming us home.

3

My First Year Back

✦ ◊ ✦

A House of Many Stories

Moving day fell on Shabbat, when even our new West Jerusalem neighborhood of Gilo observed the sacred silence that blankets all of Israel. We quietly carried our suitcases inside, mindful of the neighborhood's Sabbath peace, then made our way to our first service back together in Jerusalem. We'd arrived in Jerusalem just three days earlier and had been staying with friends my parents knew from the radio days in northern Israel. Yan and Janny were longtime friends of my parents, and they had welcomed us like family. Still, even through the fog of jet lag that made those first days feel dreamlike, there was something unmistakably special about finally having our own space.

A furnished apartment appeared so quickly—absolutely remarkable timing. I stepped onto the balcony and was greeted by huge clay pots overflowing with bright red geraniums. Their strong, sharp scent made me wrinkle my nose even as I admired their vibrant beauty. Beyond them stretched a breathtaking view of West Jerusalem spreading below us—our first taste of what life in Israel might look like.

Getting ready for our first service, I pulled on my favorite dress, the one Mom had made. The soft cotton fabric was adorned with delicate flowers, and it had a green collar trimmed with lace and touches of light pink that perfectly matched the floral pattern. As I smoothed down the skirt, I wondered if this Laura Ingalls-style dress would look out of place in Jerusalem.

My stomach tightened with nerves that went beyond attending a new church. This was about how I'd adapt to living and dressing in this ancient city where everything felt completely foreign. Within the hour, we found ourselves approaching Narkis Street Congregation for our first service. At the service, I met a girl my age with bright eyes and a quick smile, making me think we'd be instant friends. She was the first to befriend me, and for a moment, relief washed over me—that precious sense of connection in this new place.

Walking into Narkis Street Congregation was unlike entering any church I'd ever known. The sanctuary was designed like a tabernacle—a living reminder of the tent where this congregation had worshiped for nine years after extremists burned down their chapel in 1982. Through the open windows, the fragrant scent of roses from the garden outside drifted in, sweetening the air. The architecture itself told a story of resilience and faith. What struck me most was the tapestry of faces around me—a multinational, interdenominational gathering unlike anything I'd experienced in our small Wisconsin congregation.

Here at Narkis Street, my parents had found each other again after losing touch following their first meeting in Dallas, Texas. Mom had heard the Lord tell her, "The man behind you, you're going to marry," when she spotted Dad, who'd been fasting for forty days and wasn't looking his best. They'd become friends but lost contact, only to be reunited here in Jerusalem, where God's providence brought them together again.

A few months later, they married in South Lebanon, with Liz playing the accordion. Others from Narkis Street made the journey to Lebanon for their wedding. Later, when the US government wouldn't accept their wartime Lebanese marriage certificate, they had to redo the paperwork right here at Narkis Street.

Standing in that tabernacle-shaped sanctuary, surrounded by God's people from every nation, the weight of our family's history settled on my shoulders. I couldn't recognize anyone from my early childhood—I'd left too young—but I thanked God for each face I saw. These were the people who'd been part of my parents' story, who'd prayed with them together, who'd witnessed their love unfold in this city, where ancient stones held eternal promises.

Reflection: Living Stones - Finding Your Place in God's House

> *"As you come to him, the living stone, rejected by people but chosen by God and precious to him, you yourselves, as living stones, are being built into a spiritual house to be cohanim set apart for God to offer spiritual sacrifices acceptable to him through Yeshua the Messiah."* — 1 Peter 2:4-5 (CJB)

When I first walked into Narkis Street Congregation, I was struck by the incredible diversity—Jews and Arabs, internationals from every continent, all worshiping together in that tabernacle-shaped sanctuary.

Each person felt like a treasure, I wrote, *a Living Stone in God's house in the Holy Land.* I had found my treasure chest of living stones in the heart of Jerusalem.

Growing up, I had heard Dad tell the story many times of the vision that had shaped our family's calling. In June 1978, my dad, Michael, had completed a 40-day fast and spent the night in prayer at the Western Wall. He found a hostel in the old city where he could spend the night. About 15 people were sleeping on the floor. He had just asked God to take him to Heaven, because he was so exhausted from the fast. He was wide awake when he had a vision.

He was asking God why he was in Jerusalem, having completed what he thought was his duty through the fast. Suddenly, he saw the cherubim, and he was flying all over Israel, picking stones and digging them out of the ground, and carrying them so lovingly to a building—a huge house. And when he put them in the building, they lit up, and they became Living Stones.

My dad assumed that he was still alive, so he continued to pray for the people to become Living Stones. He had felt like Elijah, exhausted from the fight, and was ready to go to heaven. However, God was not prepared for him to go to heaven, and He gave him this dream to give him purpose.

Standing in Narkis Street that day, watching those diverse faces united in worship, I finally understood what Dad had seen in his vision sixteen years earlier. This was the fulfillment—Living Stones from every nation being gathered into God's house, each one lighting up with His presence.

After his vision, Dad moved to the Anglican hostel, where he stayed for three weeks. Then he stayed on the walls of Jerusalem, which were not yet fenced off. He slept below the wall on the ground and would climb up to pray on the walls for 10 weeks. After he finished his Nazarite vow, Dad met an elderly lady, Maud Bennit, who asked him if he wanted to go to a Bible study. He accompanied her to the Bible study at Saint Paul's Church. He visited the Bible bookstore, where he met Joe and Chuck, and soon began working there in September.

During this season, an American came and spoke in Jerusalem, requesting assistance in building a radio station in South Lebanon. Michael volunteered to work at the radio station. He waited a few months for the reply. He proposed to my mother on Mount Hermon on July 8, 1979, before she had to go back to the USA. Their love story is a powerful one that I hope to tell in full someday. Sometime late in the summer, he moved up to the north and started preparing the station in South Lebanon. They began broadcasting on September 9, 1979. My parents were married on November 25, 1979, in South Lebanon.

That vision sustained Dad through every step of this journey—from sleeping on Jerusalem's walls to building a radio station in war-torn Lebanon, from teaching English to broadcasting the Gospel across dangerous borders. He never forgot that God had called him to intercede for the gathering of Living Stones for His eternal house. Exactly one year after the radio station began broadcasting on September 9, 1980, I was born—another Living Stone being shaped for God's purposes.

The beauty of Living Stones is that they're not uniform. Unlike manufactured bricks that must be identical, Living Stones come in different sizes, colors, and textures from every nation and background. What makes them valuable isn't their similarity, but their uniqueness, and how perfectly they fit into the specific place God has prepared for them.

When we feel displaced or struggle to find our place, we can remember that we're not meant to fit everywhere. We're Living Stones, designed for a specific place in God's spiritual house. The very differences that make us feel foreign in some areas are precisely what make us perfect for our divine assignment.

Sometimes, we discover our place among other Living Stones who seem completely different from us on the surface, but share the same foundation: faith in the Living Stone, the Corner Stone that the builders rejected. In His house, there are no foreigners—only family members finding their way home, each one gathered with the same loving care my father saw in his vision.

However, the practical challenges of daily living—starting with learning the language—would prove far more difficult than I'd imagined.

The Ulpan Struggle

Right after we settled into our apartment, Tom and I started Ulpan—intensive Hebrew classes. The building was old and stuffy, chalk dust hung in the stale air, and our classroom always seemed to trap the afternoon heat. Our teacher was a woman with striking red hair and an even more striking personality, though not in a pleasant way. She was hard-headed and harsh, especially to my brother and me.

Days blurred into weeks, each filled with conjugations and vocabulary that seemed to slip through my mind like water. The Hebrew letters still looked foreign, and by afternoon they'd swim on the page like alphabet soup when I tried to focus—a familiar struggle for someone with dyslexia, but made worse by the unfamiliar script.

Although I'd mastered reading in English, spelling continued to be a struggle. Tackling a completely different language and alphabet felt overwhelming. We witnessed disturbing fights at the school and experienced some traumatic situations, so we were ready to try something else.

We had a positive experience when we met an Israeli family of believers who'd recently moved from South Africa. They spoke English and were charming. There were three brothers and a sister named Ruth. When they learned about the car we'd bought—an old vehicle that needed more repairs than we'd anticipated—they immediately offered to help.

"My husband works with computers," Mrs. Ackerman explained, "but our oldest is quite the mechanic." Their kindness felt like a cool breeze after the harsh heat of our Ulpan experience. The Ackermans became fast friends, and we'd often visit them in the small suburb of Jerusalem where they lived. While we were struggling with language lessons, life in our neighborhood continued to unfold.

Billy Joins the Family

In those early weeks, as we were still finding our feet, another tiny ball of fur entered our lives. We found Billy near our Gilo bus stop when he was just a kitten, probably too young to be away from his mother. He was mewing pitifully, and we couldn't leave him there.

"Can we keep him?" Tom asked, already cradling the kitten protectively. Mom and Dad agreed. Billy quickly became part of our routine. His grey Russian Blue coat was soft and plush beneath our fingers, and his tiny purr joined Snowflake's in our new little home. He was the smartest cat we ever had. He could answer the phone and talk on it. He even had a complete conversation with Grandma Rose, who thought it was Dad playing a trick on her. He was full of surprises.

Camp Connections

As the weeks passed, I attended camp at Israel's Baptist Village. The Baptist Village was like an oasis—green flat fields stretched beyond a large swimming pool in the central courtyard. Palm trees swayed overhead, and flowers were planted along the edges of the compound, creating splashes of color. I was assigned to bunk with someone named Rebecca. The first evening, as everyone was chattering about where they went to school, I mentioned, almost apologetically, "I'll be going to the Jerusalem School."

Rebecca's eyes went wide. "You're going to the Jerusalem School?!" When I nodded, she practically shrieked, "My dad is the headmaster!" When she said his name, it sounded familiar.

"Oh," I admitted, "I think I've heard of you all my life."

She mentioned to me that Grandma Rose was her sister's favorite teacher. Grandma Rose hadn't left Israel at the same time my family did when I was two and a half years old. She stayed on in Lebanon until years later, when all Americans were forced to leave. Then, she went to Jerusalem to work at the Jerusalem School. We stayed up talking until the counselor had to tell us to go to sleep. It felt like finding a piece of home in this foreign place. I found someone who knew Grandma Rose and who loved her!

Family Celebrations and New Beginnings

When I returned from camp, our family was preparing for another transition. That summer, we moved from Gilo to a suburb of Jerusalem closer to the school. Since we needed to shorten our distance from the school, we moved to the Jewish neighborhood of Pisgat Zeev, 'The Summit of the Wolf' as translated in English.

It was a very short drive from Beit Hanina, where we'd be studying. Mom had even secured a job there as a kindergarten teacher. The Saturday after camp was Mom's birthday. Tom and I had stayed up late the night before, decorating while she slept. We arranged flowers on the table and scattered little paper hearts around them, each one inscribed with messages such as: *I love you* and *You're the best!*

Mom woke up early, and at 5 AM, she discovered our surprise. Her delighted laughter was worth the exhaustion I felt all the next day. By then, we'd moved into our new apartment, and I started a prayer list of things we needed for the place. Topping that list were: a proper bed (we were still sleeping on mattresses on the floor), a real table and chairs, a couch for the living room, a stove that worked reliably, a washing machine so Mom didn't have to wash everything by hand, a dryer for the rainy season, bookcases for our books that were still in boxes, a microwave, and even just a simple coffee table. The list felt impossibly long.

The Dead Sea

Despite our material needs, we were determined to make the most of our summer in Israel. On July 19, 1994, the Herald family and friends from Haifa came to visit, and we all decided to climb Masada together. Well, "climb" might be generous; we took the cable car up.

The ancient fortress spread out before us, and we spent two hours exploring with electronic audio guides. We'd push a button, and a metallic and tinny voice would tell us about King Herod or the Jewish rebels who made their last stand there. When it was time to descend, Mom, Tom, and Mr. Herald opted for the cable car. The rest of us decided to walk down the Snake Path.

"It'll be an adventure!" Mrs. Herald said brightly. Adventure it was, all right.

The path was steep, so steep that we couldn't help but run. Our legs moved faster and faster, gravity pulling us down the mountain. We made it in nineteen minutes, breathless and laughing! Our legs were shaking like jelly.

At the bottom, we refueled with orange juice and tuna sandwiches before heading to the Dead Sea. The temperature was well over 100°F, and what had felt like dry morning air now blazed like a furnace as we approached midday. The water looked inviting, normal even. But the moment I stepped in, I understood why they called it the Dead Sea. Every tiny cut or scrape on my body burned like fire. In some areas, a strong sulfur odor hung in the air—the unmistakable smell of rotten eggs that made me wrinkle my nose. Then it happened as it inevitably would: someone playfully splashed water, and it got in my eyes.

The pain was excruciating, like nothing I'd ever felt before. I couldn't see or think, and stumbled blindly toward shore. I ran to my towel, desperately wiping at my eyes while tears streamed down my face. At least I wasn't wearing contacts. Mom said she'd gone there once with contacts, and that had been a nightmare. The sand burned my feet, heated to a blistering temperature by the desert sun.

After I recovered, I ventured back in more carefully. This time, I knew to keep my face well away from the water. I discovered the strange joy of floating effortlessly, the salt making it impossible to sink. By the time we cleaned up and changed, we were all desperate for relief from the heat. Mom bought a bag of ice, and we found a restaurant. We sat there for an hour, drinking icy beverages and slowly returning to normal body temperature.

Swimming

Later that summer, Liz Kopp drove us through the Jordan Valley to the Sea of Galilee for a day with the Baptist House youth group at the Luna Gal water park. It was my first time driving up the Jordan Valley since I was a baby. I memorized the sites as we rounded the curves—Bedouin tents, camels, and boys riding donkeys in the dusty, rocky wilderness. I spent an entire day swimming and laughing at the water park on the shores of the

Sea of Galilee, feeling like a normal kid for once.

Later, our adventure continued with a hike in the Golan Heights. We reached a dramatic overlook where jagged rocks jutted out over deep water far below. Everyone on the trip was expected to be a good swimmer, but I wasn't very good. The extra backpack and sneakers made swimming even more difficult for me. We had to jump off the cliff's edge into a pool of mountain water. There was no other way through.

I'd never done anything like that before. My heart hammered as I approached the edge. The distance looked impossible. Realizing there was no other choice, I launched myself into empty air.

The impact was shockingly cold and deeper than I'd expected, but I surfaced, proud of my courage. We swam to a wider, natural pool that felt like our own private paradise.

That's when everything changed. With the heavy backpack still strapped to my shoulders, I found myself struggling in water deeper than I'd realized. The weight pulled me down with irresistible force. My arms flailed uselessly as I fought against waterlogged fabric and gear. Panic set in as I realized how far I'd drifted from the others—too far to call for help, too far for anyone to notice my desperate struggle! The water closed over my head. In that terrifying moment, time stood still. This couldn't be how my Israeli adventure ended, drowning in a beautiful mountain pool while my friends laughed nearby, unaware of my crisis. Then, strong arms suddenly cut through the water toward me. One of the Russian-Israeli guys from our group had somehow sensed my distress. Without hesitation, he swam the considerable distance to reach me, fighting against the same weight that was pulling me under. His powerful strokes brought us both to safety!

At the time, I mumbled my thanks and tried to laugh off the incident, my cheeks burning with embarrassment. Years later, when I re-encountered him at a young people's retreat, the deeper meaning crystallized. Looking at his face, I suddenly understood what I had witnessed underwater. God had sent an angel—not with wings and robes, but in the form of a Russian-Israeli teenager with strong arms and a brave heart. In my moment of greatest need, when death seemed certain, divine love had moved through human hands to pull me from the depths. Later, I was inspired to write:

◆ ◇ ◆

When Angels Swim

◆ ◇ ◆

In the mountain pool so deep and wide,
Where shadows dance and waters hide,
My heavy pack pulled me below
To darkness that I didn't know.

The liquid darkness claimed my breath,
I felt the cold embrace of death,

The backpack dragged me deeper down,
Fear gripped me as I thought I'd drown,
Then came this boy with hair so black
Tall and strong, he pulled me back.

When through the waves came one so bold
My rescuer, with a heart of gold.
From our youth group, strong and true,
He cut the water straight and blue,
His arms like wings through water glide,
To reach me at the drowning side.

With steady stroke and fearless heart,
He pulled me from the depths apart,

And as I gasped the sweet, sweet air,
The sun caught fire in his hair.

I knew then that the heavens see
When souls are drowning, wild and free,
And send their messengers to swim
Through waters dark and waters grim.
So when the angels take their flight,
Sometimes they swim with all their might,
And sometimes wear a human face.
Delivering God's amazing grace.

Reflections

God's most profound rescues often arrive through the most ordinary hands. In that terrifying moment when the mountain pool threatened to claim my life, Heaven's response wasn't a dramatic supernatural display—it was a teenage boy who didn't hesitate to dive in. This is how God works in our lives—not always through miracles we expect, but through people who choose to act. When we're drowning, His rescue arrives through familiar faces—the friend whose call comes precisely when despair feels heaviest, the stranger who stops when we're stranded and helpless, and the family member who appears when our strength fails.

In our darkest moments, when we cry out for help, we can trust that God sees, God cares, and He will send His messengers to reach us, no matter how deep the waters or how dark the night.

4

From Thanksgiving to Uncertainty

◆ ◇ ◆

The American School in Beit Hanina

September brought a fresh challenge: my first day at Jerusalem School. I arrived an hour late in a comedy of errors that seemed ideally suited to our new life. The Arab time was different from the Jewish time, and Mom had gotten thoroughly confused. She thought she was 30 minutes early for her own teaching job, when actually she was 45 minutes late!

Mom, Tom, and I walked into our separate classrooms, shocked that we were late to school and not early. Mom said the kindergarten children were sitting at their desks waiting patiently. Mom felt mortified, but later we laughed about it. When I arrived in my classroom, heat flooded my cheeks as I stood completely exposed. My cheeks were burning for what felt like ten minutes. I realized they all were now aware that I was living on the Jewish side, while they were on the Arab side. I couldn't believe that the time zone was different just a couple of miles away!

I forced myself to focus on the schoolwork and tried to disappear into my desk. The American Jerusalem School was housed in a beautiful Jerusalem stone building that sat several stories high in the center of Beit Hanina. From our fourth-floor classroom windows, we had a perfect view of the large field where boys played soccer during breaks, while the girls watched from the sidelines.

In one of those ironies that seemed to define our Holy Land adventure, Mom ended up teaching at a school run by the very organization that had told us months earlier they had "too many" people serving in Israel already. However, once we arrived and discovered they had a shortage of kindergarten teachers, they were happy to accept her help. Funny how God works—sometimes you have to show up before people realize they need you.

What saved me that first day was seeing a familiar face—Rebecca, the girl I'd met at camp. She wasn't in my class, but in my brother's, as she was younger than me. Over the next couple of weeks, she became my bridge into a friend group that included her friends, Lulu and Haya, as well as other girls.

Our teacher was Miss Susan, a woman with red hair who was everything the Ulpan teachers had not been. Where they had been critical and harsh, she was encouraging and kind. She was humble, funny, and loving. In her classroom, I somehow felt free to be myself. I wasn't afraid to participate or answer questions. Miss Susan never once made me feel inferior—her approach was always positive, and she was always building us up rather than tearing us down.

It took me a couple of weeks to settle in and open up fully. We used the Abeka Christian curriculum, which I was familiar with from my homeschooling experience, providing a comfortable foundation to build upon. The daily rhythm of school became comforting. We started at 8:30 and stayed in our one classroom all day until 3:30, with our main break at noon and two smaller ones throughout the day. During breaks, we'd head downstairs to the kiosk, where rich Arabic coffee mingled with the boys' strong cologne and girls' heavy perfume—scents I found overwhelming but learned to tolerate, though they would bother me more in years to come. The kiosk sold falafel in pitas, Coke and Sprite, and bags of chips.

We'd take our food and gather in the field, the girls watching the boys play soccer, while we ate and talked. I was always the tallest girl in the class, and although I wasn't particularly petite, I appreciated being in an environment where appearances weren't constantly judged. Being different wasn't automatically wrong here. My classmates were kind to me—a mix of Arab students from Jerusalem, including a Turkish diplomat's son named Mustafa, a boy named Samir, and my friend Haya.

One moment that stands out was when Ahmed, a Muslim boy who sat behind me, borrowed a pencil. When our hands accidentally touched during the exchange, he excused himself to wash his hands afterward. This was entirely new for me, and while I understood it was a religious practice, awkwardness hung in the air between us. I was beginning to understand and respect Muslim customs, though I was still learning how to navigate these cultural differences.

The soundtrack of our daily life was punctuated by the call to prayer echoing from mosques throughout Beit Hanina, sometimes so loud it would practically shake us. Whether we were in class, shopping with Mom, or sitting at home, those calls were everywhere. On Fridays, we'd hear longer sermons. During periods of political tension, the mosques would broadcast protests about current events.

Sometimes, when I'd hear the call to prayer while shopping in the local markets or from our apartment, I'd quietly whisper my own prayers to Heaven in Jesus' name. This wasn't a show or demonstration—just a personal, quiet response to hearing others being called to prayer. In those moments, surrounded by a different religious landscape, I found my own way to connect with God.

Every morning, Mom would drive Tom and me to school in our yellow Russian Lada—an antique car that smelled of dust and Jerusalem heat. It was built like a tank with a huge engine that rumbled powerfully—nothing like the flimsy modern cars we'd known. As we wound through the streets of Jerusalem in that car, I'd watch the city wake up around us, still amazed that this was now our life.

The car gave us freedom to explore, though we were always aware of the risks. Just a few weeks after we'd started our school routine, a Hamas suicide bomber killed 22 people on a bus in Tel Aviv. The attack on Dizengoff Street was a stark reminder that even ordinary activities like riding the bus carried dangers we'd never faced in Wisconsin. Mom would grip the steering wheel a little tighter after hearing the news, and we all understood why she preferred driving us places rather than using public transportation.

There was one problem with our new schedule: the school met on Saturdays. I managed to attend some Baptist House youth group meetings after school hours, though I couldn't attend all of them. I loved school—a sense of belonging settled over me. I had friends who accepted me and a teacher who believed in me. The Arabic teacher wasn't there much that year—she had lost her parents and was dealing with grief. At the American School, something had shifted inside me. Maybe it was because everyone was a little bit of an outsider, coming from different countries and backgrounds. Perhaps it was because Miss Susan had a way of making everyone feel valued.

Thanksgiving Reflections

The November chill had settled into our apartment as I sat down to write on Thanksgiving Day, 1994. Outside, life in Israel continued as usual—no turkey decorations in shop windows, no mention of the Pilgrims or pumpkin pie.

However, inside our little apartment, we were determined to mark the day, even if it felt strange to celebrate an American holiday so far from America. School continued as usual. Israel doesn't recognize Thanksgiving as a national holiday, not even at the American Jerusalem School. Still, we were to have our dinner after school anyway. Our apartment had become charming in its own way. We'd arranged our few pieces of furniture to make it feel homier, hung pictures on the walls, and Mom had even sewn new curtains for the windows.

November's Unexpected Blessings

November had brought a parade of visitors that transformed our sparse apartment into something resembling abundance. It started with a lady from Texas whose mother was visiting. They appeared at our door with suitcases full of clothes. Mom's eyes filled with tears as we unpacked beautiful clothes, warm winter items, and even medical supplies. Each item felt like a direct answer to prayers.

Bob and Pam Sier arrived next, somehow managing to bring treasures from our old life: encyclopedias I missed for school projects, my carefully wrapped china dolls, soft blankets, properly fitting clothes, medicine, American food that tasted like home, and enough books and games to make our apartment feel rich beyond measure.

"It's just like Christmas!" I kept exclaiming, feeling blessed. Bob and Pam accompanied Mom to school, where Bob created balloon animals for the kids and Pam told them stories, bringing joy to everyone.

Pastor Dismore and his wife also arrived from Wisconsin, bringing novels

I had longed to read. Each tour group had brought pieces of home, transforming our apartment from empty to a truly homey space.

Book Treasures and Small Victories

Tom and I discovered treasures in the form of a book sale at Baptist House. The musty smell of old books filled the air as we browsed, and I felt that familiar thrill of possibility that comes with choosing new stories to dive into.

"Look!" Tom held up two adventure books, his eyes bright with excitement. I'd found my own selections, but I was excited to discover one of the Mandie books, which was an adventure series I loved. Like Mandie, I also had a white cat, which I had gotten after reading the books. Grandma had sent me the newest edition. It sat on my nightstand like a promise that I hadn't been forgotten.

Christmas Eve in Bethlehem

December 24th arrived with warm weather for winter. We spent Christmas Eve in Bethlehem, walking the same streets where it all began over two thousand years ago. The square buzzed with activity. Vendors sold olive wood nativity scenes, and Christmas lights twinkled against the ancient stone buildings. The air smelled of fresh falafel and sweet pastries. At the Church of the Nativity, the rich scent of incense drifted out whenever the doors opened. Christmas carols in multiple languages created a beautiful cacophony.

We'd been there for about an hour, soaking in the atmosphere, when Tom's face suddenly went pale. "I don't feel good," he mumbled, and then more urgently, "I think I'm going to be sick."

My first reaction was pure frustration. "Tom!" I grumbled. "We're in Bethlehem on Christmas Eve! Can't you just—" Yet when I saw him double over, genuinely ill, my anger melted into concern. We had to leave immediately. My heart sank. The drive home was quiet except for Tom's occasional groans.

It wasn't until the next day that we learned what had happened after we left. The family we'd been with had returned to find their car windows smashed and valuables stolen; their holiday ruined. Mom fell silent when she heard the news. "Tom getting sick might have been a blessing," she said finally. "If we'd stayed…" I thought about being angry with Tom, about the disappointment I'd felt, and guilt twisted in my stomach. Sometimes, what feels like ruined plans might actually be protection we don't even know we need.

Christmas Day Attack

Christmas morning arrived with rays of sun streaming through our windows—so different from the white Christmases in Wisconsin. Tom, fully recovered from his illness, had been awake since 5 AM, radiant with excitement. The morning unfolded in a blur of wrapping paper and Tom's delighted exclamations.

"It's 18 degrees Celsius!" he announced every few minutes, fascinated by his new temperature-telling watch. The sight of him so purely happy, surrounded by torn wrapping paper in the Jerusalem sunshine, felt like a small miracle.

I unwrapped my own treasures—the rollerblades I'd been dreaming about that my parents bought me.

"Look what came from Aunt Sherry!" Mom handed me a package from Wisconsin. Inside was a small gift and a note that simply said, *You are loved*. Those three words, written in my aunt's familiar handwriting, brought tears to my eyes. The distance from everyone we'd left behind felt especially acute during the holidays.

Then, Tom surprised me with his gift—a small handheld shaver and a photo he'd taken of the two of us on Masada, framed with Popsicle sticks he'd painted gold.

"It's perfect," I assured him and meant it. For those precious morning hours, everything felt perfect. We were together, we were safe, and Christmas joy filled our little apartment.

However, the day's peace was shattered early when news broke of another bus bombing in Jerusalem—thirteen people were injured on Christmas Day. The irony wasn't lost on us: celebrating the birth of the Prince of Peace in a land where peace felt so fragile. Still, we were determined to make it memorable for our family.

By afternoon, Jerusalem was warm and golden. Tom and I decided to play outside and skate. We went alone while my parents stayed inside. The rest of the day passed in a blur of wheels on pavement and the strange, but wonderful, experience of sunshine and heat on Christmas Day. We were laughing and skating in the parking lot below our apartment when neighborhood kids suddenly appeared, chasing us and hurling rocks and shouting names at us in Hebrew. The attack came so suddenly that we barely had time to dodge. Confusion and fear replaced our joy as we scrambled for cover. We didn't know what caused them to stone us. Later, we discovered that they had seen us at the Christian celebration earlier in the year and decided to turn their wrath on us on Christmas Day. In their eyes, we weren't just children with skates—we were symbols of the wrong faith. They thought we were the wrong kind of Christians, the kind they'd been taught to fear. This stoning was a trauma to Tom and me that we tried to forget.

Later, as we moved out the following summer, their mother came to my mother and apologized for what had happened, explaining the circumstances. She thought we were moving because of them and was sorry. She didn't want us to leave without receiving an apology and explanation.

New Dreams and New Year's Eve

In the days following, New Year's Eve arrived with an invitation to a party for the believing youth at someone's home. The party was unlike any New Year's celebration I'd known in America. Teens and kids from different countries and cultures were there. We watched *The Three Musketeers*. As midnight approached, party games began. I found myself digging through a bowl, searching for a hidden thimble—a game I'd never heard of but threw myself into with enthusiasm. "Found it!" I shouted, pulling the sticky thimble from the soda. My prize was a small stuffed kangaroo from Australia, which seemed fitting for a party celebrating new beginnings. As the clock neared midnight, someone passed out noisemakers. We counted down in a mixture of languages, and at the stroke of midnight, the room erupted in chaos. Noisemakers blared, guys and girls screamed with joy, and for a moment, it didn't matter where we were from or where we were going. We were all just kids celebrating the promise of a new year. Still, 1995 would bring yet another new beginning for our family.

New Year, New Changes

January 1, 1995. I wrote the date carefully in my journal, still getting used to writing *95* instead of *94*. The kangaroo from the party sat on my desk, a reminder of the fun I'd had.

The biggest news came from Dad that evening. He gathered us in the living room, his face showing excitement and nervousness. "I've been offered a position as a radio station manager in Metulla."

"Where's Metulla?" Tom wondered aloud.

"It's in the far north, right near the Lebanese border. It's beautiful— with mountains, cooler weather, and," he paused, "it has an ice skating rink."

"Ice skating? In Israel?" I couldn't believe it.

"Free ice skating," Dad assured us. "The whole town is different from Jerusalem. Smaller, quieter." His expression grew serious. "I'll need to move there soon to keep the station running. You'll stay here to finish the school year, and I'll come back on the Egged bus when I can. You'll join me in July after school ends."

The room went quiet—seven months without Dad.

"Will we have heat there?" I asked, remembering our cold Jerusalem nights.

Dad chuckled. "Yes, we'll have heat." He reminded us that Metulla was the village where Tom and I had lived when we were small, so it would be like going home.

As Dad's departure grew closer, familiar dread settled in my stomach. It triggered memories I had tried to forget: our San Diego apartment when I was in kindergarten, when Dad was away on military duty. I remembered Mom taking us to the police station in the middle of the night after drug addicts broke into our apartment, stealing everything of value, including Mom's wedding ring and my beloved red wagon. Mom had prayed under her breath while Tom and I slept. All of it happened when Dad was away. Now here we were again—Dad leaving, and us vulnerable in a place where neighborhood kids had already stoned us on Christmas Day. Without Dad's protection, would we be safe? That night, I sat by my window looking out at the Jerusalem skyline, the ancient stones glowing golden under streetlights. The call to prayer drifted across the rooftops, mixing with Hebrew conversations from the courtyard below.

This city had become part of me—in the confidence I had found in Miss Susan's classroom, in friendships forged over falafel and soccer games, in the quiet prayers I had whispered in response to the muezzin's call. Now it felt more fragile, more uncertain. Things were constantly changing before I could get used to them. I thought about the girl who had arrived at the American School that September morning, an hour late and mortified. She seemed like a stranger to me now, but maybe that confidence was more fragile than I had realized. The excitement about Metulla faded into the background. All I could think about was Dad leaving, and whether we'd be safe without him. At least I had something to look forward to when we would all be together again in the "Little Switzerland" village of Israel.

5

Between Jerusalem and the Mountains of the North

◆ ◇ ◆

A House Divided by Distance

Years earlier, before Dad became a believer in the Jesus movement, he had studied Russian at the University of Pennsylvania, believing it would enhance his studies in astronomy. Dad had genuinely loved his work with the Russian speakers. Every Friday night, we'd attend their church meetings together, where I'd watch his animated face as he preached in English, while his messages were translated into Russian. Sometimes he would even step in to correct the translator if something came out wrong.

Dad was leaving for Metulla. I'd known this was coming since New Year's, but somehow I hadn't believed it would happen. The radio station needed him immediately, which meant Mom, Tom, and I would stay behind in our Pisgat Zeev apartment to finish the school year.

Sometime in January, Dad was away, living at the studio in Metulla, where he managed operations, crossed the border into Lebanon, and oversaw both the studio and the transmitter site. Our apartment felt strangely quiet without his morning devotions, without his tall frame filling the kitchen doorway, and without his voice carrying through the rooms.

In the weeks that followed Dad's departure, Mom stepped into managing everything with the kind of quiet strength that I was only beginning to appreciate. She had her kindergarten teaching job at the American School, as well as daily responsibilities to attend to, and all the household chores that had been shared with Dad. We had a car, which gave us much more freedom, especially on weekends when public transportation was unavailable. Mom wasn't going to let Dad's absence paralyze us. "We need to see more of this city," she would say on weekends, and suddenly we could explore places I'd only heard about in Bible stories or history lessons.

The Friday night Russian meetings became less frequent after Dad left. My dad was a gifted teacher and preacher, and I missed his deep messages. I'd grown comfortable playing with the younger Russian children as well. Now Friday nights felt empty, just another evening in our apartment, where we were still careful about making noise on the stairs.

We were living differently since Christmas Day—more cautiously, more quietly. The stoning incident had left us all jumpier than we wanted to admit. Mom would peek through the peephole before opening our apartment door. We'd wait until the hallway was empty before leaving our apartment; timing our coming and going to avoid encounters with the neighbors whose children had thrown rocks at us. It wasn't fear exactly, but rather the kind of hypervigilance that changes how you navigate your own building.

Dad tried to return to Jerusalem on weekends when his schedule allowed. Without a car and with his responsibilities in Metulla, it wasn't always possible. When he did make it back, he'd tell us about his new life learning to run a broadcasting operation—literally living at the studio initially—and getting back into the rhythm of living in the small border town near the Lebanese frontier.

Yellow Chariot to Ancient Worlds

We drove our yellow Lada "chariot" around the city and through the country. One of my favorite discoveries, during those early months in Jerusalem, was the Israel Museum, perched on its hill in Givat Ram like a treasure chest waiting to be opened. I was mesmerized by the Shrine of the Book with its distinctive white dome reflected in the surrounding pool—a building designed to look like the very pottery jars in which the Dead Sea Scrolls had been discovered.

Inside, I stood transfixed before manuscripts older than anything I could imagine, words written by hands that had touched the same stones Jesus walked on. The black basalt wall, situated across from the white dome, told its own story of sons of light and sons of darkness, a visual reminder of the spiritual battles that had raged across this land for millennia.

The museum became an annual pilgrimage for me. A place where I could wander through the reconstructed synagogues in the Jewish Art wing and trace my fingers along the edges of ancient pottery in the Archaeology wing. Each visit revealed new exhibitions, new connections between the ancient and modern worlds I was learning to navigate. I loved discovering how these artifacts made history tangible—not just stories from Sunday school, but real objects touched by real people who'd lived and loved and struggled in this same land centuries before.

The replica of Jerusalem during the Second Temple period fascinated me endlessly, letting me see exactly how the city looked when Jesus walked its streets. Outside, we always stopped to take photos by Robert Indiana's

AHAVA sculpture—the Hebrew word for "love" rendered in bold red letters, a perfect symbol of what this land meant to our family. The Bible Lands Museum also became one of our favorite destinations.

However, it was our visits to the Rockefeller Archaeological Museum that truly captured my imagination. The building itself was magnificent, featuring white limestone with Eastern and Western architectural elements that blended seamlessly. In the courtyard, Tom and I would pose for pictures with the archaeological lion fountain and compare them to our baby pictures we'd taken there so many years ago. Seeing ourselves now—thirteen and eleven—compared to the toddlers and babies we'd been at that same fountain, made me realize how much we'd grown. How this place had always been part of our story, even when we were too young to remember it. The museum still had its original 1930s displays—old-fashioned showcases with handwritten English labels that made everything feel like stepping back in time. The 8th-century wooden panels from Al-Aqsa Mosque, the Crusader marble lintels from the Church of the Holy Sepulchre, and artifacts from Jerusalem, Megiddo, and Ashkelon—each piece told a story of civilizations rising and falling.

Our friend from church was involved in Dead Sea Scrolls research at the museum. Seeing her inspired me, and suddenly archaeology didn't seem like something that only happened in movies or books. It was real, happening right here in Jerusalem, carried out by real people who were excited about uncovering pieces of the past. I started imagining myself as a female Indiana Jones, making dramatic discoveries and solving ancient mysteries.

One warm afternoon, our family drove to Ashkelon, where we swam in the Mediterranean Sea. The water was gentle and welcoming, unlike my previous aquatic experiences. Not as salty as the Dead Sea, and no dangerous mountain pools. Just normal family fun, floating in the waves and feeling warm sand between our toes.

The Russian car sometimes created complications. On a couple of trips to Jericho, locals saw our distinctive yellow Lada and, assuming we were Russians, told us to leave and never to return. Rather than argue with them about our nationality, we simply left. It was another reminder that even our choice of transportation carried political implications in this complex land, where everyone seemed to be categorizing those around them.

Pisgat Zeev

Soon, I discovered I didn't need to visit museums to see archaeology in action—it was happening right outside our apartment. Throughout our neighborhood in Pisgat Ze'ev, active excavations were revealing the ancient past buried beneath our modern suburb.

Every morning, riding to school in the yellow Lada, I'd press my face to the window to check the progress of the archaeological digs. They were uncovering incredible things: Jewish ritual baths from the Second Temple period, featuring steps that allowed large numbers of people to undergo purification simultaneously; age-old wine presses with mosaic-covered stomping floors; the remains of a Byzantine monastery that had operated for centuries on the highest point of our hill.

Day by day, week by week, I could track their careful progress as they revealed structures that had been buried for two millennia. The archaeologists worked methodically, brushing dirt from weathered stones, measuring and photographing each discovery. I'd watch them bent over their work, and think about how patient and precise real archaeology was, so different from the dramatic treasure-hunting of adventure movies. Sometimes on Shabbat, when everything was quiet and the work had stopped, Tom and I would walk over to get a closer look at what they'd uncovered during the week, if the sites weren't sealed off.

Pilgrimage Through the Holy City

Thankfully, the same car that brought us trouble also took us to special places. Beyond the museums and archaeological sites, Jerusalem called to something deeper in my spirit. This wasn't just sightseeing—I was getting to know Scripture and its Hebrew roots, and I knew more clearly what Jesus meant in context. At fourteen, I was beginning to understand that I wasn't just a tourist in Israel: I was a pilgrim.

The Pool of Bethesda, where Jesus had healed the paralytic, became one of our stops. The archaeological site with its twin pools and five porticoes was still being studied and interpreted, and Byzantine and Crusader church ruins were scattered around the area. The Church of the Holy Sepulcher became sacred ground for me. The church was dark and mysterious, filled with the scent of incense and the quiet prayers of pilgrims from around the world. There, in a hidden chamber beneath the traditional site of Calvary, I placed my hand on the split rock, the very stone that had cracked in two at the moment of Jesus' death. The rock was cool under my palm, and I could trace the fissure with my fingers, imagining the earth shaking as darkness covered the land. The guides led us through hidden caves in the back of the church, passages that most visitors never took time to see. Centuries-old Christian symbols were carved into the walls, and the air felt heavy with the weight of centuries of prayer and pilgrimage. They pointed out additional secret locked tunnels that held more mysteries. "There's so much more down there," one guide whispered.

I also visited the Garden Tomb, with its peaceful garden setting and tomb carved into the rock face. It felt more like the place I'd imagined from Sunday school stories—quiet, contemplative, and surrounded by greenery.

The Old City's maze of historic streets drew us in, where vendors sold olive wood nativity scenes and fresh falafel to an endless stream of pilgrims. Walking through the Via Dolorosa led us along the path Jesus had walked, carrying His cross, with each station marked by plaques and prayers. At the Wailing Wall, I watched Orthodox Jews pray with an intensity that with a beat I could feel. They moved their heads and upper bodies up and down for ages in a rhythm as they prayed. Our exploration also took us to the base of the Golden Gate until we were told to leave the area by the Muslims on the Temple Mount.

Our days in Jerusalem were filled with many exciting sights. Walking through Jerusalem's holy sites as a confused teenager, wrestling with faith, I experienced this:

◆ ◇ ◆
Teenage Pilgrim Blues
◆ ◇ ◆

Why am I here in this ancient maze
Where stones remember what I forget?
Walking through two-thousand-year-old days
While my heart's still trying to reset
From Wisconsin woods to Jerusalem stone,
From peace to this stranger falling apart.

Dad's gone north, Mom's holding on,
And I'm just a kid with a questioning heart.
Show me why I'm here, God,
In this ancient, holy place
Where pilgrims weep and vendors shout,
And I'm seeking Your embrace.

Through the sacred and the mundane,
Through my doubt and desperate prayer,

Walking where You walked in pain,
Finding You are everywhere.

I touched the rock that split in two,
Felt the earthquake in my bones,
Crawled through caves that hide Your truth
While I'm drowning in unknowns.
They showed me tunnels going deep—
"More mysteries," they said with a grin—
But I can't find the peace I seek
In this strange place I'm living in.
Maybe I'm just young and scared,
Maybe fourteen feels so small,
But You've promised You'll be there
When Your weary children call.

'Cause in the Via Dolorosa crowds,
In the Wailing Wall's ancient tears,
Something whispers through the doubts:
"I'm walking with you through your fears."
Now I see why I'm here, God,
In this ancient, holy place
Where pilgrims weep and vendors shout,
And I'm finding Your embrace
Through the sacred and the mundane,
Through my doubt and desperate prayer,
Walking where You walked in pain,
Knowing You are everywhere.

Yeah, I'm walking where You walked in pain
And finding You're still walking there
With a teenage pilgrim in the rain
Who's learning how to breathe Your air.

BETWEEN JERUSALEM AND THE MOUNTAINS OF THE NORTH

I couldn't articulate it then. I only knew God was walking with me through experiences I did not fully understand.

Years later, while studying anthropology, I would learn the difference between a tourist, an immigrant, and a pilgrim. A tourist visits places and returns home. An immigrant moves from one home to another. But a pilgrim? A pilgrim is on a sacred journey where the displacement itself becomes holy ground. The sacredness isn't waiting at the end; it's woven through the journey, where adventure and calling meet you along the way.

Traditional pilgrims travel to holy sites such as Jerusalem and Rome. Jesus didn't waste the journey between destinations. He healed people along the way: the Samaritan woman at the well, the demoniac in the Gerasenes, the bleeding woman who touched His cloak in a crowd. The in-between places, the border territories, the roads connecting one town to another - that's where much of His ministry happened.

What if the journey's displacement is what God uses to move you out of your comfort zone and get you to obey Him? What if that displacement is where the glory cloud resides and where the pillar of His presence leads? The displacement pushed me into pilgrimage, not just physical travel, but a spiritual journey to the heart of God Himself.

At fourteen, I only knew this: I belonged fully to none of these places, yet each taught me something essential about God. The displacement wasn't a problem to solve. It was the pilgrimage itself.

The Old City deepened my understanding of pilgrimage, but God was with me everywhere—in our apartment, at school, and even while watching archaeologists work in our neighborhood. The sacred sites simply made His constant presence feel more vivid and connected to history. Even during separation and spiritual searching, God had moments of pure joy waiting for me.

Shalom Jerusalem Concert

March 1995

Spring brought unexpected joy in the form of a concert that would become one of my treasured memories. The Hosanna Concert, *Shalom Jerusalem*, on March 24th turned out to be one of those sparkly nights that you know you'll remember forever. The venue buzzed with excitement, as voices in Hebrew, English, Arabic, and a dozen other languages filled the air. I'd somehow ended up with five local girls that I knew living in Jerusalem. We claimed seats near the middle where we could see everything. The lights dimmed, and the first notes rang out across the auditorium. The music washed over us, powerful and moving, transcending language barriers in a way only music can. "Come on!" Ruth Ackerman grabbed my hand as a particularly energetic song began. "Let's dance!" We made our way to the side aisle, where others were already moving to the rhythm of the music. I felt self-conscious at first, but Ruth's enthusiasm was infectious, and soon I stopped being embarrassed. We spun and clapped, raising our hands in joyous praise.

The Silence

After that night at the concert, something strange happened. My journal went silent. For months—from March 24 until September 8, the day before my fifteenth birthday—I stopped writing entirely.

Perhaps, some experiences are too immediate to capture in words. Maybe the constant stress of Dad being away most of the time made reflection feel dangerous. Combined with the lingering fear from the Christmas stoning incident, I didn't feel safe to write. There was just too much I couldn't put into words.

I couldn't tell my classmates—a mix of Muslims and Arab Christians—at the American School about our planned move to Metulla, a Jewish village in the north. So I kept the secret, participating in end-of-school activities, while knowing I wouldn't be returning in the fall.

My father would come back from Metulla on weekends, but not every weekend. He would tell us about his work at the station, about the small town where he was now living, and about the studio where he was preparing for our arrival. Mom continued teaching her kindergarten class and managing our household alone during the week. Tom and I attended school, did our homework, and went about our daily activities in Jerusalem. Seven months of Dad's absence created feelings I couldn't articulate then. Writing this memoir, I can finally give voice to what that season felt like:

◆ ◇ ◆
Deployment of the Heart
◆ ◇ ◆

Dad enlisted in God's army long before I understood what it meant to be deployed to the front lines of faith. Broadcasting light into Lebanon's darkness while his family held the home front in Jerusalem's ancient streets. Like military wives throughout history, Mom learned to carry everything—teaching kindergarten by day, driving the yellow Lada through archaeological wonders, and keeping us steady when the silence stretched between his weekend leaves. I was a soldier's daughter learning that some wars are fought with radio waves and some battles won with Gospel words transmitted across dangerous borders, while families wait and pray and trust that love spans mountains. The months were

January to July, a deployment of the heart where duty called louder than our need for his presence at the dinner table, in our evening prayers, and in the small moments that make a house a home.

However, God's army families know something civilians don't: that separation is sacrifice, and that distance is devotion, that when you're fighting for eternal victories, temporary loneliness is the price of purpose. Weekend visits became small resurrections—Dad's stories from the station, updates from the front, and plans for our reunion in the northern outpost where our scattered unit would reassemble under one small roof. I stopped writing in my journal because some seasons of waiting and wondering are too classified for teenage words, too sacred for ordinary language. The silence wasn't empty—it was full of growing, learning to be strong while missing him, learning to trust the mission that took him from our daily life. Like army brats who measure childhood in deployments and moves, I learned to call temporary places home, to pack light but love deep, to understand that serving God sometimes means your father crosses borders you can't cross, fights battles you can't see, and carries burdens you can't share.

The truck was loaded with our Jerusalem year—canopy beds and Syrian tapestries, museum pamphlets and holy memories, washing machines and answered prayers, and everything we'd gathered. Finally, the orders came through: "Pack up, move north, join the deployment, the family reunites." Soon we'd be together in that tiny house he'd prepared for us. A forward operating base where love could reassemble, where pilgrims could rest between missions, where a soldier's family could be whole again in the mountains of the north. This is what I learned in the silence: God's army marches even when families divide. Every deployment ends in homecoming for those who serve with faithful hearts and trust the Commander who orders their steps from Jerusalem stones to northern mountains where reunion waits, like morning breaking over the gates of promise.

The mountains of the north were waiting. I had learned to expect the impossible from this land, where archaeology was not a dream but part of everyday life, where teenage pilgrims discovered that God walks with them through every kind of wilderness.

6

Gates of the North

✦ ◊ ✦

Preparing for Reunion

As spring turned to early summer, my father's coworker at the broadcasting facility helped him find a tiny two-bedroom house to rent after school had ended. He moved out of the studio and into this little place, preparing for our reunion.

In late June, school finally came to an end. Another academic year completed, another transition, another period of adaptation behind us. Looking back on those months of transition in Jerusalem, God shaped my heart through hardship and wonder combined. As a teenage pilgrim, I had touched the split rock beneath Calvary and explored hidden caves. I had learned what it meant to live with fear, creeping up the apartment stairs. I had discovered the particular loneliness of keeping secrets from classmates who wouldn't understand where our journey headed next. Still through it all—the months when Dad was away, the weeks when Mom managed everything alone in Jerusalem, and the silent spaces—God had been faithful.

The girl about to climb into that truck for Metulla wasn't the same scared kid who'd arrived in Jerusalem months earlier. She was braver now, ready for whatever adventure came next in this crazy, wonderful land. She was headed to the village where she spent her first years.

The man from the Mount of Olives who helped us move came with his truck. We loaded everything we'd accumulated during our year in Jerusalem. There was the canopy bed Dad had made for himself and Mom. Mom had sewn tapestries she had gotten from the Old City, which originated from Aleppo, Syria, into the bedspread and curtains, making them true works of art. We also loaded proper beds for Tom and me, the bookshelves Dad had built while we lived there, and all the appliances we'd purchased in Pisgat Zeev: washer, dryer, refrigerator, and dining room table. Everything that had been on our prayer list that cold November day when we'd had so little was checked off. It all fit into one truckload!

The truck that carried our belongings wound north through landscapes that took my breath away. This wasn't Jerusalem's ancient stones or even the Judean wilderness I'd grown accustomed to; this was biblical territory in its full glory. Cedar trees dotted the mountainsides, their branches reaching toward heaven like the ones Solomon had used for the Temple. In the distance, I could see the snowy peaks of Mount Hermon, the heights that the psalmist had sung about.

"Look," Dad said, pointing ahead as we rounded another bend. "There it is—Metulla."

I pressed my face to the window, drinking in my first glimpse of what would be our new home. The town seemed to nestle into the mountainside like it had grown there naturally, serene and peaceful. This was a *moshav*; essentially a farming community where families owned their own land but shared certain activities. The houses still featured typical Israeli architecture, with ceramic floors, cement walls, and Jerusalem stone tiles, but here they were accented with wooden beams and chalet-style elements that were not typically seen in Jerusalem. These alpine touches, combined with the fact that you could actually ice skate here (one of the only places in Israel where that was possible at the time), gave the place its nickname of "Little Switzerland." What struck me most was how Metulla sat between two hills, as if we were approaching the gates of the north, a threshold between worlds.

The hillsides themselves were mostly bare, and the cottages that would later dot them hadn't been built yet. Beyond it, mountains stretched toward Lebanon, creating a dramatic backdrop. Below the town, I could see the green of what I'd later learn was the Nahal Ayun Nature Reserve, with its seasonal waterfalls and streams flowing down toward the Jordan Valley.

"From Metulla to Eilat," Dad said with a grin, quoting the famous Israeli saying. "We're going as far north as you can go in this country."

We stood at the very edge of Israel, looking toward a country that was technically still at war with us. The weight of that geography settled over me as we drove into town. We were moving to the frontier, to a place where the complexities of Middle Eastern politics weren't abstract newspaper stories, but daily realities.

When we finally arrived at the house my father had prepared for us, the first thing I noticed was how small it was compared to our apartment in Jerusalem. However, he was there, grinning widely, ready to show us around his workplace. After months of separation, we were finally together again. Dad drove us around the town and showed us the two little cottages we had lived in when I was just a baby and toddler. I was beginning to see how this was our story, and this village was a deep part of me.

The changing of the guard was already underway when we arrived. The previous American manager's family had already departed, though he remained for a time to help with the transition. There was one other

American Christian family in Metulla as well, but they, too, were preparing to leave. Something about this exodus felt eerie and forboding—all these Americans heading for the exits just as we were walking in the door.

If they couldn't make it here, how will we? What went wrong that we don't know about yet? We were back after all these years, willing to risk everything to broadcast the Gospel into Lebanon. Still, I couldn't shake the unsettling feeling that we were stepping into something others had found impossible to handle.

Metulla

Near the Community Center, there was also the radio studio on the Israeli side of the border where Dad would work daily. But our new home on the northern side of town was a little old bungalow, its cement siding covered with moss and peeling paint that revealed faded yellow underneath. The space was so cramped that Tom and I had to share a room, with him sometimes sleeping on the couch when we needed space.

That summer, when Grandma Rose came to visit, the space became even more challenging. Grandma and I shared the room with me while Tom slept on the couch.

There was something extraordinary about being here—we only had to walk down the block to see that we were right on the border of Lebanon. Nearby was the famous Good Fence crossing at Fatima Gate, where for years Lebanese workers had crossed daily to work in Israeli fields and orchards, and where Lebanese civilians had come for medical care during the civil war. The crossing had become a symbol of the humanitarian relationship between the two countries, though it would be closed when Israel withdrew from Lebanon in 2000. More importantly, Dad was here every evening, instead of just on weekends. However, he'd leave for Lebanon at 5 AM if he were working there that day. We were together again, even if "together" meant more cramped.

If the house felt small, the sounds reminded us daily of our surroundings. Metulla was quiet most of the time, but the border was never far away. Helicopters would thunder overhead, and sometimes we'd hear the rumble of tanks moving along the frontier. The war in Lebanon wasn't just news here. It was the backdrop of daily life, the reason Dad crossed that border every morning to broadcast into a country torn apart by conflict.

As we began to settle in our new home, I was fortunate to meet Eron, the daughter of the other American Christian family who was preparing to leave. She was much younger than I, about seven years younger, but she had the easy confidence of someone who had spent years navigating this unique border town.

"Want me to show you around?" she offered, and I eagerly accepted. This was exactly what I needed—a little local guide who could help me understand my new world.

Our walking tour of Metulla was a revelation. The main street featured the town's *makolet* (a small local grocery store) along with several hotels and restaurants that felt both Middle Eastern and European at the same time. There was also a community center where local events, such as Passover celebrations, were held. Eron pointed out the synagogue, explaining the rhythms of the small Jewish community that called this frontier town home. Yet it was when we reached the Canada Center that I stood amazed.

"There are swimming pools and ice skating rinks!" Eron announced proudly. "There's also a gym and a shooting range."

After a year in Jerusalem, where recreation meant walking through archaeological sites or swimming occasionally in the Mediterranean, the Canada Center felt like a secret kingdom we were discovering. As my birthday approached in September, all I could think about was getting my own pair of ice skates, though we'd soon discover they were nearly impossible to find for sale in Israel.

Finding Our Rhythm

The neighbors mostly kept to themselves, and we did the same. In the border town, everyone had their own reasons for being there and their own ways of coping with the constant low-level tension. Privacy seemed to be an unspoken courtesy everyone extended to everyone else.

For our practical needs—banking, shopping, and fellowship—we'd make regular trips to nearby Kiryat Shmona, just a short drive south. Several times a week, we'd wind down from our mountain perch to this larger town where we could find everything Metulla's small main street couldn't provide. More importantly, it was where we connected with other believers, finding the community and support that would become essential during our years on the frontier. Dad would even lead a small Russian-English house church that became another thread connecting our new life to the work God had given him.

We also started Hebrew *ulpan* classes in Kiryat Shmona, though it wasn't the best experience. The classes were overcrowded, with nowhere to sit, and one day the Russians blocked us from having seats, so we ended up leaving the *ulpan* entirely. It wasn't hostility so much as survival. The room was overcrowded, and in the jostle for chairs, we were the outsiders.

Yet I did make one important friend there, Denis, a speed skater from Ukraine who had been a champion in his home country before immigrating.

His slender figure made him look like a bullet on the ice! He and his older brother were incredibly fast. I had no idea then that Denis and I would eventually skate together; yet meeting him planted another seed of possibility for my growing love of the ice.

There were encouraging signs as well. Mom reconnected with a friend from her earlier days in Metulla, who lived nearby. We met her and her children at the park during those first weeks. Her son, Sam, and daughter, Sarah, were friendly enough. I didn't know then how significant Sam would become in my life. We'd eventually end up on the same hockey team when I pursued my growing passion for skating.

Soon, I would learn about the Hill of the Doves, where Dad managed the transmitter site in a buffer zone that was technically part of Lebanon but accessible only to the Israeli military and authorized people like our family. Dad would take us there to show us around, and I'd often accompany him on his weekly trips so he wouldn't have to go alone. It was here I began to understand what it meant to live with constant tension, having access to this restricted place where most civilians could never go.

The ice rinks that had seemed like fairy tales from Dad's stories began calling with increasing urgency. By September, I could no longer ignore the pull.

Ice Dreams

As I approached my fifteenth birthday, something had shifted inside me. The silence that had gripped my journal for so many months was finally breaking as I began to write. I wrote about hoping to attend an upcoming convention in Jerusalem, about the ice skates I desperately wanted, and about slowly finding my place.

Then October arrived with a possibility I hadn't dared imagine: tryouts for the ice hockey team. Standing at the rink's edge, watching the boys practice, I felt something fierce awaken. This wasn't just about skating anymore—it was about fighting for my place. I was nervous but determined; one of only two girls attempting to join what was clearly a boys' sport. To my amazement, I was accepted onto the team, despite still skating on rental skates and having yet to learn a proper hockey stop. (I was still using the toe pick like a figure skater.)

To steady my nerves, I even scribbled a chant in my journal that was half pep talk, half battle cry:

> *Step on the ice, this is gonna be a fight.*
> *You're gonna have a long, hard night.*
> *Get up, we haven't started, we're just getting right.*
>
> *SKATE TO THE LEFT! SKATE TO THE RIGHT!*
> *You'd better make sure your skates are laced up good and tight.*
>
> *Oh, it's hockey time, we're gonna feel the burn,*
> *You're gonna crash and learn.*
> *It's hockey time, no turning back.*
>
> *SKATE FORWARD! SKATE BACKWARD!*
> *You gotta move like lightning, it's hockey time.*
>
> *Don't run home, you gotta skate like a wildcat*
> *Or like a bat in attack,*
> *But you'd better make sure you got that helmet tight.*
> *You gotta skate like you mean it!*
>
> *Oh, it's hockey time, time to go fast,*
> *You'd better not be last.*

Hockey time again, you'd better move with power
Or you'll be counting every hour.

Practice makes perfect if you want the respect.
SKATE FORWARD! SKATE BACKWARD!
You gotta skate like thunder.
SKATE FORWARD! SKATE BACKWARD!
You'd better make sure your skates are laced up good and tight!

This wasn't just about learning to skate; it was about proving I belonged on that ice, about fighting for my place in a world that didn't expect girls to play hockey. Every line pulsed with the Rocky-style intensity I felt, knowing I had to work twice as hard to earn respect on a team of boys.

Yet even as I found my footing on the ice and began learning to fight for respect, my dreams were growing darker. The same sensitivity that helped me anticipate plays on the rink was picking up undercurrents I couldn't yet name. Something was coming.

November Darkness

November 4th arrived like any other evening. Our family squeezed together in the small living room of our bungalow, the television flickering with images from Tel Aviv. Prime Minister Rabin stood before a massive crowd at the peace rally, speaking in support of the Oslo Accords. The camera panned across thousands of faces, young and old, all gathered in Kings of Israel Square.

I watched the sea of people, feeling something I couldn't name building in my chest. Then it hit me—not like a thought, but more like a physical blow. A knowing so deep and certain it shook me to my core. The words ripped from my throat before I could stop them. "They are going to kill him!"

My family turned to stare at me, their faces a mixture of concern and irritation. "Don't be so dramatic," someone said. "He's surrounded by security."

"Why would you say something like that?" Mom asked, her voice gentle but worried.

I couldn't explain the crushing weight in my spirit, the absolute certainty that had seized me while watching those crowds. It wasn't a thought—it was knowledge, heavy and inevitable, pressing against my ribs. "I just know," I whispered.

Exhaustion hit me like a wave. The weight of carrying something I couldn't explain left me suddenly too tired to argue or even watch anymore. I mumbled goodnight and escaped to my shared room, pulling the covers over my head, hoping desperately that sleep would prove me wrong.

I woke the next morning to devastating news on two fronts. Billy, our beloved cat who could talk on the phone and had such a personality, had been killed by poison set out by the city council to eliminate street cats. His big appetite had been his downfall. He'd eaten the poisoned food meant for strays. I was heartbroken, as I cradled his still form and remembered all the joy he'd brought to our family.

Then came the news that shook me to my core: Prime Minister Rabin had been assassinated at 9:30 the night before, shot by a Jewish extremist as he left the very rally we'd been watching. My words echoed in my mind with a weight I wasn't prepared to carry at fifteen. *I had known. Somehow, impossibly, I had known!*

Looking back, I can see that the dual loss of Billy and Rabin on the same dark night drove home the reality that living at the gates of the north meant dwelling in an enchanting, yet dangerous place where beauty and danger walked hand in hand. This was the frontier, where the complexities of a broken world pressed in from every direction.

As November's darkness settled over Metulla, I was carrying something heavy, something that set me apart in ways I couldn't explain to anyone. I had always been a dreamer, but these warnings scared me. I was unprepared for the weight of intercession and prayer that I felt I should have done. False guilt rose within me that I hadn't done enough to prevent what I'd somehow seen coming, a feeling that would become familiar whenever I had these dreams. Sometimes I'd try to intercede and pray that it wouldn't happen, and occasionally the outcome would be different from what I'd seen. However, this time with Rabin, I had simply gone to bed tired and unsettled.

The next morning brought a sobering realization. My parents hadn't taken my prediction seriously the night before, but in the morning, they remembered my words and acknowledged that I had been right. They saw it as foreknowledge. At breakfast, we'd share our dreams like other families shared the weather. It felt normal to us, but I was beginning to realize how strange it would sound to other kids my age. Tom did not have these experiences at the time, so he had a harder time understanding me. What I was only beginning to understand was that there were no other born-again teenagers in our section of the north that I knew of.

◆ ◇ ◆

Gates of the North

◆ ◇ ◆

I was fourteen when the truck climbed north
Toward gates I couldn't name,
Carrying our boxes and our calling

GATES OF THE NORTH

To a place between two hills
Where the Promised Land kissed Lebanon
And ice rinks gleamed impossible
Under the Middle Eastern sun.

Cedar trees reached heavenward
Like Solomon's temple beams,
Mount Hermon crowned in white
While we wound through valleys
Ancient beyond memory,
Sacred ground beneath our wheels.

At the northern edge, we arrived
Where the Good Fence once opened
For Lebanese workers crossing daily
To tend Israeli orchards,
Where hope and history mingled
At the threshold of two worlds.

I didn't know that I was arriving
Not just at geography's border
But at the threshold of myself
Caught between seen and unseen,
Between innocence and burden,
Between the girl who dreamed
And the one who would see too much.

The hills held us like cupped palms,
Metulla, Little Switzerland in the Holy Land,
Where chalet beams accented
Ancient Jerusalem stone
And the Good Fence bore witness
To humanity's hunger

For connection across divisions.

I was learning what it meant
To dwell in the in-between
Between Israel and Lebanon,
Between innocence and knowing,
Between the girl I'd been
And The Stranger Lovely
Awakening within these mountain walls.

Here, where two nations touched
And waterfalls sang toward Ayun's springs,
I would discover that some callings
Plant you precisely at the edge,
In the beautiful, dangerous spaces
Where earth meets heaven
And celestial belonging transcends all borders.

In the aftermath of that dark November night, I began to understand that our move to Metulla hadn't been about geography alone. God had positioned us at a threshold where the seen and unseen worlds touched, where a fifteen-year-old girl would learn to carry both dreams and prophecies. Metulla wasn't just our new home; it was the place where I would learn what it meant to live with one foot in heaven and one on earth.

> *From Metulla to Eilat, we had reached the very edge of modern Israel, but I was beginning to understand that we were also standing in the heart of biblical Israel that God had promised Joshua: "I am giving you everyplace you will step on with the sole of your foot All the land from the desert and the L'vanon to the great river, the Euphrates River will be your territory."* **—Joshua 1:3-4, CJB**

GATES OF THE NORTH

Metulla might be at the frontier today, but in the time of David and Solomon, Lebanon and these very mountains had been under their kingdom's power. We weren't just living on the edge—we were living in the center of God's ancient promise.

As 1995 drew toward its close, I was learning that life at the gates of the north carried both wonder and sorrow, prophecy and loss. The ice rinks that had seemed like dreams were real, but so was the darkness that could snuff out both a beloved pet and a nation's leader in a single night. I was discovering gifts I was still learning to understand, the ability to see what others couldn't. I couldn't have articulated it then, but the *Stranger Lovely* was awakening within me, though I didn't yet have words for what that meant. I only knew that in this enchanting, yet dangerous place between two hills, where cedar trees reached toward heaven and ice rinks gleamed under the Middle Eastern sun, I was learning to live with spiritual sight and a heart that felt everything too deeply.

The gates of the north had opened to receive us, but they could not protect us from the universal sorrow of a world broken by sin. Here, at the edge of the modern-day Promised Land, I was beginning my education in being a stranger in every earthly home while belonging fully to a Kingdom that transcends all borders.

Dwelling as Strangers in the Promised Land

"By faith Abraham obeyed when he was called to go out to the place which he would receive as an inheritance. And he went out, not knowing where he was going. By faith he dwelt in the land of promise as in a foreign country, dwelling in tents with Isaac and Jacob, the heirs

with him of the same promise; for he waited for the city which has foundations, whose builder and maker is God." — **Hebrews 11:8-10 (NKJV)**

Here was the father of our faith, the one to whom God had promised this very land, yet he too lived as a stranger within it. Like Abraham, we can find ourselves feeling foreign even in places God has called us to inhabit. The Land of Promise doesn't always feel promising when you're navigating cultural barriers or learning to belong in unfamiliar communities. Abraham's example reminds us that displacement isn't a sign we're in the wrong place—it's often evidence we're living by faith rather than by sight. Abraham waited for "the city which has foundations, whose builder and maker is God."

When we feel like strangers in the very places God has led us, we're walking in the footsteps of the faithful. Our temporary residences become altars of trust, reminders that we belong to a Kingdom that transcends all earthly borders.

7

Between Fire and Ice

✦ ◊ ✦

The New House

We were upgraded. We moved just a block away, but we had more room! Three bedrooms! After months of cramped quarters, Tom and I each got our own space.

This felt like a real home at last. The house had a tiled roof and a welcoming porch, surrounded by a beautiful green yard. From our yard, we could see the Hill of the Doves in the distance, a daily reminder of Dad's important work at the transmitter site. I finally had my own room again, with two lemon trees right outside my windows that were always heavy with fruit.

Yet it was the ice that transformed my world. Somehow, I'd made the hockey team. Not just made it, I was actually playing, actually part of something. The Canada Center had become my world, a place where acceptance was earned through sweat and determination. Yet like all societies, it had its own unspoken rules, its champions and outcasts.

The week before the holidays in December brought an opportunity I could never have imagined. Seventy of the world's best figure skaters came to Metulla for an exhibition, and our hockey team had been chosen to participate in the opening ceremonies.

"You'll carry an Israeli flag too, Lydia," our coach explained. "The whole team will skate out together, everyone with a flag."

The night of the performance, the arena was packed with more people than I'd ever seen in Metulla. Music pumped through the speakers, and lights swept across the ice in patterns. When our team was announced, we skated out onto the ice. The cold air hit my face, and suddenly everything felt perfect. I raised my Israeli flag high, skating with my team as we all carried our flags, and the crowd roared. For those few minutes, I was part of something bigger, representing a country that was becoming mine with each step I took and each day I skated.

Tom told me later that I looked like I was trying to touch the sky with that flag. "You were the best one out there, Lydia," he said, and even though he was my little brother and probably biased, I treasured those words.

After our moment in the spotlight, we made way for the figure skaters, petite girls in sparkly dresses who spun like tops, and older skaters who jumped and landed as if gravity were optional. I collected autographs, my hands shaking with excitement as Olympic medalists smiled and signed my program.

The Dark Side of Dreams

Triumph has a way of making you forget that, in border towns, shadows are never far away. As winter deepened, I would learn that every dream has its dark side, and hockey was no exception. The triumph of the flag ceremony couldn't erase the daily struggles that came with being the outsider trying to prove herself worthy of belonging.

My rental skates, before the blessed hockey skates arrived, had been instruments of torture. They were cheap, ill-fitting things that left bubbles and blisters from the rubbing. One particular spot on my leg, just above the ankle, refused to heal. My passion for skating was so intense that not even this pain could stop me from skating. I kept going despite the blisters. "Just put bandages on it," I told myself each day, wrapping the wound and hoping it would finally close.

Then came the day that changed everything about my understanding of champions and allies. We were scrimmaging, and I'd made a mistake—passed to the wrong player, lost the puck in a way that made our team look foolish. The usual comments started flying in Hebrew, sharp and cutting. However, this time, someone stepped forward. "Enough," Sam said, his voice carrying across the ice with quiet authority. He skated over to where I stood, shoulders hunched with shame. "She's learning. We all made mistakes when we started." The criticism stopped. Not because of what he said, but because of who he was—one of the best players on the team, respected, liked. When Sam spoke, people listened. "Don't let them get to you, Lydia," he said quietly, just to me. "You're tougher than they think."

In that moment, Sam became my champion. He was simply a good friend and teammate. My heart was set on finding someone who shared my faith, so I never thought of Sam as a boyfriend. Instead, he became something equally valuable—the person who stood between me and the worst of the cruelty, who translated when coaches spoke too fast, who helped me understand not just the game but the unspoken rules of belonging.

I had needed a defender like that more than I realized. The spiritual loneliness I'd felt since moving to this frontier had only increased through the winter months. Hockey became my refuge from that isolation and the growing signs of war in our area. The cold air numbed the constant ache of being between worlds. On the ice, we were not on the edge of a battlefield on the northern border—we were in another kingdom altogether, and I got lost in it.

The physical exhaustion felt good and helped me find a release. I loved to skate freely, even when I wasn't playing hockey, and would skate for hours, backward and forward, and in circles. Sometimes I would bring my Walkman and have modern worship playing; other times, I would skate with '90s music playing on the loudspeakers, which seemed to be on repeat every day.

Sam may not have understood my spiritual struggles or what it meant to live as a follower of Messiah in this place. Yet somehow, he reached out to me anyway, maybe because he recognized something in my fierce determination. Whatever the reason, he began looking out for me in ways that felt like answered prayer.

Winter Training

As the weeks passed, the ice became my world that winter. Sam was genuinely helpful and kind, always willing to slow down when the rapid-fire Hebrew on the ice left me confused and struggling to keep up.

"The judge is calling a timeout," he'd explain patiently, giving me the Hebrew translation to memorize, or, "That's what the goalie position is called." All the hockey terminology that the other boys took for granted was still foreign to me, especially since it was in a second language.

One afternoon, he had an idea. "What if we made a tape?" he suggested, his eyes lighting up with excitement. "You could listen to it at home and memorize all the terms. I could help you record it."

The radio studio was just across the street from the Canada Center, and Sam was eager to see where Dad worked. We went over to the studio, and Dad let us record the key terms I needed to memorize in Hebrew while we had cookies and juice. Sam was clearly having fun. I was grateful to have someone to guide me through this. This kindness meant everything to me.

Through the winter months, our friendship deepened. When the second hockey performance came, skating before 1,500 Canadians, we glided out together as a team, carrying our flags. When I got real CCM hockey skates to replace my rental torture devices, Sam was the first to notice how much better I was skating.

I was still the only believing teenager I knew in our section of the north. On the ice, with Sam's encouragement, I began to believe I might actually belong somewhere. That sense of belonging was about to be tested in ways I could never have imagined.

Kibbutz Dafna

January 1996

The new year brought a major change in my education—one that would shatter the comfortable world I had begun to trust. When we started attending the private school at Kibbutz Dafna in January, I'd made two girlfriends within the first few weeks.

However, it was Sam whose friendship would become more complicated. On the hockey team, he'd been one of the guys who'd defended me when the coaches were tough and helped me when things got lost in translation. At school, our friendship felt different. He'd sit with me on the bus, sharing his snacks. However, the moment we stepped off the bus, distance would creep between us.

Noa, one of the friends I'd made at school, was a figure skater who was very different from me. We often argued and viewed things differently, but we both shared a love of skating that united us. Noa would confide in me about things. We always had something to talk about with the drama at the skating rink and in our classes.

The Education That Changed Everything

I had settled into comfortable routines at this small school, where my foreign origins made me an object of considerable fascination. I felt like some kind of *Stranger Lovely*, and people seemed to gravitate to me. The local students were curious about me, eager to hear about distant lands and practice English with someone who spoke it natively. I was starting to feel like I belonged, which made what happened next even more devastating.

It was with considerable shock that I found myself summoned, along with fellow students, to receive Mrs. Rothschild's instruction. This lady's professional qualifications in psychological matters had convinced the administration of her fitness to address topics that, in my previous educational experience, had been considered the province of parents and clergy.

There exist certain subjects which, however necessary they may be deemed by progressive educators, are calculated to produce the most uncomfortable effects upon any classroom's moral atmosphere.

The particulars need not be detailed in their entirety, save to observe that her approach displayed a frankness that would have scandalized even the most worldly community leaders. Her manner of presentation, delivered with the clinical detachment of one discussing agricultural procedures, treated as commonplace those intimacies which I had been taught to regard as sacred mysteries reserved for marriage.

"It is perfectly natural," declared Mrs. Rothschild matter-of-factly, "for young persons of your age to begin exploring these physical expressions of affection. Indeed, statistics indicate that the majority commence such activities by their fifteenth year."

My stomach clenched as I watched familiar faces transform before my eyes. The effect upon my assembled classmates was immediate and pronounced. Several received this news with cringe-worthy excitement, while the boys present seemed to suddenly regard their female companions through an entirely altered lens. I found myself wishing most fervently for the power of invisibility, perceiving in glances directed toward my person a speculation that had been absent in previous interactions, and hoped to escape before anyone might attempt conversation upon subjects so recently aired. Yet I could not avoid observing the animated discussions that immediately commenced among my peers, nor the disturbing alteration in their general deportment.

"I intend to find someone suitable for experimentation," announced one girl with boldness that would have made her grandmother faint. "Perhaps Tal from the senior class would prove agreeable to such an arrangement." The words hung in the air like smoke from a fire that would consume everything in its path. Where I came from, we talked about waiting, about these matters being sacred. At my previous school, when I passed a young man a pencil, he would wash his hands afterward because, as a Muslim, he couldn't touch a girl's hands. Here, the instructor was practically encouraging experimentation among fifteen-year-olds.

It was in the aftermath of this educational catastrophe that I first observed a troubling change in Sam's behavior toward me. The friend who had once stood up for me was about to become my greatest threat.

The False Champion Reveals Himself

After that disturbing class, Sam began making inappropriate suggestions on our bus ride home that left me horrified. I was completely unprepared for this transformation. His conversation had shifted from sports and academics to topics that made me deeply uncomfortable. The particulars need not be detailed here, but his frankness would have appalled anyone. He treated sacred matters I'd been taught to revere as casual jokes.

When I responded with horrified silence, Sam interpreted my reaction as bashfulness requiring encouragement rather than genuine revulsion. "Come now," he would say, "surely you're not as innocent as you pretend. All the girls here are thinking about it—the teacher made that quite clear."

I went home and confided in my mom about what was happening. She was so disturbed that she talked to a preacher in Tiberias during the week. That Shabbat, during our congregational meeting, he preached a message about inappropriate education in schools, not mentioning names. His entire sermon focused on what I had experienced, becoming another argument in favor of homeschooling. Even though he didn't name me, I felt deeply embarrassed and ashamed. It felt as if I had done something wrong just by being there. This false shame carried me into the next season.

Desert Trials

Despite the growing tension with Sam, life continued with its demands.

In February, our school organized a trip to the Negev Desert. We walked 70 kilometers over several days through the harsh desert landscape. The physical challenge was intense, and by the time we returned, I had lost 5 kilos. However, I made it through, and the experience gave me a sense of accomplishment and a growing appreciation for the desert and its stark beauty and resilience. I remember seeing sands of brilliant colors that some use as artwork. I'd never seen that before. The desert flowers were already blooming in the spring, and it was gorgeous.

When I got back, there was another performance at the Canada Center with 1,500 people in attendance. We had numerous photos taken of us, and the visiting Canadian team generously donated a substantial amount of equipment to our hockey program. I received an autographed hockey shirt, puck, and autographs from the Canadian players.

During this time, Dad began teaching me to operate the soundboard at the radio studio. We also had visitors from Holland come to see the station, and we showed them around the area. Still, even as life continued with its normal rhythms, the tension with Sam was building toward something I couldn't yet name.

Separation Anxiety

It was during this increasingly uncomfortable period that Mom announced her departure for the United States. She was going to see family in Missouri, Wisconsin, and Texas. "It's only for the month of March," she kept saying as we drove to the airport in the dark. "I'll bring back lots of things, and you will have fun with Dad and Tom."

I knew what she was not saying—she was homesick too for her family in the USA, and considering our aunts and uncles were ill, she had to see them.

I depended on my mom, and she had never gone away for a month before. Usually, it was Dad who went on trips. At the airport, I hugged her so tightly that she laughed. I felt vulnerable with her gone. However, we were accustomed to this kind of lifestyle, and we would make it work. Then she was gone, disappearing through security, and we were down to three.

The Lies I Didn't Comprehend

With Mom gone and tension rising in the region, stress was mounting. Sam's inappropriate jokes continued, but I still thought that they, as teenage antics, would eventually pass. I had no idea what was really happening behind my back. I thought he just had a crush on me and was being annoying about it. The meaningful glances between teammates, the occasional suppressed laughter—I noticed these things, but never connected them to Sam's behavior.

Living Under Threat

The personal drama was soon overshadowed by external danger. Mom had barely landed in America when the world exploded. On March 30th, two Lebanese civilians were killed by an Israeli missile while working on a water tower in Yater, a village less than two kilometers from the border. Hezbollah responded by launching 20 rockets into northern Israel.

The talk of giving back the Golan Heights sent ice through my veins. From our house in Metulla, we could see those heights. If they gave them back, we'd be sitting ducks. The Syrians would be able to see everything, target everything.

Then came the Katyusha rockets. The sound—a whistling shriek followed by an explosion that rattled windows—became sickeningly familiar. We'd huddle in our bomb shelter, Tom and I trying to act brave.

One night, a rocket hit just 50 meters from the radio station and 100 meters from our radio transmitter. Still, external dangers, terrifying as they were, couldn't prepare me for the betrayal that was about to combust my world from within.

✦ ◇ ✦

The Day I Learned the Truth

The rockets weren't the only explosions coming my way. Sometime in mid-March, the day began with no warning of what was to come. I arrived at the rink as usual, completely unaware that my reputation had been under attack for some time.

It was a boy on our hockey team, maybe fourteen, who first gave voice to the lies that Sam had been spreading. I was lacing up my skates, focused on the routine of preparing for practice, when he started making accusations about what Sam and I had supposedly done together. The words landed with the force of a slap. This was my first public attack on my character, and my Hebrew was not strong enough to mount an articulate response. I could only stare at him, stunned, my mind reeling as I tried to process what he was saying.

"Everyone knows what you and Sam have been doing, Lydia," he declared with the confidence of someone who believed he had the entire team behind him. "There's no point in pretending innocence when half the team has heard the details."

The casual way he spoke lies, the pleasure he seemed to take in my shock—it was like watching someone set fire to your house while smiling. I looked around the rink, suddenly seeing my teammates through new eyes. *Do they believe him? How long had this been circulating behind my back?*

I stood stunned by the sheer audacity of these accusations, my mind struggling to comprehend how lies I'd never even heard before could have gained such widespread acceptance. The injustice struck me like a physical blow—accused of things that had never happened, that existed nowhere but in Sam's malicious imagination. Sam and I had never even held hands or kissed. The only time we'd spent outside the rink or school was that single afternoon in the studio with my dad.

The Battle Erupts

We were gathered at the edge of the ice, bent over our half-laced skates, the clatter of blades and chatter of teammates filling the air. I was the only girl in that circle, intent on lacing my boots, when the first accusation was flung with the force of a slap. Their laughter sharpened into deliberate taunts, and before long, the jeers turned to coarse curses. Hemmed in, with the rink on one side and the bleachers at my back, their words came at me like darts. I felt the peculiar terror of isolation—that of a single girl facing a company of boys united in mockery.

I tried to answer with the meekness my upbringing had instilled in me. "It's not true. It's a lie," I managed in Hebrew, my voice trembling with the effort of restraining the storm of emotion that threatened to overwhelm my composure. This young disciple of malice, intoxicated by the power that Sam's lies had placed in his hands, proved unwilling to be deterred by such simple denial. Indeed, my attempt at defense seemed only to inflame his appetite for the sport of public humiliation.

"Don't play the innocent with us, Lydia," he sneered with the confidence of one supported by popular opinion. "Sam has told us everything about your eager participation in the activities that the teacher recommended for our consideration."

It was at this moment that something within my spiritual constitution underwent a transformation as sudden as it was complete. All the accumulated frustrations of my young pilgrimage—the countless instances of exclusion, the systematic undermining of my character by one I had trusted as a friend, the injustice of being condemned for things that had never happened—crystallized into a single, overwhelming impulse toward direct action.

The first blow was delivered by my own hand, though I could scarcely believe myself capable, as my fist connected with the surprised face of my tormentor. All the careful instruction in peacemaker forbearance seemed to evaporate in the face of this ultimate provocation, replaced by an instinct for self-defense that appeared to spring from some deeper source than my conscious will.

This young agent of slander responded with equal force, punching me in the eye and launching into the kind of all-out fight that would have shocked anyone watching. What followed was no ordinary disagreement; it was a raw battle between his lies and my desperate need to defend the truth, fought with an intensity that showed just how much damage Sam's campaign had done.

During this struggle, which drew the horrified attention of all who witnessed it, I found myself fighting not merely against a single antagonist, but against the entire web of lies. When other players threatened to join the assault against me, I discovered within myself reserves of righteous fury that I had not known I possessed. *Let them try*, I thought with a boldness that surprised even myself. Several other players ganged up on me, and I was fighting several boys at once. Each blow I struck carried months of accumulated frustration and injustice, while each blow I received confirmed what I was beginning to understand: I was completely on my own in this fight.

Sam, author of my torment, stood by in elegant idleness, watching the conflict his lies had begun. He did not defend me as a friend he had once claimed to be, nor did he attempt to correct the falsehoods that had set the fight in motion. Only when the venom of their derision turned upon him did he rouse himself—not for me, but for his own honor. And then the fight swelled into chaos, pulling everyone in.

The coaches came to break it up, with Avi leading them. The worst part came after—when the adrenaline faded.

Divine Intervention

In the aftermath of the fight, I ran to the ladies' bathroom and locked myself in, sliding down the wall as tears came. When my hockey coach knocked and told me, "Hurry up, Lydia," I couldn't move. Then came a gentler presence from the other side of the wall.

It was Avi, an older American-Israeli player I looked up to. He was fully integrated, bilingual, and accepted in ways I aspired to be. For the rest of the evening, he kept checking on me, being kind in a way that gave me the strength to endure the hockey practice that still had to happen. He told me he didn't believe the lies and that what they did was wrong.

His presence felt like Divine Providence, whose character had outgrown the crude entertainments of his younger companions. In that moment of crisis, God had placed a champion of authentic virtue right where I needed one to be.

Yet even as I felt grateful for Avi's kindness, I was still reeling from what had just happened. The immediate shock and hurt were overwhelming, and all I could do was try to pull myself together enough to get through the rest of practice.

In the Quiet of My Room

That night, lying in my bed with the windows open and the sweet smell of the two lemon trees drifting into my room, something more profound began to crystallize in my heart.

This wasn't merely about hockey or teenage drama—***this was the moment I began to understand who I really was.*** Sam hadn't just been attacking my reputation; he had been trying to drag me into his worldly fortress. When I wouldn't cooperate, when I refused to compromise my standards, he lied and claimed I had anyway—perhaps to boast, perhaps to save face. I'll never know what he thought he could accomplish.

I realized I would never truly belong to that kind of fortress, never be one of them, because I was called to walk in holiness as a follower of Messiah. It was my very refusal of Sam's suggestions—my stubborn fidelity to truth—that marked me as different and set apart.

In that moment of deepest humiliation, ***I began to understand that I was meant to be a stranger in this world,*** lovely only to the One who called me His own. I belonged to a different Kingdom entirely, and no amount of earthly acceptance would ever be worth abandoning that sacred calling.

THE DIARIES OF A TEENAGE PILGRIM THE EARLY JOURNEY

8

The True Champion

◆◇◆

Wrestling with the Aftermath

In the days that followed, I couldn't stop replaying the fight. Had I done the right thing? They had ganged up on me—the boys surrounded me as their verbal attacks grew more vicious with each moment. When I couldn't take anymore and threw the first punch, it triggered a swarm—suddenly I was fighting several of them at once. I had finally refused to accept lies as truth and humiliation as deserved.

I also remember trying to bleach my hair blonde. I doused it with hydrogen peroxide, left it in, and then lay in the sun for several hours, following a method that was foolishly recommended. I took all the pain I had experienced and set out to be someone different. Like Anne of Green Gables, my hair-dyeing attempt didn't turn out right. Somehow, instead of blonde, it turned streaks of orange, but not the lovely red Anne had. I remember going to the rink and Sam laughing at me.

I wasn't sure if I had done the right thing that day, fighting back, but as the only girl left on the team, I had spoken in a language only hockey players could understand. God, it seemed, had used this breaking point to draw me closer to Him. I desperately needed to remember that I wasn't alone in this battle.

Souled Out

My hair still had several different hues, but I went to the youth conference with Tom in the last week of March, just after everything had transpired. I remember not wanting to participate. Still, it felt like exactly what I needed: a chance to be around other teenagers who were believers, people who might understand the spiritual battles I was facing.

I was struggling with the overwhelming sense of not belonging that came with depression. I was even having a hard time at the conference getting out of the spiral and doing the trust exercises that I felt were silly. However, the preaching was the best part for me, and the worship, which was like manna from heaven in the desert of my soul. Experiencing these conferences for the community of believers of this land was so encouraging to our faith, as many of us were living on the edge and in need of fellowship.

I met twins who seemed nice, and also a Jewish believer with the last name of Klein, which was similar to my Grandma's maiden name, Cline. My friend Ruth was there, but we didn't have much time to catch up, which was disappointing.

The conference was encouraging, though. I heard that Michael W. Smith was coming to Israel, and I really wanted to go to that concert. Eventually, I did get to go to his concert in Jerusalem at the YMCA, though I can't remember exactly when it was. Being around other believers reminded me that I wasn't completely alone. However, returning to Metulla meant facing the practical consequences of everything that had happened.

Decisions

When the dust settled, my parents made the difficult decision to pull me from hockey. They could see the toxic environment and chose to protect me, even though it meant giving up something I loved. They said I could finish the year, which would be a couple more months. Since I would not be able to play hockey next season, they asked me if I might want to join the speed skating team instead.

I was sad but grateful—sad to lose my identity as a hockey player and some of the adventures that came with it. Yet I was grateful that I could still skate, even if it meant trying something completely new.

By the time Mom returned on April 4th, something had shifted in me. Maybe it was surviving the rockets, the fight, and the accumulation of small victories and defeats. I felt tougher somehow.

When Champions Become Enemies: Finding God in Betrayal

> *"If an enemy were insulting me, I could endure it; if a foe were rising against me, I could hide. But it is you, a man like myself, my companion, my close friend, with whom I once enjoyed sweet fellowship at the house of God, as we walked about among the worshipers."* — **Psalm 55:12-14 (NIV)**

> *"Cast your cares on the Lord and he will sustain you; he will never let the righteous be shaken."* — **Psalm 55:22 (NIV)**

David knew the particular anguish of betrayal by a trusted friend. Ahithophel had been his close counselor, someone who walked with him in fellowship, who shared his bread and his burdens. When Ahithophel joined

Absalom's rebellion against David, it wasn't just political treachery—it was personal devastation.

"If an enemy were insulting me, I could endure it," David wrote. We can prepare for enemy attacks, armor ourselves against and even expect them. However, when the assault comes from someone we trusted, someone who knew our vulnerabilities because we had shared them in confidence, the wound cuts deeper than any sword.

This is the betrayal that steals sleep, that makes us question our judgment, that tempts us to build walls so high that no one can hurt us again. The Psalmist David felt it, and I felt it that winter in Metulla. You may have felt it too—the shock of discovering that someone you trusted was working against you behind your back.

However, David's psalm doesn't end in despair. In the midst of his anguish, he makes a choice that changes everything: *"Cast your cares on the Lord and he will sustain you; he will never let the righteous be shaken."*

The Hebrew word for *"cast"* here means to hurl, to throw with force. David isn't suggesting a gentle laying down of burdens—he's advocating for the spiritual equivalent of hurling your pain at God's feet with all the force your betrayed heart can muster. God can handle our fury, our confusion, our desperate need for justice.

What David and I discovered is that earthly champions will fail us, but our Heavenly Champion never will. Human defenders may turn into accusers, but Jesus remains *"the same yesterday and today and forever"* (**Hebrews 13:8**). The betrayal that feels like it will destroy us often becomes the very thing that drives us deeper into the arms of the only Champion who will never fail.

David learned to trust God as his defender rather than relying on human champions. His betrayal by Ahithophel taught him that the approval of men is fleeting, but *"the Lord watches over the way of the righteous"* (**Psalm 1:6**).

Forgiveness and Moving Forward

A few days later, an unexpected opportunity for closure presented itself. On April 8th, just a few days after Mom's return, Sam asked me to lend him my hockey stick. I realized it wasn't really about the equipment; he wanted to see me again, to somehow bridge what had happened between us.

Giving Sam my hockey stick after everything that happened was my way of saying I forgave him. I was still shaken that he had started the lies about me, and kept my distance. Eventually, I regained my pride and learned to walk down the village streets without the false shame I'd been carrying. I'd forgiven him, but we didn't have much to do with each other anymore.

I thought I found a champion.
In the bathroom stall I crumbled,
Tears and rage and broken trust,
All my hope in human champions
Crumbling into bitter dust.
But then Heaven sent a whisper,
Not in anger but in peace,
Yeshua's voice within the darkness
Promised pain would find release.

I could build walls around my heart,

Never trust or hope again,
Or I could seek a Champion
Who transcends the world of men.

There's a Champion who won't fail me,
Who won't spread lies in my name,
Who defends me in the shadows,
And who bears away my shame.

He's the One who knows my story,
Every wound and every scar,
Who fights battles I can't see
And who loves me as I am.

When earthly champions betray us,
When our trust lies shattered here,
We can run to Heaven's Champion
Who will never disappear.

He's my Advocate eternal,
My Defender and my Friend,
The Champion who won't abandon,
On whom I can depend.

So I'll skate into His presence
When the world becomes too cold,
Finding warmth in His protection,
Finding truth that won't grow old.

Thank You, Jesus, my true Champion,
For the love that never fails,
For the victory You've given
Over lies and their travails.

In Your fortress, I am safe,
In Your love, I am secure,
You're the Champion I was seeking,
And Your faithfulness endures.

The Deeper Truth

At the time, I didn't realize how deeply this experience impacted me, so I chose to blank it out of my mind. It remained in my subconscious, and a year later, back in the Missouri Ozarks, it surfaced in a poem called "Stranger Lovely." I was looking through my journals many years later and cried when reading about this. I had blocked it all out and forgotten how hurt I had been.

This betrayal deeply wounded me, but also helped me to stand for the truth. I had been ashamed of fighting back, but recently I saw it through different eyes. I saw it through the eyes of writers like John Bunyan and Jane Austen—who also wrestled with truth, integrity, and rejection.

We are from another fortress, not one of worldly achievements, but one of Hope. God wants us to return to that Fortress of Hope and know that we belong to Him. Let's not place our hope in false champions who want their own glory as they pursue worldly achievements. We need to know that they may exclude us for not playing their games. All the rejections are worth it if we can keep running after the King of the Kingdom. Those who belong to no earthly fortress might be especially equipped to serve a Kingdom that transcends all human boundaries—an eternal Fortress of Hope.

9

Between Thunder and Ice

War

April 1996

"We are at war!" I wrote in my journal. The urgent and jagged words marched across the page. Israeli forces had launched a military operation against Hezbollah, conducting airstrikes on Beirut, and ordering the evacuation of forty villages in South Lebanon.

The reality of life on the frontier had never felt more immediate than during those seventeen days of Operation Grapes of Wrath. What had been a theoretical danger—the knowledge that we lived between two countries technically at war—became visceral, immediate, and inescapable.

Many children in northern Israel are fleeing to southern cities, I continued writing, trying to process what was happening around us. We weren't among those fleeing, but I understood why families were choosing to evacuate. For us, the idea of leaving was never even discussed. The radio ministry had to continue - the Gospel broadcasts into Lebanon were too important to abandon, no matter how dangerous it became. The sound of helicopters had grown constant, a mechanical thunder that never quite faded from the background of our days.

The night that crystallized everything for me was when nature and war seemed to conspire against us. *Last night, we experienced a severe thunderstorm, accompanied by lightning, Katyusha rockets, and helicopters. It was scary!*

I remember lying on my narrow bed, the soft cotton blanket filled with cotton stuffing pulled up to my chin, listening to the layers of sound: the crack of thunder mixing with the whistle-shriek of incoming rockets, the rumble of helicopters overhead, and the rain pounding against our windows. It was apocalyptic, as if the very sky was at war with itself. In those moments, the boundary between nature and violence completely dissolved.

A rocket hit near our radio station in Lebanon! Dad's work suddenly seemed more dangerous than ever. Every morning when he left for the transmitter site or to travel to the radio station in Marjaayoun, I wondered if he'd come back. The Gospel broadcasts were also making us visible to those who saw any foreign presence as enemy activity. *Still, we are strong with God's love*, I wrote. I wrote lines that revealed how deeply the isolation was affecting me:

> *Do you hear me calling? Do you hear me calling?*
> *Do you hear me crying? Do you see if I am crying?*

The repetition, the desperate rhythm of it, showed how much I needed to be heard, to be seen, to have someone acknowledge what we were going through.

After the Ceasefire

May 1996

Three weeks later, the short war was over. *I am back in school and working hard to avoid falling behind.* The return to normalcy felt surreal. How do you go back to algebra and Hebrew grammar after weeks of rocket attacks and constant helicopters? School felt like playing house, going through the motions of normal teenage life while carrying the weight of experiences most teenagers would never have.

Life in the borderlands taught us to compartmentalize, to function normally in the spaces between emergencies. The ceasefire held, and gradually, the helicopters became less frequent. The tension in Dad's shoulders eased slightly.

Our electrician from Lebanon was nearly killed when he was shocked by the high voltage from the radio towers. *He should have died, but God saved him! I was in the next room at the Hill of the Doves when it happened!* The Hill of the Doves, where Dad managed the transmitter site in the security zone between Israel and Lebanon, had always been dangerous territory. This incident brought home just how many people were risking their lives for the sake of the radio ministry. The electrician was Lebanese, working to maintain the equipment that broadcast the Gospel into his own war-torn country. *This had happened to him twice, and he survived both times. God loves him dearly. It is dangerous to work with these high voltages! He risks his life for the Gospel!*

Our calling involved more than just our family. A whole network of people believed the message was worth the risk. The electrician returned to work after nearly dying twice. His dedication humbled me. While I was struggling with teenage social dynamics, grown men were risking electrocution to keep the Gospel broadcasts running.

Comfort and Joy

June 19

The arrival of summer brought unexpected blessings. *In June, Tom got a puppy from the believers who are now living in Metulla. My brother loved the puppy.* The arrival of new believers in Metulla was a blessing. After feeling so spiritually isolated, having other followers of the Way living nearby was a gift I hadn't expected. The puppy they gave my brother became a source of joy in our small household, and I could see how much he needed something innocent and playful after the intensity of the past months. Watching Tom with his puppy reminded me that we were each processing the stress of life in the north in different ways. While I was wrestling with spiritual burdens and social betrayals, he was just a kid who needed to play, laugh, and love something uncomplicated.

The End of Hockey

July 1996

By midsummer, my athletic journey reached a turning point. Even after all that drama, I continued to play hockey through the spring and into early summer. That final game against Tel Aviv represented the end of an era—I was the only girl among fifty hockey players, still fighting for my place in a world that had shown me how quickly acceptance could twist into betrayal. With that final game, a chapter of my life closed, leaving me to face an uncertain future.

Summer

August 1996

With hockey behind me, what was left of the summer stretched ahead empty and uncertain. August had arrived with its relentless heat. *That summer had not been the best summer of my life.* After the toxic environment at the school and the complications that had followed, my parents chose to homeschool me. However, it also meant schooling at home, having even less connection with other teenagers, and more time alone with my thoughts and struggles.

We are hoping to move into a bigger house soon, one that can accommodate both the Israeli radio studio and our home, eliminating the need to rent two houses. Finding adequate housing, managing expenses, and creating space for both family life and ministry work—these logistics shaped our daily reality as much as rockets and political tensions.

I am longing for another youth conference or something. It's been a lonely summer. This final line captured the heart of my struggle. I wanted friends who shared my beliefs, and a sense of community and understanding that only comes from other teenagers who share my faith.

The summer of 1996 felt like a season of endings—the end of my hockey dreams, the end of my childhood illusions about friendship and belonging, and the end of feeling safe in the world. I didn't yet understand that sometimes things have to end completely before something better can begin.

10

Wind

✦ ◇ ✦

Sweet Sixteen

September 1996

Your attention, please! This is a sixteen-year-old writing! I wrote those words with a flourish in my journal, feeling the weight and wonder of finally being sixteen. The declaration seemed important. I was claiming my voice, my perspective, my right to be heard, instead of being just some kid getting dragged along. My sixteenth birthday brought new glasses with magnetic sunglasses that attached to them, a practical gift for the bright Israeli sun.

The Woman on the Road

Then came the night that reminded me who my mother really was. Mom found a woman beaten and bloodied on the roadside—she had been pushed from a car by a man who didn't want to be seen with her. She was a prostitute, broken far deeper than her physical injuries.

"She's sleeping in your room tonight," Mom told me matter-of-factually.

"I've called our Dutch friend to examine her, then we'll help her get to Teen Challenge."

I watched this stranger settle into my bedroom—long black hair hanging limp, movements slow and zombie-like from drugs. She was bloodied, traumatized, and desperate. My emotions tangled with pride, fear, and frustration. After the Sam situation, I was hypersensitive about what people thought of me. Having a prostitute in my bedroom felt like handing ammunition to anyone wanting to judge our family. Watching Mom pray with her changed something. Her voice was tender, offering hope to someone society had thrown away. I felt proud to have a mother who actually lived the Gospel.

The woman stayed for a while until Mom drove her to Teen Challenge in Haifa for treatment and a fresh start. She ran away after one day because she couldn't stop smoking.

The disappointment hit harder than expected. I had wanted to see God's dramatic rescue. Instead, she chose familiar bondage over difficult freedom. "We'll keep praying for her," Mom said. The incident left me with complicated feelings. I was proud of Mom's compassion but frustrated by my conflicted response. A part of me wanted to welcome strangers without worrying about reputation, while another part was tired of being different and explaining our family's choices that others found incomprehensible.

I was beginning to understand that following Jesus like my parents did, meant accepting that most people wouldn't understand. Understanding it was one thing. Living it myself was another.

Speed Skating

October 1996

October 13th marked a new beginning as autumn arrived. I officially joined the short-track speed skating team. The sport demanded everything from me: balance, precision, and fearlessness. Though the learning curve was steep, I found unexpected joy in the rhythm of blades cutting through ice. The team members welcomed me with genuine warmth, though the language barrier made deeper connections challenging. The transition from hockey felt like shedding an old skin. The hockey coach wanted me to return my hockey skates as part of the changeover, but I wasn't ready to surrender them until my speed skates arrived.

Even this fresh start carried echoes of familiar challenges. The speed skating team was intimate, with fewer than ten of us, and had mostly Russian cultural dynamics. My friend Denis had been my bridge into that world, but with him competing at the USA Championships, I felt like an outsider again. Around this time, I colored my hair back to its original color and got a new haircut, which drew unexpected attention and compliments. Meanwhile, my brother flourished at Hebrew school, forming friendships that I could only observe from a distance.

New House, New Hope

December 1996

As winter approached, we finally moved into our larger home. It was the biggest villa we would ever have the chance of living in, bringing new possibilities and fresh hope. The radio studio was across the hallway from my bedroom, so I would be very close to the action.

I got my short-track skating boots on the day after Christmas. My dad's colleague delivered them. I couldn't wait to finally use them! Boris, my skating coach, was busy, and I hoped he could help me put the blades on. *I held my skating boots. They were custom-made, unlike anything I had ever seen before. I had made a mold copy of my feet to send to the company, and they sent me back custom-made skates. It was amazing, considering all the rental skates I had used, especially with having such a difficult-to-fit foot.*

Now I just needed to have the blades mounted. I'd officially be a speed skater, not just a hockey player trying something new. Maybe on the ice I could find a place that was purely mine. The place where I learned to fly. Speed skating served as my sanctuary, the one place where I could escape all the complexity and move forward. On those blades, I found a safe space where nothing mattered except speed, grace, and the rhythm of my own heartbeat.

✦ ◊ ✦

Warrior to Wind

✦ ◊ ✦

I was the girl among the boys who battled,
Now I'm the wind that cannot be rattled,
Round the curves like thunder rolling,
Watch my destiny unfolding!

Bending low, I touch the ice,
Speed and grace beyond all price,
Through the turns my fingers trace

WIND

Lines of power, lines of grace!

Team moves like birds in formation,
This becomes my transformation,
No more fighting for my place
I had found my saving grace!

Round the track in sacred flight,
Learning how to trust, not fight,
Racing not for earthly prize
But for what transcends the skies!

Hockey warriors watch and wonder
At this girl who breaks like thunder,
Once their teammate, now I rise,
In His love, I touch the skies!

I was the girl among the boys who battled,
Now I'm the wind that cannot be rattled,
Pilgrim racing toward the Light,
Slicing ice with Heaven's might!

The poem captured everything I couldn't yet put into prose - how speed skating had transformed me into something more graceful.

Expanding Horizons

January-February 1997

The new year brought fresh opportunities for connection and growth. In January, my grandma arrived for a visit, bringing with her the comfort of familiar love and the excitement of having someone witness my new life in Israel.

The Canada Center had another show. I skated with the speed skating team. Over 1,200 watched, including new immigrants who had been invited to observe our demonstrations. The transformation was complete. I was a speed skater now. I had my place. Denis' father gave me some instructions on daily training exercises, guiding me in how to improve even when Denis himself was out of the country competing.

In February, Grandma, Mom, and I ventured to Mount Hermon and Majdal Shams, while another day found us at a ladies' meeting at Stella Carmel. These opportunities to travel and connect with other believers appeared like windows opening in my previously isolated world.

When Denis finally returned from his international competition schedule, the entire team buzzed with excitement. He looked stronger, more focused—the weeks of competition had refined every movement. "Want to race?" he asked during practice, and I felt that familiar flutter of nerves. Denis was the champion, after all, with years of elite training carved into muscle memory.

We lined up for a forward sprint. "Ready?" he called out.

I gave everything I had, but Denis pulled away effortlessly, his technique flawless, his speed devastating. I couldn't beat him skating forward - not even close. He finished lengths ahead, barely breathing hard while I gasped for air. "Good effort," he said kindly, but I felt the familiar sting of not being fast enough, good enough.

"Let's try backward," I suggested, surprising myself with the boldness. It seemed almost like a joke. Who races backward on the Olympic track with these long short-track blades? We lined up again, this time facing the opposite direction. The long speed skating blades made backward skating much more challenging than hockey skates had ever been - especially navigating the curves backward, having to do crossovers with these extended blades that were prone to tangling with each other. Yet I found my rhythm quickly; something about skating backward felt natural to me, as if my brain worked differently in reverse.

"Ready?" Denis called out again.

Something amazing happened. My blades found rhythm on the ice; my body found its flow. I was flying backward. Faster than I'd ever moved. I managed the crossovers on the curves despite those long blades. Out of the corner of my eye, I saw Denis struggling, his technique faltering in reverse. I won. I'd beaten the champion. Everyone was amazed, including me. The irony wasn't lost on me—I was even dyslexic on the ice, and I'd just mastered racing backward with long short-track blades on an Olympic track. Denis shook his head in disbelief, grinning. "How did you do that?"

When I told my family later that evening, my voice rang with a pride I hadn't felt in months: "I can skate backward faster than the champion—even with those long speed skating blades!" I had found my element in the rhythm of blades on ice, in the meditation of endless laps, and in the quiet companionship of teammates. This felt healing after the aggressive sport of hockey and all its drama. Speed skating seemed to be what I was made for, giving me wings to soar and the freedom to become something unconstrained.

11

Flood

✦ ◊ ✦

Flood

March 13, 1997

The peaceful rhythm of spring was shattered by something I couldn't have anticipated. That morning, I had the dream that would stay with me forever. As the dream began, I could hear the 1995 Jars of Clay song "Flood" playing, a contemporary Christian rock song I loved, one that would become the haunting soundtrack to what I was about to witness. The music played throughout the entire prophetic experience; the lyrics about floodwaters somehow fitting the deluge of violence and blood I was being shown.

I was flying—not in a plane, but somehow suspended in the air like a camera, moving over the familiar landscape of northern Israel. Below me spread the shimmering waters of the Sea of Galilee, its surface catching the morning light as I soared above Tiberias.

The flight felt purposeful, as if I was being guided to witness something specific. I moved over the Jordan River Valley until I arrived at what I would later learn was the Island of Peace—a joint Israeli-Jordanian tourist area under Jordanian rule.

What I saw next was horror beyond anything my mind could have imagined—school girls. Seven of them, around my age, thirteen and fourteen years old. They were on what should have been an ordinary field trip, laughing and talking as teenagers do, when gunfire erupted. I watched from above as a Jordanian soldier opened fire on these innocent children. The blood was everywhere—on their clothes, pooling on the ground, staining the very earth of this place, ironically called the Island of Peace.

I woke up crying and visibly shaken. My hands trembled as I tried to shake off the vivid images. The blood, the terror on those girls' faces, the senseless violence—it had been so real, so immediate. I stumbled to the kitchen, my heart still pounding, trying to convince myself it was just a horrible nightmare.

A few hours later, the news broke. Seven Israeli schoolgirls from Beit Shemesh had been killed at the Island of Peace by a Jordanian soldier named Ahmad Daqamseh. The details matched my dream exactly—their ages, the location, and the horrific nature of the attack. As the reporters described the scene, I felt sick knowing I had already seen it all.

I couldn't stop crying. Mom found me sobbing, unable to explain why this news affected me so deeply. How could I tell her I'd watched it happen in my dream before it occurred? How could I explain that God had somehow allowed me to witness this tragedy prophetically, in advance? I did ultimately tell her, but it was hard to tell anyone. I felt so horrible that I couldn't prevent the attack.

King Hussein of Jordan would later travel to Israel to personally apologize to the grieving families, telling them, "Your daughter is like my daughter.

Your loss is my loss." It was a huge step. This king humbled himself as an Arab and went to a neighboring country to sit in mourning with the families. *It was a breakthrough for the kings.* His humility offered us comfort, and his gesture of crossing borders to mourn with Jewish mothers showed that some leaders understood the sacred nature of innocent life.

Still, the questions tormented me. *Why had I been shown this? What was I supposed to do with such a terrible dream? Why would God allow me to experience the horror of something I couldn't prevent*—to see violence before it happened, to know tragedy was coming, but be powerless to stop it.

As the Jars of Clay song continued to play in my head for days afterward, I understood that some floods wash away more than just the landscape. *Some floods change the very soil of your soul.* Maybe God was calling me to intercede and pray for the girls in my generation. These girls were hurting and drowning in a flood of tears. God loved them and wanted to rescue them from sinking.

So I played that song on repeat hundreds of times and prayed for the girls in Beit Shemesh and around the country who needed God in this flood. *Perhaps the dream was not for me to stop it, but rather to bear the burden of interceding and praying for the aftermath.* The dream wasn't meant to make me a hero who prevented tragedy. It was meant to make me an intercessor who carried the weight of others' pain.

For weeks afterward, I found myself weeping for girls I'd never met, praying for families whose names I didn't know, yet perhaps that was the point. Perhaps God needed someone young enough to feel the full weight of grief for her peers, someone who understood what it meant to be a teenage girl in this violent world, someone to stand in the gap through prayer when standing in person was impossible.

Carrying Others' Pain: The Weight of Intercession

"Bear one another's burdens - in this way you will be fulfilling the Torah's true meaning, which the Messiah upholds." —**Galatians 6:2 (CJB)**

"I have great sadness and unceasing anguish in my heart. For I could wish that I myself were cursed and separated from the Messiah for the sake of my brothers, my own flesh and blood" —**Romans 9:2-3 (CJB)**

There are moments in the life of an intercessor when God pulls back the veil and reveals pain that isn't your own, but somehow becomes yours to carry. The dream wasn't just a glimpse into tragedy; it was an invitation into the heart of God, who sees every injustice, feels every loss, and weeps over every senseless death.

Paul understood this burden when he wrote about his *"great sadness and unceasing anguish"* for his people. It was the natural response of a heart that God had enlarged to hold more than its own concerns. When we're called to intercede, we're called to step into the gap between heaven's heart and earth's brokenness. That space can feel impossibly wide.

I wasn't prepared for the weight of seeing violence before it happened. Carrying the grief for girls I'd never met, of feeling responsible for tragedies I couldn't prevent. Yet this is the mysterious calling of the intercessor: to bear burdens we didn't choose, to weep tears that aren't only ours, to stand in the gap for those who don't yet know they need someone to stand for them.

The burden felt crushing because it was real. God doesn't give us sanitized, easy-to-handle glimpses into the world's pain. He shows us raw reality because He needs someone with skin on to care about what breaks His heart.

As the Spirit, *"pleads on our behalf with groanings too deep for words"* (**Romans 8:26, CJB**), so we're called to groan with Him for a world in desperate need of redemption. God sought for someone who would *"stand in the gap before me on behalf of the land"* (**Ezekiel 22:30, CJB**), and sometimes He finds that person in the most unlikely places—a teenage girl in a border town. My heart was responding the way His heart responds to injustice.

Intercession isn't a spiritual gift for the strong: it's a calling for those willing to be broken open by love. When we carry others' pain, we're participating in the sufferings of Messiah, who bore not just our sins but our sorrows. We're joining the chorus of creation that groans for redemption.

The tears I wept for those schoolgirls weren't weakness: they were intercession. The prayers for their families weren't burdens to escape but bridges of love spanning the gap between heaven and earth. God needed someone young enough to feel the full weight of grief for her peers, someone who understood what it meant to be a teenage girl in a broken world.

If you've ever felt overwhelmed by the pain you see, if you've ever wept for strangers, you may be experiencing the call to intercession. It's not a comfortable calling, but it's a sacred one. When we carry others' pain to the throne of grace, we become part of God's answer to the very problems that break our hearts.

Understanding

March 1997

In the wake of such spiritual heaviness, divine intervention arrived in the form of a math tutor in Kiryat Shmona who specialized in working with students with dyslexia. Trying to advance my mathematical skills in

Hebrew had left me feeling defeated and confused. This woman saw past my struggles to the intelligence trapped beneath, making me feel not just capable, but brilliant.

> *Her presence profoundly blessed me. She understood the way my mind worked. In her patient guidance, I recognized a helper sent from heaven to help me learn in a way that honored rather than fought against my differences.*

Time in Haifa

As April approached, I had been making frequent trips to Haifa, gradually building connections with local youth. Grandma had been volunteering at the Teen Challenge center, and during my visits to stay with her, I found myself part of a broader community of faith.

Adventures and Challenges

Spring 1997

Practical challenges continued shaping our training. Our coach had spent the entire month in Japan. The Zamboni driver's refusal to properly clean the ice was damaging our blades.

That spring, I attended a camp, but I did not write about it. Far more memorable was our rare family vacation with Grandma to Ein Gedi and Eilat. Our camping adventure turned into comedy when fierce desert winds launched our tent across the Red Sea with us inside, soaking us as we tumbled into the water. The pre-dawn rescue mission became a family legend. Our visit to Eilat's underwater observatory on May 23rd proved more successful, revealing an alien world of coral gardens and tropical fish through submerged chambers.

Back home, I found solace in four hours at the Canada Center, lost in the rhythmic sound of blade against ice. Grandma even skated with me, and I was thrilled she wanted to explore my world.

The next day brought a new American intern who was eager to learn Dad's radio work. His arrival coincided with Metulla's annual bike race, where my participation ended abruptly. My bicycle broke down near Mayim Baruch during the mountain descent. Stranded without communication, I experienced genuine vulnerability before my parents—guided by mysterious parental radar—appeared to take me home.

The Conflict Continues

June 1997

On June 10th, the ongoing conflict reminded us that peace remained elusive. An anti-tank missile struck Metulla, and rockets were fired at nearby Kiryat Shmona. The attacks shattered any illusions that the relative quiet since Operation Grapes of Wrath might last.

After the war and my difficult season with the hockey players, I had been hardened to the rocket attacks. At that time, I didn't have much sympathy for those who were afraid. Something in me calloused to protect myself. I tried to show I was not scared by refusing to go down to the shelter. Sometimes, I would go for a walk with the dog instead. I was defiant and didn't want to be caged. I decided that if the farmers were still on their tractors in the fields, I wasn't going to hide in the bomb shelters. Only in my journals did I let loose some of the pain I was hiding internally. The attacks in June served as an ominous reminder that our precarious peace could shatter at any moment. As summer deepened, the weight of living with constant uncertainty began to take its toll. The external pressures were building toward something I couldn't name. My internal defenses were starting to crumble.

As summer intensified, so did my internal struggles, until everything I had been holding inside finally erupted. On July 2, 1997, the accumulated weight of loneliness and displacement finally overwhelmed me. *I don't recall asking for this calling!* I wrote in my journal, the words carrying all the frustration of a teenager who felt trapped by circumstances beyond her control.

I Didn't Ask for This

I didn't ask for rockets overhead, or dreams that fill me with dread, I didn't ask to see what others can't see, or carry burdens too heavy for me.

I didn't ask to be the foreign girl in every place my restless feet unfurl, I didn't ask for lies to steal my name, or false champions who'd set my heart aflame.

I didn't ask to live on the border's edge, where peace and war dance on a razor's ledge, I didn't ask to fight for every friend, to wonder if acceptance has an end, I didn't ask for this calling, Lord, this weight, this pain I can't afford. I'm drowning in despair, why must I be the one to carry this burden?

But then You whisper soft and low: "My child, I know you didn't ask, but I have equipped you for this task. The very things that make you weep are gifts I've planted buried deep.

Your tender heart that feels much, it mirrors Mine with healing touch. Your stranger's eyes that see between the hidden hurts that go unseen. I didn't call you to be strong, I called you to depend on Me when all goes wrong.

I didn't call you to belong to earthly kingdoms, you're my garden and I am your song. The rockets that make others flee teach you to run straight to Me.

The dreams that shake you in the night are glimpses of My perfect sight. You think you're broken, think you're wrong. I have made you for this song to sing My love in border lands, to hold My peace in trembling hands.

You didn't ask, but I still chose to plant My garden where thorns grow. You didn't ask, but I still knew that I could trust this heart to you. So when you feel too weak to stand, remember, this was always planned.

Not your idea, but Mine alone, to make a Stranger Lovely, known. Because you bear the Light of the celestial city within. I'll be your strength when strength runs out, I'll be your peace when filled with doubt, I'll be your home when home feels far, my precious child, that's who you are. You didn't ask for this calling, dear, but I asked you, and I am here.

By August, dozens of Katyusha rockets would rain down on northern Israel, the first significant escalation since the 1996 ceasefire. Even before that escalation, the mounting pressures had become unbearable.

We are saved by the blood of the Lamb and the Word of our testimony. I write these things and bare my soul, so that those who have experienced frustration, displacement, loneliness, or brokenness may know my testimony of the pilgrimage I was on. I want you to know how He can take someone broken and renew their mind, and heal their heart. He approaches each of us differently. At that moment, I was drowning in despair.

Years later, I'd recognize the exquisite precision with which teenage insecurity was weaponized against my sense of belonging. I had arrived at, what seemed a thoroughly reasonable conclusion, that I was the defective component in our family's divine calling.

My struggles, my spectacular failure at social integration, and my episodes of despair: all seemed irrefutable evidence that I had no place in their story.

The lies sounded entirely sensible. *Your parents would achieve so much more without constantly managing your emotional crises,* they whispered. *You're an impediment to their effectiveness. You're making everything harder. They'd be better off without worrying about you.*

Beneath my practical rationalizations lay a deeper wound, the conviction that I was too much for them to bear. I departed carrying anger I could neither name nor untangle, hurt that seemed too enormous for my adolescent vocabulary. I carried the bitter satisfaction of a martyr who believes she's solving everyone's problems by removing herself from the equation.

After much prayer and family discussion, my parents decided it was time for me to live with my grandmother in Missouri and complete high school there. The plan represented everything I had dreamed of during my darkest moments—escape to normalcy, to a place where I could be just an American teenager. I would leave my *Fortress of the North* to finish my education in the Ozarks. August 13th was set as my departure date.

I was running away, hurt and angry at Israel—that beautiful, impossible country that had made me perpetually displaced, never quite fitting into its rhythms and expectations. I was angry at God, whose love for me had become a theological concept I could recite but no longer feel with certainty.

Yet even as I prepared to leave, I carried my mother's parting wisdom like a compass: "To have a friend, you have to show yourself friendly." I was determined to become Lydia Friend, a friend to many, someone who could start fresh and learn to love and listen to the Voice of God. I would turn seventeen shortly after arriving, and perhaps this season of spiritual revival would begin in the heart of the Ozarks, in the safety of my grandmother's house.

As departure loomed, questions thundered through me.

> *Was I running toward freedom or fleeing from destiny? Could I shed the Stranger Lovely I had become like an outgrown coat? Could I pretend I'd never carved ice with my fingertips as I flew around curves, never beaten the champion while skating backward? How could I deny the orchards where I had walked among ancient apple trees, lifting their worship to heaven? The campfires where Hebrew melodies danced with flames? The home that pulsed with Arabic hymns from dawn to dusk? How could I forget our radio studio, learning to broadcast the Gospel across borders, or climbing to the Hill of the Doves where transmitters sent God's voice into the darkness? Or could I forget the Negev's burning sands, where I had laughed with classmates, and the oil lamp I'd unearthed from no man's land. A relic of civilizations lying in the rain in the buffer zone between life and death? Could I forget my Friend family and all the friends that I had made and would make?*
>
> *Would I forget the pilgrimage I was on in this land, and the people living in darkness who needed someone to shine a light for them? Would I escape the land of the valley of the shadow of death to live in the Ozark sun and abandon the ones who needed hope?* **(Isaiah 9:2)**

These weren't postcards to be packed away. These were the stones that had built my soul, the faces that had carved themselves into my heart, the places that had claimed me as their own. I was running away from where God had placed me, but perhaps He would still run after me. I knew I was a stranger in a strange land, but maybe America would teach me how to be Lydia Friend. The question lingered: *Would I always remain the Stranger Lovely, even as I learned to be Lydia Friend?*

12

Return & Revival

✦ ◊ ✦

The Journey to Independence

August - October 1997

T he decision had been made. It felt both brave and terrifying. I would leave what I'd come to think of as the *Fortress of the North* to further my education. The plan was clear: I would go live with my grandmother in the Ozarks and complete high school there. Dad's only request was that I shouldn't come back without a driver's license.

Grandma was what I called a "Night Watcher." Someone who prayed through the nights as God burdened her heart. Her small apartment would become both a refuge and the beginning of a spiritual revival I couldn't yet imagine. She was born in Texas County, Missouri, just as her grandmother had been before her. This was my heritage, my roots calling me home, though I didn't yet understand how deep those roots actually ran.

Ben Gurion Airport hummed with the familiar chaos of departures. Hebrew announcements echoed off tile floors. I stood with my family near the security checkpoint, my boarding pass growing damp in my palm, watching other teenagers say casual goodbyes to parents they would see again in a few weeks.

This was different. My flight to Chicago would carry me toward a life I'd chosen but couldn't quite imagine. It was my first real step toward independence. I could see the sadness in Tom's eyes.

When the time came to leave, Mom cried as she held me. "I'm going to miss you so much," she whispered.

"Ruth, she'll be fine," Dad said gently. I could see the emotion in his eyes, too. "This is what she needs to do."

"I know, Michael, but she's so young…" Mom's voice broke. Dad placed his hands on my shoulders and prayed for me, blessing me with words that carried both paternal love and divine commission.

This felt far more complicated than other times I'd moved. Mom's parting advice became my mission: *I would be Lydia Friend, a friend to all. I would start anew in the heart of America. Whatever awaited me in Missouri, I would face it as someone new. Someone who could be a friend.*

Like Jacob, who traveled to Haran in search of safety and family connection, I was traveling to the Ozarks. I was in search of my heritage. I wanted to uncover who I was and where I came from. Grandma was my "Night Watcher", and she would help me as I began to fight not with humans but with angels.

The First Lesson in Independence

The fluorescent lights in Chicago's O'Hare International Airport buzzed overhead as I splashed cold water on my face, trying to wash away the exhaustion of the transatlantic flight. My reflection stared back hollow-eyed and disoriented, caught between the girl who had boarded a plane in Israel and whoever I was supposed to become in America.

I gathered my carry-on and headed toward the exit, legs still unsteady from twelve hours in the air. The terminal stretched before me. It was a maze of gates and moving walkways, filled with people who seemed to know exactly where they belonged. Halfway to baggage claim, panic hit.

My passport. Where is my passport? I ran against the flow of passengers, heart hammering. There on the tiny shelf by the sinks, my blue passport lay forgotten, as displaced as I felt. Clutching it to my chest, I realized this was my first lesson in independence. Sometimes you have to retrace your steps to move forward.

Grandma waited with tears streaming down her face. Behind her stood my cousin Jimmy, who'd grown so tall that even at my height, I felt like Alice in Wonderland after drinking the shrinking potion.

The twelve-hour drive to Missouri stretched through landscapes I'd never imagined. We passed rolling hills. I had no idea I was heading into cowboy country, a place where rodeos were regular entertainment. In fact, many of my future classmates would turn out to be actual cowboys. Somewhere around hour ten, we crossed into the familiar rolling hills of the Ozarks.

All the emotions I'd been holding back erupted. I sobbed as we drove into Licking—great, ugly sobs. The reality slammed into me: here I was, seventeen, carrying the memories of fifteen different homes. It was like watching my whole life flash before my eyes—seventeen years of goodbyes, of packing up and starting over. Now I was leaving my family for the first time, caught between the memories of my past and the promise of my future.

New Beginnings

The next day brought the familiar ritual of American high school registration, but nothing about this felt familiar to me. Licking High School was built like a fortress of Ozark stone with modern hallways and worn linoleum floors. It carried the comfortable shabbiness of a place where everyone knew everyone else's business. After the intensity I'd known in Israel, this felt refreshingly human-scaled.

The guidance counselor shuffled through my transcripts with a bemused expression, as if trying to solve a puzzle. I handed him report cards from the Arabic-English International School, the Hebrew school, and my English homeschool program. At least two were in English, but the Hebrew transcript made him squint at the foreign script.

"Hebrew," he murmured. "We'll start you in the usual classes," he continued, pencil moving across forms with practiced efficiency. "Algebra, English, biology, history. You mentioned art and athletics?"

"Art, yes. I'd like to try cross-country if possible." The words felt tentative. In Israel, joining a team meant navigating complex social dynamics and proving yourself worthy of inclusion. Here, I hoped, it might be simpler.

The real test came in music class, when we were all required to stand and introduce ourselves to our new classmates. I hadn't rehearsed this moment. I was put on the spot and had no time to analyze what I would say.

"I'm Lydia," I began, my voice clear and without any trace of a foreign accent.

"I'm a speed skater from Israel. The most incredible thing I did this summer was coming here."

The words hung in the air for a moment. I could see them trying to process the information. Israel. Speed skating. The combination seemed to puzzle them in the same way it had puzzled administrators. The truth was both complex and straightforward. I had come from Israel, which was true, though I wasn't an Israeli citizen. I had been born there and lived there for over three years since becoming a teenager. I'd also lived there nearly three years as a baby. Still, explaining all that seemed impossible in the moment.

"What country did you come from?" someone called out, as if I hadn't just said.

"Israel," I repeated, then added helpfully, "In the Middle East."

A guy, who I think was named Derek, asked me, "Would it be okay if I called you Israel? I can't remember your name."

The question caught me off guard. Not because it was rude, but because of what it represented. Here I was again, being renamed for the place I'd left. It felt more comfortable for others than learning who I actually was. My name was not unusual, nor was it difficult to pronounce or remember. Yet somehow that simple fact would be lost on many in my high school.

"That's fine," I heard myself say, though something in my chest tightened. I had left Israel because I couldn't find a belonging there. Now I found myself becoming "Israel" to people who would never quite see me as simply American.

What I didn't know was that this nickname would spread through the school like wildfire. Students, even people who had heard my actual name multiple times, would start calling me "Israel" instead of Lydia. It was as if my real identity had been erased and replaced with a geographical label that carried meanings I couldn't control. In hindsight, I should have told everyone something different. I should have said I was an American expat who had just returned from overseas. Now, everyone thought I was a foreign exchange student. I hadn't yet realized how they viewed me, as I was still grappling with my own identity.

The irony wasn't lost on me. I was carrying the name of a country that had both shaped and wounded me, in a place where I hoped to finally belong. It felt like a paper cut that shouldn't matter, yet somehow bled far deeper than anyone could see.

◆ ◇ ◆

Returning to What I'd Forgotten

A few days after school started, Grandma took me to visit Aunt Helen, who lived in the Success area not far from Licking. I had no specific memories of Licking itself. As we drove into Success, something stirred in the deepest parts of my consciousness.

"You lived around here when you were little," Grandma said gently as we pulled into Aunt Helen's driveway. "Before all the military moves."

"Lydia! Look how you've grown!" Aunt Helen exclaimed when she saw me, pulling me into a warm hug. "Rose, she's gotten so tall!"

"I know." Grandma smiled. "It's hard to believe this is the same little girl."

As we sat in Aunt Helen's home, she turned to Grandma with concern. "Rose, how are you managing with her staying with you? That's a big responsibility."

"Helen, it's been a blessing," Grandma replied. "Michael and Ruth know she's in good hands."

During our conversation about family and the years that had passed, memories began to surface. The old trailer off Boiling Springs Road where we'd lived when I was barely five. I remembered playing in the sawdust near Uncle Bud's farm. In my mind, I smelled the sweetness of wood shavings and felt the crunch beneath my small feet.

I remembered letting the cows escape by accident and watching Uncle Bud chase them around the yard. I remembered his frustration. The memory was so vivid I could almost hear the cows lowing. Uncle Bud's voice calling after them. My great-grandma Ann Friend met me soon after we returned from Israel when I was nearly three. She died not long after.

There were kittens, and my brother and I had played with them for hours. One little black one we had named Lyla, meaning Night. My clearest memory was of music. I remembered singing in that old beat-up trailer with Mom's cassette player. My voice lifted over whatever songs she'd chosen, feeling the pure joy of sound filling a small space.

I could remember jumping off a rope into the water. The thrill of letting go and hitting the cool surface. There had been snakes in the water, too, and the fear that came with them. I wasn't sure if it had been at Boiling Springs, Dog's Bluff, or another river. The memory was clear: the rope, the jump, the snakes, the fear.

These weren't memories of Licking specifically, but of Texas County, Missouri. The landscape that had held my earliest years back in the USA, after returning from Israel. This was before Dad joined the military and we began the long journey through California, Texas, Georgia, and Wisconsin that would eventually lead us to Israel and then back here again. Sitting in Aunt Helen's kitchen, I realized I was returning to my past and to where my Grandma had gone to high school as well.

Finding My Pace

Cross-country became a blessing. Here was something beautifully simple. Put one foot in front of the other, breathe steadily, and let the Missouri landscape teach me what I needed to know. The coach didn't bother with me much, and that was fine. He kept us off the track as much as possible, preferring that we run on grass around town and through ball fields—anywhere the ground was softer and the scenery more interesting than endless oval loops. I preferred it too. There was something freeing about running through Licking's streets, past houses where people waved from their porches, through neighborhoods where the rhythm of daily life played out.

My teammates were mostly farm kids who had been running these roads for years. I was still adjusting to the difference from sea-level Israel; still learning to read the weather patterns that could change from blazing heat to sudden storms in the space of an afternoon. We talked as we ran, finding our pace together and sharing stories about where we'd come from and what we hoped for.

During our longer runs, especially the ones that took us through Deer Lick Park, I found myself thinking about the land itself and what had drawn people to this place. Grandma had told me the story of how Licking got its unusual name, explaining that there had been a natural salt lick here—a deposit that attracted buffalo and deer, who would gather to lick the ground for essential minerals. Early settlers had recognized this natural phenomenon, and the community that formed around it became known as "The Settlement of Lick," eventually shortened to simply "Licking."

Running through the park where deer still came to drink, I thought about how that salt lick had provided something vital that the animals couldn't find elsewhere, something their bodies needed to survive. Maybe that's what I was doing here, too, finding something essential I couldn't yet name, but deeply needed to survive.

The Art of Sacred Making

During this season, the art room became my refuge. Clay dust hung in shafts of afternoon sunlight, and the familiar smell of earth and water welcomed me like an old friend. Rory had claimed the stool beside mine with that easy way he had of gravitating toward my workspace.

Today, I was working on the large oil lamp. My hands moved with the certainty that comes from creating something that matters. The clay responded to my touch, taking shape under fingers that remembered this ancient form from museum visits in Jerusalem.

"That's really something," Rory said, his voice softer than usual. He'd set aside his project.

"It's Hebrew," I said simply when he asked about the script I was carving. *"Your word is a lamp unto my feet and a light unto my path."* **Psalm 119:105**

Something shifted in his expression, as if he were seeing past the clay to something more profound and more significant. In that moment, the art room became a sacred space, not because of what we were creating, but because real questions were being asked and genuine answers were being offered.

"Do you really think God cares about regular stuff?" he asked quietly. "Like, not just church stuff?"

The question hung between us, vulnerable and real. This wasn't the Rory who would later whistle at me across the track field or perform for audiences. This was someone genuinely seeking something rarely talked about in a place where faith was often worn like Sunday clothes—but separate from real life.

"I think God cares about everything," I said carefully. "Especially the things we create when we're trying to understand something bigger than ourselves."

We worked in comfortable silence after that, but something had changed. For once, Rory wasn't performing or hiding behind his friends' expectations. He was simply seeking.

Our quiet conversation was interrupted by the roar of military jets passing overhead, American aircraft on some training mission. The sudden noise made everyone in the class look up, and then, inevitably, look at me.

"The Israelis are coming!" someone called out jokingly, and the whole class laughed. I managed a weak smile, but the comment stung more than I expected. It was another reminder that no matter how American I was, no matter how much I belonged here by heritage and citizenship, I would always be seen as somehow foreign.

The Identity Crisis

The "Israel" nickname had spread through the school, and with it came questions I didn't know how to answer. Are you Jewish? The question followed me through hallways and cafeteria lines; asked with curiosity, suspicion, and sometimes something darker.

I hated that question, not because there was anything wrong with being Jewish, but because I couldn't answer it honestly. I secretly wanted to say yes, wanted to claim that identity that felt so much a part of my heart, but I had no proof. We'd never been able to definitively trace our family roots, despite names in our genealogy that could be Jewish or could be something else.

Mom had always said she had a "Jewish heart." Someone once told her that if she claimed to have a Jewish heart, that meant she was Jewish. Yet God had made one thing clear to her before she could go to Israel: she could not go unless she loved the Arab people, because God loves the Arabs. She hadn't understood how she could love both people, but she told God, "If I meet an Arab, maybe I will like them. I like everyone, usually."

God told her to get on a bus, and she would meet her first Arab. She went to the bus station, got on the bus, and found it completely empty. She waited, and as the bus was pulling out of the station, a man came running up, yelling, "Wait for me!" in an Arabic accent.

She asked him if he was Arab, and he said yes. They became friends, and she ultimately led him to the Lord. After that, she felt she had both a calling and a love for both Arabs and Jewish people. It all started with her Jewish heart, and then she developed an Arabic heart, discovering that her heart was big enough for both.

For me, it was the same. I loved both people, but I always struggled with answering whether I was Jewish because I felt like Mom; we had no proof of bloodlines, just family names that might mean something or might not. The feeling remained that we might be Jewish deep down. I was a real American mix, but I didn't want to deny the possibility of being Jewish while also not wanting to lie and claim something I couldn't prove.

So I developed a standard answer: "I'm a Christian born in Israel." It was safe, honest, and usually satisfied people's curiosity. Still, the constant questions wore on me, especially when they came from unexpected places.

Confronting Hatred

Not everyone at Licking High School was a farm kid or cowboy. Some students from bigger cities brought different attitudes. I noticed a group of kids who wore black trench coats and dark glasses, cultivating an image that set them apart from the rural simplicity of most of their classmates. It was some of these kids who cornered me one day, asking the familiar question but with an edge: "Are you Jewish?" Their tone made it clear this wasn't idle curiosity. These were kids with white supremacist attitudes, and they wanted to know if I was someone they needed to hate. I looked at them steadily, drawing on reserves of courage I didn't know I possessed.

"Jesus was Jewish," I said. *"Do you have a problem with that?"*

The question stopped them cold. Whatever response they'd been expecting, it wasn't a theological challenge. They mumbled something and walked away, and they never bothered me again. The encounter stayed with me, a reminder that the identity questions I wrestled with weren't just personal; they touched on deeper issues of prejudice and hatred.

While it would have been easier to dismiss it, I didn't want to. I wanted to confront the prejudice. Even though I trembled sometimes, I tried to always face things and bring truth out into the open when I could.

Processing Identity

This identity wrestling would continue for years to come. At seventeen, I was just beginning to grapple with the complexity of belonging to multiple worlds while feeling fully at home in none of them. The questions that followed me through Licking High School's hallways were only the beginning of a much longer journey toward understanding who I really was.

I wanted to belong in Israel since I was born there. I wanted to prove somehow that I was Jewish, since Christians like me didn't receive automatic citizenship by birth. Even though I played with the idea in my mind, I never wanted to convert or anything—I was solid in my faith as a follower of Messiah. I was just curious to find out if I did indeed have Jewish heritage, which I have so far never been able to prove.

All I knew was that I felt foreign everywhere. I was too foreign for some Americans who called me "Israel," yet too American for Israelis when I'd lived there. I was too different for small-town Christians who had never left their county, and too Christian for the secular world. I was too uncertain about Jewish identity to claim it, and too connected to it to dismiss it completely.

13

When Darkness Births Light

✦ ◊ ✦

Five Minutes of Wonder

October wrapped the Ozarks in brilliant reds and golds, and I found myself settling into rhythms I'd never expected to love: coffee with Grandma before school, afternoon miles on country roads that taught my legs about endurance, evening hours at the apartment doing homework, reading the Bible, and poetry.

The state cross-country meet in Jefferson City brought triumph, fun, and kindness. Thursday, the day before the race, everything seemed to go wrong. We were scheduled to go out to eat as a team, but my ride didn't arrive on time. The coach and other runners were ready to leave, and it looked like I'd be stranded there alone, waiting for my ride. That's when one guy stepped forward. I don't even remember his name, but I remember his simple declaration: "I'll wait with her." Just like that. No big deal to him, probably, but to me it meant everything. Someone cared enough not to let me be abandoned. Someone was willing to sacrifice their own plans to make sure I wasn't left alone.

Before we left for ice skating after the race in Jefferson City, Libby had approached us at church. "Rose, would it be all right if my daughter and I joined you in going ice skating in Jefferson City?"

"Of course, Libby," Grandma had said with a smile. "The more, the merrier." The sharp bite of arena air and the familiar scrape of blades on ice felt like coming home. I laced up the too-small rental skates. I moved onto the ice with muscle memory, and suddenly I was flying backward around the rink. Libby's little daughter skated happily with me, creating a fun and beautiful moment. The rink was busy with families from Friday night public skating, wobbling around the perimeter, along with teenage couples holding hands and giggling.

Then I saw him. He moved across the ice like he'd been born to do it, every stride fluid and powerful, his hockey skates cutting sharp turns that sent ice spray glittering under the arena lights. While everyone else navigated around each other with varying degrees of awkwardness, he flowed through the crowd like water. He never seemed to slow down yet never came close to a collision.

Now that's someone who understands ice, I thought, pushing myself to match his pace. I was halfway through my own set of crossovers when he glided up beside me. Up close, I could see he was probably college-aged, with kind eyes and the easy confidence that came from genuine skill rather than arrogance.

"You're fast," he called out as I passed him on the next turn. "You compete?"

"Speed skating," I called back, not slowing down. "Short-track."
"From around here?"

"Israel," I said, and saw his eyebrows rise.

"You play hockey?" I asked when we found ourselves skating side by side.

"I do," he nodded. "Though I'm taking some time off right now." We fell into an easy rhythm, traveling parallel while the recreational skaters swirled around us. There was something special about that moment.

"I'm living down in Texas County with my grandmother," I said, then added the explanation that usually came next: "My family is in Israel. I came here to finish high school."

If the international backstory surprised him, he didn't show it. Instead, he asked, "Have you done much traveling?"

"Some," I said, then found myself curious about his own story. "What about you?"

"Some," he echoed with a smile, then added casually, "I spent last summer in Romania. I helped build a church there."

I nearly missed my next stride. "You built a church?"

"Well, helped build one." His face lit up with the memory. "Mostly, we swung hammers and mixed concrete."

The image hit me with unexpected force. This skilled athlete could have spent his summer at hockey camps or training programs, but instead chose to serve Romanian believers by building a place of worship. Here was someone who understood what I was still learning: that our gifts weren't just for our own advancement but for something larger.

"That's incredible," I breathed. "What was it like?"

His face glowed with genuine joy. "Hard work, but amazing. There's something about creating a place where people can worship together." He paused, seeming to search for words. "It felt like the most important thing I could do with those months." We skated in comfortable silence for a moment, both lost in our own thoughts. Here was someone who understood ice and faith, someone who saw athletic ability as a gift to be stewarded rather than an identity to be worshiped.

"Do you miss it?" I asked. "Romania?"

"Every day," he said. "But I think I'm supposed to be here for a while, figuring out what comes next. Sometimes God puts you in a place to prepare you for where you're going."

The words resonated in my chest like a bell being struck. *What was God preparing me for in these Missouri hills?*

"I should probably head out," he said as we completed another lap. "Early morning tomorrow."

"Of course," I replied, though I wanted to keep skating, keep talking, keep existing in this bubble where I'd found someone who spoke both the language of ice and the language of faith.

"It was great meeting you," he said, extending a gloved hand.

"Thank you," I managed.

With that, he skated toward the exit, moving with the same fluid grace that had first caught my attention. I watched until he disappeared through the rink doors, then continued skating alone, my mind spinning with more than just the circular motion of the ice.

As I finally headed toward the rental booth, I found myself praying a different kind of prayer than usual. This was a prayer of gratitude for unexpected encounters and the way God could use a stranger's five minutes to remind you that you weren't as alone as you thought.

The drive back to Licking passed in a blur of streetlights and possibilities. I might never see that hockey player again, might never have another conversation quite like that one. Yet, in that brief encounter, I'd glimpsed something I'd been searching for without knowing it. You could be serious about your faith without being boring, athletic without being shallow, adventurous without being selfish. *This was someone I wanted to be like.* Here was proof that it was possible to be both fully committed to following Jesus and fully engaged with the world.

◆ ◊ ◆

Spotlight

The weeks passed in a blur as I settled into new routines. I'd been successfully blending in at Licking High School for a while, content to be just another student navigating hallways and homework despite the "Israel" nickname. Some days, everything seemed designed to make me feel like an outsider all over again.

One Friday, I wore a lovely floral dress to school, something that made me feel feminine and confident as I walked through the doors that morning. I'd worn dresses before without incident, but somehow this particular morning, everything conspired to make me stand out in ways I hadn't intended.

In English class, Mrs. Brown decided to make me an example. "Class," she announced, "I want you to notice our student, Lydia, today. She's gifted in knowing a different language, Hebrew, and represents the kind of international perspective we rarely get to experience firsthand."

My cheeks began to burn. This wasn't the gentle acknowledgment I might have appreciated; this felt like being put under a microscope for qualities I wasn't sure I possessed. My dyslexia had made language learning a struggle, not a gift. Dad was the real linguist in our family, the one who deserved praise for his facility with multiple languages.

"Lydia, would you say something in Hebrew for the class?"

Twenty-five pairs of eyes turned toward me, expectant and curious. My mind went completely blank except for one phrase that seemed to emerge from my embarrassment: *"It's hot in here,"* I managed in Hebrew.

The class laughed, not unkindly, but I felt exposed in a way that had nothing to do with my dress and everything to do with being singled out for talents I didn't feel I owned.

"Why did you wear a dress today?" one girl asked afterward, as if my clothing choice had been some sort of declaration against the norm.

"My jeans were dirty," I said simply. The dress had made me feel confident, ready to face the day. Now it felt like a spotlight I couldn't turn off. The girls complimented the dress, but their attention made me uncomfortable. I'd spent weeks learning to blend in, and one clothing choice had undone all that careful camouflage. I was visible again as the interesting outsider.

Walking home, I realized I'd learned something important about belonging: sometimes what makes you stand out is exactly what keeps you from fitting in. The dress wasn't the problem; the problem was my fear that being noticed meant being judged, that visibility would always lead to disappointment.

The Fall

The weekend brought a different kind of pain. Something happened outside the church after the service that devastated me. I was playing on the ice with two sisters from the congregation—just slipping and sliding around in our regular shoes, laughing and having fun on the frozen surface behind the building.

Then I fell hard and severely hurt my knee. The two sisters I'd been playing with said they would get help because I was clearly in pain, lying there on the cold ground, unable to get up easily. What came out the door was not what I'd imagined. An older teenage boy emerged from the church building, someone I'd noticed earlier and thought was cute.

"I'm okay," I said, trying to manage through the pain as he approached. He looked down at me with an expression I couldn't quite read, then shrugged with casual cruelty.

"I wasn't worried about you anyway."

The words hit me like a punch in the gut. I'd been prepared for the physical pain, but not for the emotional dismissal. In that moment, lying there on the ice in terrible pain, I felt the full weight of how alone I was. To make matters worse, I thought he was cute, which made the rejection cut even deeper. The spiral began that night.

Into the Darkness

That Sunday, even worship couldn't lift the heaviness that had settled over me since falling on the ice. I'd managed to hide the worst of my pain, both physical and emotional, but by Monday, the weight of depression crashed over me like a wave.

I stayed home from school, telling Grandma I felt sick. It wasn't entirely a lie. I had been feeling under the weather since the race on Saturday.

The car had broken down again. I had algebra and biology to catch up on, assignments that felt overwhelming in my current state. Still worse than the practical problems was the spiritual darkness. Lying in Grandma's small apartment, staring at the ceiling, I felt abandoned in a way that made me question everything I thought I knew about God's faithfulness.

"God, I need help," I whispered into the silence. "Send someone to love me. I move and move and move, and I'm still alone."

The prayer felt pathetic even as I spoke it, but it was the most honest thing I'd said in days. I was tired of being strong, tired of adjusting, and tired of being the interesting outsider who never quite belonged anywhere. It was in that darkness, when hope seemed impossible to find, that the words began to come. Not answers exactly, but the beginning of understanding. That night, overwhelmed by everything I was feeling, the words poured out of me like a prayer:

Abba Father

Abba Father,
You protect me, never neglect me,
Even when everything grows dark and cold.

When I look up to You and pour out my heart,
Your love surrounds me.
Always there when no one cared

My one true friend.

All my secrets, all my pain, all my joy
I've shared with You.
When things don't go my way,
You're the only one I turn to.

When I feel like crying all my tears away,
I'll sing a song for You that day.
All my fears will fade away, Lord
You are everything to me.

After a life of moving and losing,
I have discovered there is only One
Who has been where I have gone
And where I want to be.

The words poured out of me like water from a broken dam, each line a recognition of something I'd known but never articulated: through all my displacement, only one constant had remained. And with that shift came another song. What poured out this time was a prayer of dedication:

✦ ◊ ✦
I Want to Be Like You
✦ ◊ ✦

I want to be like You
Light blazing in my face,
When they see me walking by
They see Your grace.

Fill my cup,

Make it flow,
Splash Your love
On all below.
Set us free in Jesus' name!
We need You like DNA,
Can't breathe without Your name,
Break these cells,
Break these chains

We can't live without You!
We can't breathe without You!
JESUS, JESUS, JESUS!
Set us free!

These stones need Your fire,
Living stones need to fan the flame,
Broken but still
Breathing
Jesus, end our shame!
You're our DNA!
You're our DNA!
We're dying without You!
Save us today!!
Save us all,
Before we die,
We need You, Lord,
You hear our cry!

Make us Living Stones!
Even the rocks cry out!
Hosanna come and save,
Hosanna come and save,
Jesus! Have Your way!

WHEN DARKNESS BIRTHS LIGHT

✦ ◊ ✦

Writing both pieces in that dark time felt like breaking through to the air after being underwater too long. Everything started feeling better after that. The depression wasn't gone completely, but I had words for it now, and more importantly, I had a vision of what might come from it.

Singing in Chains: When Darkness Births Worship

"Around midnight, Paul and Silas were praying and singing hymns to God, and the other prisoners were listening to them." — **Acts 16:25 (CJB)**

There's something mysterious about the songs that emerge from our darkest hours. Paul and Silas, chained in a Philippian prison, their backs bleeding from beatings, chose to sing hymns at midnight. Not because their circumstances had improved, but because something deeper than circumstances was rising up within them.

The words from "I want to be like You" weren't born from happiness or spiritual victory—they were carved out of raw need, desperate gratitude for the one constant in a life of continual change. What emerged wasn't just personal comfort, but a recognition that would reshape everything: *"After a life of moving and losing, I have discovered there is only One who has been where I have gone and where I want to be."* This wasn't theology I had learned in Sunday school; this was truth I had discovered in the trenches of teenage depression and cultural displacement. Where the first song had been about finding God faithful in my personal darkness, the second was about becoming a light for others who were struggling.

Paul and Silas's midnight songs didn't just comfort them; they shook the foundations of the prison and opened every door. Their worship in chains became the soundtrack for breakthrough, not just for themselves but for everyone within hearing distance.

When we sing in our chains—whether they're made of circumstances, depression, displacement, or rejection—we discover that worship has the power to reshape not just our perspective but the very foundations of what holds us captive.

14

The Weight of Distance

✦◇✦

From a Distance

November 1997

As Thanksgiving approached and I remained in Missouri, the gulf between me and my family felt oceanic. The guilt I carried for leaving them crystallized one gray morning as I sat at Grandma's small kitchen table with my journal open. The lament began:

Yeshua, please let me bless my family. I want to thank them for everything they have given me. They are part of me, and I am part of them. I feel guilty for leaving. I feel I wasn't finished with my story there. I'm afraid that I am growing up and will never be the little girl who fills their home with laughter and noise.

Finding Sanctuary

The Pentecostal Holiness Church became my anchor during those heavy November days. I spent a lot of time at the altar, pouring out my heart to God. **The altar calls weren't just for giving your heart to Jesus: they were for bringing everything to Jesus.** Almost every Sunday night, I was drawn to walk to the front, kneeling at the worn wooden altar where so many others had wrestled with God and found peace.

Wednesday nights brought youth group meetings where Jacob and Libby served as our leaders. Jacob had a special way of making everyone feel heard, while Libby brought enthusiasm. She was both my youth leader and the school librarian, bridging my church life and school life in ways that made me feel more integrated.

The two sisters I had befriended, Ruby and Anna, welcomed me into the group like I had always belonged there. My cousin Lisette and her husband, along with their boys, also attended church there. Every Wednesday night, the youth group would gather in the small classroom behind the sanctuary for discussions that felt more real than anything I was learning in regular school. We'd dive into Scripture and wrestle with questions about how to live out faith in a complicated world.

Sterling and his wife, Melodin, also attended church there. I remember how Sterling would later visit us in Israel. We would meet him in Tiberias, and I'll never forget how emotional and excited he was to see us in the Holy Land. That was still to come in the future. For now, they were just part of the church family that was teaching me what it meant to belong somewhere.

Essential in Unexpected Places: The Salt Lick Calling

"You are salt for the Land. But if salt becomes tasteless, how can it be made salty again? It is no longer good for anything except being thrown out for people to trample on." — **Matthew 5:13 (CJB)**

"But you are a chosen people, a royal priesthood, a holy nation, a people for God to possess! Why? In order for you to declare the praises of the One who called you out of darkness into his wonderful light. Once you were not a people, but now you are God's people; before, you had not received mercy, but now you have received mercy." — **1 Peter 2:9-10 (CJB)**

Learning about Licking's unusual name gave me a new perspective on my own journey. That salt lick had provided something essential that buffalo and deer couldn't find elsewhere—something their bodies needed to survive. They would travel great distances, following an instinct toward what they needed most.

Standing in those Ozark hills, feeling foreign yet somehow essential to someone I hadn't met yet, I began to understand what Yeshua meant when He called His followers *"salt for the Land."* Salt doesn't exist for itself; it exists to preserve and to enhance whatever it touches. A salt lick doesn't apologize for being in an unexpected place; it simply offers what creatures desperately need.

The very experiences that had made me feel displaced were actually equipping me to belong with anyone who needed someone to understand. Being called "Israel" instead of Lydia wasn't just about other people's inability to see my real identity—it was about learning to carry the weight of a name that wasn't mine, preparing me to help others discover their true names.

Through my identity crisis and my faith in Messiah, I was becoming someone who could offer what others couldn't find elsewhere: the ability to love across divisions, to understand multiple perspectives, to build bridges in places where others only saw walls.

Every place I had lived, every rejection I had experienced, every moment of feeling like I didn't quite fit—all of it was creating something essential, not for my own comfort, but for others who would need someone to understand their hunger for home.

As the autumn leaves fell, I learned things I couldn't have discovered any other way. Depression was real, but not final. Sometimes God's greatest gifts come wrapped in our deepest pain. Sometimes the very experiences that break you become the foundation for everything you're meant to build.

The identity crisis was far from over. The complexity of loving both Jewish and Arab peoples while belonging fully to neither would shape choices I couldn't yet imagine. Still, maybe being foreign everywhere meant I could offer something essential to people who were breaking cultural boundaries.

My journey from displacement to purpose was teaching me that sometimes you have to lose your place in every human category to find your place in God's plan. **Sometimes God positions us in unexpected places not because we'll thrive there, but because someone else desperately needs what we carry.** We become human salt licks, offering what travelers who have journeyed far from home desperately need. Not someone who belonged perfectly anywhere, but someone who could provide sustenance to others, others who were also searching for what they needed to survive.

15

Home for the Holidays

◆ ◇ ◆

School

December 1997

As November's introspection gave way to December's demands, I found myself busier than I had been since arriving in Missouri. End-of-term exams consumed my days, and the winter concerts with our choir added rehearsals to an already packed schedule. I stood in the back row with Brittany and Derek, our voices blending in holiday harmonies that filled the auditorium.

In Doc's biology class, I continued my ongoing wrestling match with evolution. Doc was a Christian who believed in evolution, and while I occasionally argued with him, I also genuinely tried to understand his perspective. Few students engaged in these kinds of discussions. I needed to understand how faith and science could intersect, even if it meant engaging in challenging conversations.

My social life was expanding in ways that surprised me. Mira, my biology classmate and study partner, had become a real friend. She invited me over to watch movies, and I even spent the night at her house.

Brittany from choir class and I did lots of activities together. Amber, the niece of one of Grandma's friends, had also become a good friend. We attended the same school, and I would see her at church and occasionally around town. I even attended her baptism at the river. The busyness activity kept me from journaling much that month. I was too busy living life to write about it—probably a healthy sign.

Tickets

As December progressed, one truth became inescapable: I needed to go home for Christmas. Not just wanted to, needed to. For seventeen years, Christmas had meant family, and family had meant being there with no exceptions.

My family handled the practical details, ordering tickets online like we'd done countless times before. Unfortunately, something went wrong somewhere between their computer screen and my front door. The tickets never arrived, leaving me to face the uncertainty of holiday travel with nothing but hope and a confirmation number.

Home for the Holidays

There's something sacred about an unbroken tradition. Standing at the St. Louis airport, watching the ticket agent's face become a study in bureaucratic stone, I felt that sacredness threatened. For one hour, he held my future hostage while I stood there, dignity dissolving with each "I'm sorry, but you cannot travel today."

When I finally got a boarding pass, I was too exhausted for relief. Flight 1884 lifted off into winter skies, carrying me toward the ancient crossroads of the world. Ice crystals decorated the wings, and somewhere in the galley, meals had gone missing. My fellow passengers became accidental companions in this aerial pilgrimage, their easy conversation a balm for my frayed nerves.

Twelve hours of transit lay ahead, and I prayed constantly for strength to face another transition. The friendly passengers beside me had no idea they were sitting next to a seventeen-year-old who was becoming an expert in international displacement.

Israel received me two days before the celebration of another traveler, who had found no room at the inn. In this land where swords once rang against stone, I dreamed of stories yet to be written, the beauty of a place where heaven and earth seem to touch. I walked through castles with my brother, Tom, over the holiday, the ancient stones whispering stories of kingdoms and conquests. I felt the familiar frustration—how could someone with dyslexia ever hope to capture these stories in words? This was before spell-check was common.

However, something else had changed, too. My family had adjusted to life without me. I felt a bit like a visitor in what had once been my own home. The holidays brought joy, but also some unexpected feelings.

My father's sermons were powerful, his passion for ministry lighting up the small congregation in a way that reminded me why people loved him and my mother, Ruth.

The Weight of Goodbye

January 6, 1998

I stood with my family near the security checkpoint. "It was wonderful being here," I said, trying to fill the silence that felt too heavy. It had been, mostly. Still, the visit hadn't been the homecoming I had dreamed about during those lonely nights in the Ozarks. I was conflicted and confused about life.

Mom held me close at the gate, her voice quiet with concern. "Are you sure about this?" she asked. "You could still change your mind."

"I know," I said. "But I promised Grandma I would finish the school year."

She nodded, though I could see the worry in her eyes. "Just remember you always have a home here."

The goodbye was hard, but we both knew this was something I needed to do. She was right. For a moment there, I had imagined canceling my ticket, unpacking my suitcase, and sliding back into the familiar rhythms of home—family dinners and Snowflake purring on my bed. However, I had a purpose to fulfill in the Ozarks.

"I love you so much, Mom," I said, standing up.

Yet it was Mom's goodbye that nearly broke my resolve. "I don't know how to let you go," she whispered.

I hugged my brother and received one of his usual bear hugs in return. "Take care of them," I whispered in his ear.

I went up the escalator, shaken. Ahead of me lay another interminable flight, another connection, another landing in a place where I was still figuring things out. Mom was crying openly now, Dad's arm around her shoulders. Tom looked older than his fifteen years. They watched until I disappeared up the escalator, and I carried the image of them with me: my anchor, my roots, my first definition of home.

As I settled into my window seat and watched Tel Aviv shrink beneath the aircraft wings, something else emerged too: the terrifying, exhilarating weight of being on this journey, even when it led away from everything I had ever known.

The plane lifted into the Mediterranean sky, carrying me back toward the Ozarks. This time, I was heading away from the Holy Land, but I was beginning to understand that the God of sacred places could meet me anywhere. His Spirit was everywhere, ready to meet us in our moments of greatest need.

16

Between Two Worlds

Toronto

January 1998

The Toronto airport stretched endlessly in every direction, a cathedral of steel and glass. My connection had been canceled due to winter weather. The next available flight wouldn't leave until the evening. I was stranded here for the entire day.

> *I'm so tired. I'm worried Grandma won't find me. I hope my luggage doesn't get lost. I haven't brought much in my hand luggage. It feels like eternity. I can't believe I can't fly because of the weather when the snow isn't even sticking.*

A family with children had also been delayed, and we struck up a conversation while we waited. Meeting new people had become my way of passing the time during travel, though the anxiety still gnawed at me. Would Grandma have trouble finding me at the airport back home with all these delays?

I was returning to Missouri with mixed emotions. Mom had almost convinced me to cancel my ticket and stay in Israel, but I couldn't break my promise to return. The truth was complicated: I loved my family desperately, and if I could have stayed to finish school there, I would have. My promise to Grandma called me back to finish what I'd started.

I'm beginning to wish I hadn't left home in Israel. I'm on the other side of the world already. I wish I had a flying saucer right now so I could get to my destination.

Eventually, I found a quiet corner near the windows and settled in with my book, watching planes taxi past on the tarmac. The exhaustion hit me in waves—emotional, physical, and spiritual.

For months, I had run on adrenaline and teenage determination. Now, suspended between two worlds with nowhere to go, I felt the weight of every choice I had made.

> *God,* I prayed silently, *I don't know if I'm doing the right thing. Take away my burdens and save me. Help me trust that this path leads somewhere good, even when I can't see where.*

Outside, snow fell but didn't stick to the ground, white flurries against the January sky. Soon I would be on a plane, flying back toward an uncertain future. First, I had to survive this airport, this day, this moment of being utterly alone with the consequences of my choices.

Return to Missouri

I landed in Chicago, and Grandma was waiting at the gate, her familiar face creased with worry and relief. She wrapped me in a hug. Even her warmth couldn't chase away the bone-deep exhaustion that had been building since I had walked away from my family at Ben Gurion Airport.

The drive back to the Ozarks passed in a blur of winter-stripped fields and small towns that looked exactly like they had when I had left three weeks ago. Nothing had changed here, though I felt completely altered inside.

I slept for fourteen hours straight and woke up feeling like I had been hit by a truck. My internal clock was completely scrambled. By evening, jet lag was hitting me in waves, but I had promised to return to church. The Wednesday night youth group was supposed to practice for some upcoming service. They had asked me before I left to share about my trip when I got back.

That evening, I shared my experiences with the church group. "You came back," said Crystal, one of the girls who was a good friend to me. "Even though you could have stayed."

"I came back," I confirmed, though I wasn't entirely sure why. "I made a promise."

After the meeting, I walked to Grandma's car through the Missouri cold, my breath visible in small clouds that dissipated as quickly as they formed. Above me, the winter sky was vast and clear, studded with more stars than I had ever noticed before my trip.

The Warrior Dream

The first few days back in Missouri passed in a blur of readjustment. I reset my internal clock, caught up on missed assignments, and reconnected with the rhythm of small-town life. On my third night home, however, sleep brought something unexpected.

My heart hammered as I woke, the taste of gunpowder and fear still metallic on my tongue. The dream clung like smoke, vivid and urgent in a way that made my ordinary Ozark bedroom feel thin and fragile. What was that?

I pulled my knees to my chest in bed, trying to make sense of the images that had torn through my sleep like shrapnel. It had started so normally: my friends and I from Metulla, the border town in northern Israel, where I had lived. We were at the mall in Kiryat Shmona, doing typical teenage things—shopping, laughing, trying to forget about the tensions that always simmered just beneath the surface of life, near the Lebanese border.

Then, someone whispered the word that could freeze any Israeli's blood: "Bomb." The explosion, when it came, was more feeling than sound—a pressure wave that seemed to collapse reality inward.

In an instant, the mall shifted into something out of a war movie. Teenagers scattered like startled birds as chaos erupted around us.

The army that pursued us wasn't human. Even in the dream, I sensed the wrongness in the way they moved—coordinated, malevolent, ancient in purpose. *Demons*, my sleeping mind had labeled them.

When their leader cornered his prey, his face composed of all sharp angles and burning eyes; nothing human remained in his expression as he raised his weapon. The bullets hit, and I felt each impact—the shocking force of it—but somehow, I remained standing. Somehow, death didn't come.

The machine gun appeared in my hands as if summoned by desperate prayer. I could still feel the weight of it, the way the metal grew hot as I fired round after round into the demonic camp. I ran in circles, shooting, driven by divine strength! A warrior instinct I had never known before that moment, until the bullets ran out.

The two small demons that chased me next were somehow worse—an army of child-sized mockeries of innocence, their pursuit relentless and personal. *Then the girl appeared,* my mysterious ally, and suddenly the fight wasn't mine alone anymore.

The mall had become a labyrinth then, escalators and elevators transforming into escape routes as we fled deeper into the building's mechanical heart. My companion moved with supernatural grace, leading me through passages that shouldn't have existed, away from the chattering pursuit of our enemies.

The stone wall at the end presented both an obstacle and a test. I climbed desperately, muscles burning, only to spot the *woman with the cat* in my peripheral vision. She had looked like a helper, like some kind of guardian posted to protect refugees from the battle below.

Evil distorted her face when I looked directly at her. The same wrongness I had sensed in the army, disguised but not hidden.

The *real angel* who appeared next was different, cleaner somehow, his presence like sunlight after storm clouds. His words echoed in my memory: *"It was a test of discernment."* In the dream, the distinction had been visceral, unmistakable.

The vehicle ride that followed was the strangest part of the experience. The dream kept shifting, as dreams often do—one moment I sat in the passenger seat, the next I was running alongside at impossible speeds, then clinging to the outside as we hurtled through landscapes at 200 miles per hour.

Countries flashed by like pages in a flip book. Everywhere, the enemy's work was visible: shadows creeping across cities, darkness seeping into hearts, the systematic corruption of everything beautiful.

We pulled over when hostile forces passed, hiding like resistance fighters in occupied territory. We took shelter in abandoned buildings, where I made preparations for battles that I didn't understand but somehow knew to be crucial.

The final scene was the most telling: *I raised a weapon to fire at retreating enemies, only to be stopped by the angel's urgent warning.* The girl wearing the enemy's uniform was on our side, despite appearances.

> *How many times have I misjudged people that way, making assumptions that someone was against me because they looked different, spoke differently, or acted differently?*

"*This is spiritual warfare, not physical,*" the angel said, and the words felt like a key unlocking a truth that I had always felt but never voiced.

Now, sitting in my Ozark bedroom as dawn crept through the curtains, I tried to understand what the dream had been trying to tell me. The dream felt too coherent, too purposeful to be random neural firing—it felt like a message.

> *Perhaps the dream was showing me that the real battles aren't fought against flesh and blood but in the spiritual realm, and I knew that God was calling me to a life of spiritual warfare, prayer, and intercession.*

At times, He would awaken me through dreams, allowing prayer to flow for countries and principalities. He made it personal through the dream when the familiar faces of kids in Metulla appeared. I felt that this dream awakened a warrior of a different kind of prayer.

I reached for my journal, and words began to flow, capturing the dream's vivid intensity before it faded. Outside my window, Licking, Missouri, was waking up to another ordinary day, farmers and ranchers heading to early chores, the school bus warming up in the district lot, and teenagers like me getting ready to navigate the small battles of high school life.

The dream's strange gift had left its mark, and I felt different now—a prayer warrior in training, *learning to recognize the real enemy and fight the battles that mattered.* The taste of gunpowder was finally fading from my mouth, but the prayer warrior's heart, which the dream had awakened, was still beating strongly in my chest.

Maybe these Ozark hills were preparing me for battles not yet visible. Beneath the surface, I now knew that deeper battles were being fought, spiritual warfare that required a different kind of courage. Whatever battles lay ahead, I was learning to trust the One who equips His warriors.

17

The Architecture of Displacement

✦ ◊ ✦

The Foundation of Understanding

Looking back now, I can see that every painful moment was teaching me something I couldn't understand then. Human belonging would always be partial, always conditional. Yet, divine belonging was constant, crossing every border, surviving every move.

Take away my burdens and save me, I had prayed in the Toronto airport. However, the burdens weren't taken away—they were transformed. My prayers evolved from desperate pleas to deeper recognition, and finally to mature surrender. The burden of being between worlds became the blessing of seeing more clearly. The burden of loneliness was transformed into the grace of deep dependence on God. The burden of difference became the strength of a unique perspective.

I was learning that sometimes the miracle isn't finding where you belong, but discovering that *belonging itself can be reimagined.* I learned that home can be a person rather than a place. I discovered that identity can be rooted in heaven, while your feet walk across the earth.

The Complexity of Return

The journey between Israel and the United States was marked by complexity. I was simultaneously escaping and abandoning, saving myself while potentially hurting those I loved. My return to America wasn't simply going home—it was entering a new kind of displacement where I was too Israeli for America, and too American for Israel.

Even when surrounded by friends in the Ozarks, I carried a loneliness that surprised me. This wasn't a failure of faith or friendship—it was something deeper being refined in me. My loneliness proved to be generative—it produced poetry, prayers, and eventually purpose.

My parents had given me the unexpected gift of speed skating after they told me I couldn't continue with hockey. Gliding alone around that Olympic oval track, finding my rhythm in solitude, I discovered that sometimes your greatest strength emerges from learning to endure in the wilderness-moments-of-life.

We're all speed skaters, in a way, circling the track of our lives in search of something we can't quite articulate. **My pilgrimage was toward the very heart of God**—not an angry deity, but the *Relentless Beloved Shepherd*

King. My Beloved had been pursuing my restless soul since before I knew His name, romancing me on walks in the Galilean mountains and beneath Ozark sunsets.

From this vantage point, I can see His hand in every lonely moment, every difficult transition, every time I felt caught between worlds. Those wilderness seasons weren't empty spaces in my story—they were sacred ground where God was captivating my heart, teaching me to recognize His voice above the noise of my fears and desires.

Even years later, God has gifted me, during extreme hardships, with dreams of skating on the Celestial Sea of Glass. These dreams gave me hope that one day I will join my Savior in a land where I truly belong. His kingdom requires no passport, only a new name written in the Lamb's Book of Life.

The Invitation

He's calling to you, too, wherever you find yourself in life's wilderness. **There's a dance He's inviting you into**—a relationship of deep intimacy and trust. It's a bridal dance where He leads with perfect love, and we learn to follow with growing faith. The invitation has always been the same: ***Will you dance with Me?*** The choice is ours: to accept His outstretched hand, to discover that true freedom comes not from controlling our own steps, but from trusting the Relentless Beloved who sees the complete picture.

18

Spiritual Warfare and Growing Faith

January-February 1998

As winter deepened in Missouri, I found myself writing poetry that captured my emotional landscape:

Winter Soul

The cold invades my soul,
Winter has set in,
And I long for the meltdown.

So, slowly with face bent upward,
I wrap myself in a patchwork quilt.
Gazing past the mountains and trees
To the never-ending oceans and seas,
Where seagulls drift high in the breeze
And palm trees sway along the beach.

I feel the sunbeams bore into my soul.
Along the sandy beach,
I run until the sun sets.
Then my sight travels back
Through the trees and mountains,
And I'm still snuggled in my patchwork quilt.
I give a startled look
As I feel someone tap my shoulder.

The Nightmare

Thursday morning, the nightmare clung to me, refusing to be washed away by the pale Missouri dawn filtering through my bedroom curtains. In the dream, I had seen him—the devil himself—not some cartoon figure with horns and a pitchfork, but a presence so evil it made me shake. He had been after my family, and I could see the fear in their faces, could sense their terror as if it were my own. The worst part was the helplessness, the knowledge that precious people were under attack, and I felt powerless to protect them.

I sat on the edge of my bed, shaking. I knew with absolute certainty this wasn't just my subconscious processing anxiety. The oppressive feeling that had settled over me was foreign, invasive—like some evil spirit sent to torment me.

When the phone rang early that morning, I nearly jumped out of my skin. "Hello, sweetheart," came a familiar voice from the other end. It was one of Grandma's friends. "I sensed I needed to call and check up on you and your grandmother."

The relief nearly brought tears to my eyes. "I had a terrible dream," I whispered, as if speaking too loudly might summon back the darkness.

"Tell me about it, honey."

So I did, pouring out the nightmare's details, while she listened with the patient attention of someone who understood that some battles weren't visible to the naked eye.

When I finished, she prayed over the phone—not a quick, perfunctory prayer, but the kind that called down spiritual reinforcements and reminded us we weren't fighting alone. Across the phone lines, two women separated by decades were united in faith. By the time we hung up, the oppressive weight had lifted.

At school, I wore my usual smile like armor. Biology class, American history, geometry—I moved through my schedule with cheerfulness. To my classmates, I was the girl with an interesting life, always upbeat.

"Why are you always so happy?" asked Jennifer, a girl who sat near me in biology. She'd been watching me during our lab work, probably wondering how someone could be genuinely enthusiastic in the first hour.

The question caught me off guard. *Happy? If she only knew about the nightmare that had stalked me all morning, about the way I sometimes cry into my pillow at night, and how I miss my family with an ache that feels physical.* She was right, in a way. I was happy, not because my circumstances were particularly joyful, but because I had deeper joy than circumstances could touch. I had Jesus living inside me, and even when I faced nightmares, His presence kept me afloat. He helped me overcome the terrors of the night. He shone His light and renewed me with His love.

"I guess I have reasons to be joyful," I said, trying to find words that wouldn't sound preachy. "Even when things are hard, I know they're not permanent."

She looked at me like I was speaking a foreign language, which, in a sense, I was. The language of faith was as foreign to most of my classmates as Hebrew, maybe more so.

The rest of the day passed in a haze. By sixth period, the sky had turned dark and ominous, matching the spiritual atmosphere that still lingered from my nightmare. When the announcement came over the intercom that school would be canceled the next day due to a flu outbreak, relief and restlessness mixed within me.

Pocket Money

Friday morning arrived with the promise of independence wrapped in the simple act of earning pocket money. When Grandma mentioned that the Ingalls family needed help with house cleaning, I jumped at the chance.

The drive to their house took us through the rolling Missouri countryside. Winter-bare fields stretched toward the Mark Twain National Forest, where pine trees towered against the sky. Visiting David and Diane Ingalls had always meant stepping into a piece of American literary history—David being the closest living relative of Laura Ingalls Wilder—but they meant so much more to our family than that connection.

After my grandfather died from radiation exposure during his Air Force service, David and Diane stepped in as pillars of strength for my mother and uncle. They were our cousins, and they carried that bond with love and laughter. David's humor could fill a room, and Diane's lovable nature made her just as fun to be with. Being with them wasn't just a family visit; it was stepping into warmth and belonging that helped carry us through.

They'd both worked at the Christian school where my mother and uncle had studied, and through all the years of our family's wandering, they remained beacons of love and hope.

"You've grown so much since we last saw you," Diane said as she handed me a bucket and cleaning supplies. "Missouri has been good to you."

Working alongside Grandma and Diane was healing after the spiritual and emotional heaviness of the previous day. By noon, the house gleamed, and I had twenty-five dollars in my pocket, earned through honest work.

"You're quite the helper," David said, his eyes twinkling. "You remind me of your mother at that age—always eager to pitch in."

Diane's sister, Sheryl, was also a cousin of mine. She had a daughter, Tammy, who was a bit older than me and worked as a hairdresser. I was so blessed to go to their home one day, and she knew how to trim curly hair and style it perfectly. It was an amazing feeling, getting my hair trimmed out in the green Ozark country at my cousin's house. After moving around the world and not being near family, I treasured these memories.

Drivers Permit

The drive to Rolla was like a pilgrimage toward adulthood. At the DMV, I studied my driver's education manual one final time, the pages worn from repeated reading. The test questions seemed straightforward enough—right of way, stopping distances, traffic signs—but I was still nervous, as I always was for exams.

"Missed three," the examiner announced when I finished. "That's a pass. Congratulations." The learner's permit was like gold in my hands—tangible proof that I was becoming someone who could navigate this country.

Daydreaming

English class blurred around me that afternoon. My thoughts drifted like smoke, and when I couldn't focus anymore, I let my pen follow where my spirit was already wandering:

Thoughtful Thoughts

I am here, but constantly there.
My thoughts are always something fairy tale.
I think I ought to let myself listen to my thoughts.

So, I now begin:

The wind blows, my hair flows,
And I become entwined with all that's around.
Constantly listening to every possible sound.

Chasing some gazelle,
Wandering through ancient castles,
Looking for lost desert camels,
Counting sheep and shepherds,
Looking at leaping leopards,
Walking through ravines and valleys,
Seeing Roman soldier rallies,
Listening to bird calls,
Seeking the secret waterfalls,

Awed by the Golan Heights,
Hearing the Lord say, "Let there be light!"
Feeling the awesome presence of Holy Mountains,
Sometimes, a snow-covered fountain.

There is such a view from this telescope I've made.
I wish that the glass would never blur nor fade.

For some days, I recall how life seemed so hopeless.
But when the hour has changed, so have I;
I must say that one hope still remains.

Here am I, I could constantly kiss the sky,
Yet wonder why it takes so long
For me to find what I am and will be.
I now know all is not in vain—
There must have been a brilliant Creator involved.

So, I sit here at my study seat.
Trying my best to chain myself down.
As I want to run outside, to taste creation's very best side.

Later that night, I found myself writing another poem about the locks around my heart:

Opening Mind to Memory

I open my mind to new and old,
To places memory told,

Following ancient paths
Until I see sacred buildings
And read the royal epitaphs.

Real artwork, I see as I feel—
The Creator's paintbrush sifting through my soul.
Until my voice comes out of the darkened well
And leaps to the trees,
Then prances through sea reefs.

When silence comes, hear me whispering,
Running through the paths so green.
Wishing someone human with me
To hold my hand and pull me through
These broken trees and scattered leaves.
But I am here alone without you.
I hear you whisper, "I'll come another day
To hold your hand and help you pray."

Saturday night before bed, I read a verse that seemed to glow on the paper:

"He who hears you hears me, he who rejects you rejects me, and he rejects me rejects him who sent me." — **Luke 10:16**

I realized that when I am rejected, I am not the only one standing. Also, since the Son and the Father are being rejected, Jesus takes on everything I take.

The revelation hit me like lightning. All this time, I had been taking every rejection personally, wearing each dismissal like a stone in my backpack.

This verse completely changed the entire narrative. When people rejected me for my faith, they weren't just rejecting me. They were rejecting the Jesus I carried within me. It was comforting to know that Jesus was experiencing it with me and that I was not alone.

Super Bowl Sunday Solo

Sunday came with its challenges and revelations. After church, Grandma patiently taught me to handle the clutch on her car, coaching me through the delicate balance of gas and clutch that would eventually become second nature. My stomach stayed in knots the entire time—from fear of stalling in traffic and from what I planned to do that evening.

That evening, despite my stomach churning with nerves, I decided to sing during the Super Bowl Sunday service. It had been years since I had done a solo. I sang "If This World" by Jaci Velasquez. The song spoke to feelings of displacement and being left out in the cold by a world that doesn't understand you. The lyrics also proclaimed hope in a God who offers comfort and love when you feel rejected and alone. As I sang about finding refuge in God's embrace despite feeling like an outsider, the words ministered to my own heart. Even in the midst of what felt like rejection, I was reminded that there is a God I can trust who sees my pain and offers His unfailing love and comfort.

The lyrics had moved me for weeks as I memorized them, and they touched deep places in me. Just after I started singing, Storm—the big, dark-haired guy who had been cruel to me when I fell on the ice—got up and left. I could hear every step, louder than my own voice. He gathered his jacket deliberately and walked straight down the center aisle, his footsteps echoing in my mind.

While my heart was crumpling, I held on to the lyrics and kept singing. Somewhere in the middle of my humiliation, I remembered the verse from that morning, Luke 10:16. This rejection wasn't just about me—it was about the Jesus I was trying to honor with my song.

When I finished, I returned to my seat, cheeks burning, fighting the familiar urge to make myself invisible. The altar call came at the end of the service, and I found myself walking to the front again—not to perform this time, but to kneel. The tears flowed freely as all the hurt, anger, and loneliness I had been carrying spilled out before God.

I prayed for the strength to keep trying, keep singing, and keep showing up even when it hurt. God's presence surrounded me, reminding me that I was never alone. I wasn't the only young person who had come forward. Others my age were also crying out to God. We were all there together, wrestling with God, with doubt, with pain, and pouring out our hearts in the same sacred space.

I want to wrap myself in blankets from heaven, to let Him know how holy He is. For He is the one who was, is, and is to come. Praise, glory, and honor to the one who is on the throne forever and ever, amen.

January 28, 1998

A Burden for John

The following week brought unexpected connections.

> *After school, I ran a mile and talked to Ruby from church. I saw one of my new friends skating, and she let me skate in her brother's skates. She is a neighbor, and her brother is in my biology class. She told me her brother had attempted suicide twice. Ever since she told me, I have been so burdened for him. I keep praying that God will use me to be a*

friend to him. However, I didn't think he needed a friend, because he seemed to be very popular. Still, maybe God opened my eyes to this for a reason. How can I make a difference?

I'm beginning to realize that it doesn't matter if you are popular or not; you can still be struggling. I hope to share the love of Jesus more. Give me eyes to see, Lord, what you see. I once didn't know Jesus, but now I listen to His words and strive to be what He wants me to be.

Seeing True Colors

Choir class had become one of my favorite parts of the day. Brittany and I had developed an easy friendship. The kind where we could dissolve into giggles over the smallest things. We still managed to hit our harmonies when the choir director called for attention. That Tuesday, we were being particularly silly, whispering jokes during warm-ups, and trying not to laugh.

I should have seen Derek coming from across the room, but I was too focused on making Brittany laugh. When he appeared beside us, his presence immediately shifted the energy. Derek had a way of taking up space that went beyond his physical size. He moved as if he owned the room.

"Having fun, ladies?" His voice carried that practiced charm that probably worked on most girls our age.

"Just working on our breathing technique," I said, trying to keep things light.

Derek was already moving closer, that smile never quite reaching his eyes. He had been bothering me for a few days. I didn't know how to handle his flirtatious remarks when he already had a girlfriend who was a good friend of mine.

Before I could step back, his hand was around my neck, fingers fumbling with the chain of my necklace with an intimacy that made my skin crawl, his fingers cold against my throat.

"What's this say?" he asked, leaning in close enough that I could smell his cologne—too strong, overwhelming.

My hand flew to my throat, both to protect the necklace and to put distance between us. "It's Hebrew," I said, my voice sharper than I had intended.

"Hebrew, huh?" His tone changed and became colder. "Figures."

Then, came the comment. I won't repeat the exact words he used about Jewish people, but they were designed to wound, to diminish, to make me feel small and foreign and unwelcome. The casual cruelty of it took my breath away—hatred against the Chosen.

My response came from somewhere deeper than thought. My foot stomped on his, hard enough to make him yelp and step back.

"What was that for?" He looked genuinely puzzled, as if he couldn't imagine what he had done wrong.

"You know exactly what that was for," I said, my voice shaking with anger.

Derek's face showed nothing. This was perhaps the most chilling part of the entire encounter.

The choir director was calling for attention at the front of the room, and Derek took advantage of the distraction. In one smooth motion, he put his arm around Brittany's shoulders—and mine. The presumption of it, the way he claimed both of us simultaneously, made my stomach turn. I wanted to shrug away immediately, but we were supposed to be paying attention to our teacher, and causing a scene would only draw more unwanted attention.

Derek seemed to sense my discomfort and used it against me, his hand moving from my shoulder to my back, his hand spread wide across my spine in a touch that was possessive and wrong.

"Sorry about before," he whispered in my ear, but his hand remained firmly in place. "You forgive me, right?"

The words came out automatically, having been trained by years of being told to be polite. "You're forgiven." Even as I said it, though, rebellion stirred.

Derek wasn't sorry—he was testing boundaries, seeing how much he could get away with. The prejudiced comment hadn't been an accident or a moment of poor judgment. It had been calculated, designed to put me in my place and establish his dominance. When class finally ended and Derek moved away to rejoin his friends, I could still feel the imprint of his hand on my back. Even as I walked to my next class, the sensation remained—as if his touch had left some mark I couldn't wash away.

"You okay?" Brittany asked as we gathered our things. I wanted to talk to her about the comment, about the fear that was growing in my chest, hard and cold as a stone. But how do you explain to someone that their boyfriend gives you the creeps?

"I'm okay," I said, shouldering my bag. Then, I rushed out the door. As I walked to my next class, one thought kept circling through my mind: *Derek scared me in a way that went beyond his inappropriate behavior. There was a predatory quality about him, calculating and cruel, that he kept hidden beneath that charming smile. He was comfortable revealing it to me.*

Derek had nicknamed me "Israel," and it spread throughout the school, with everyone calling me that and asking if I was Jewish.

His hatred told me everything I needed to know about his character. I was learning to trust that cold feeling in my stomach, that instinctive recoil that occurs when someone reveals who they truly are. Derek had shown me his true colors, and I couldn't help but try to avoid him.

Homecoming

What a wonderful and busy day I have had. Today was homecoming. When I entered the room, I greeted John. He murmured back but seemed pleased. We had a biology exam that day. The day went on, and by the seventh hour, spirits were high for the pep rally.

I found myself changing seats three times during the rally, hoping to catch sight of Brittany, but she was nowhere to be found.

Instead, it was John who caught my attention. When I had greeted him that morning, he had murmured back with what seemed like genuine pleasure, though his shyness made it hard to tell. As students filed out after the pep rally, I spotted him a few feet away and took a chance.

"Are you going to the game tonight?" I asked.

"No," he answered, and we went our separate ways.

Still, something about that brief exchange stayed with me. As we prepared to leave school, I found myself praying for another opportunity to talk with him. I had heard from his sister something that made my heart burdened—the weight of that knowledge pressed against my heart as I walked ahead of him toward the exit.

Then he caught up with me. What followed was one of those conversations that reminds you that you're exactly where you're supposed to be. As we walked home together, John opened up in ways that surprised us both. Despite his extreme shyness—a quality that reminded me of my brother Tom—there was something remarkably bright about him, an intelligence that shone through his quiet demeanor.

"I want to go to Israel," he told me, and I could hear genuine longing in his voice. The pieces of his story emerged gradually. As we talked, I saw something else—hope, curiosity, and a spirit that hadn't been completely extinguished. I made a mental note to give him the Hebrew book I had at home. It might feed his interest in Israel and, perhaps, open doors to deeper conversations about faith and purpose.

My cousin Lanny surprised us with a visit that evening. He joined us for dinner before we all headed to the homecoming game. Grandma settled in with my great-uncle Alanson and Great Aunt Margie. I found a spot near Rynata from our prayer group, close enough to the cheerleaders to feel the energy of the crowd. Watching Lanny get some playing time added to the evening's joy.

When the game ended, most students headed to the homecoming dance. I chose to leave instead, walking away from the music and laughter spilling out of the gym. Part of me wondered if I was missing out on something important—the kind of normal teenage experience I had been seeking since returning to America. However, dancing was not allowed for me according to the rules at Grandma's house.

Tomorrow, I wanted to get to know those Gothic girls I had been noticing.

They seemed as displaced as I sometimes felt. If I was learning anything in this season, I was starting to see that God had placed me here not just to find my own belonging, but to help others discover theirs, too.

Walking Home

I hadn't written in my diary for almost a week, and there was a good reason. Sunday had brought one of those inexplicable depressions that settled over me like fog, leaving everything gray and muted. Tuesday made things worse. I pushed myself through a two-mile run despite my body's protests, only to have my back go out of alignment.

Wednesday of that week brought its own kind of trouble. John and I had fallen into the habit of walking home together when our schedules aligned. He was easy to talk to. That afternoon, we were discussing his fascination with ancient history when a beat-up truck pulled alongside us, music thumping from its open windows.

"Hey, John!" one of the guys called out, his voice carrying that particular edge that made my shoulders tense. "Why didn't you ask for a ride home?"

John's steps slowed, and I could sense the change in his energy—the way he seemed to shrink into himself. The driver leaned out his window, his eyes locking onto me with an intensity that made my skin crawl.

"Who's this?" he asked, as if I weren't standing right there.

"Just a friend from school," John mumbled.

"I'll see you tonight at your house," the driver said, and it wasn't a question. The way he said it made my stomach drop. This wasn't a casual suggestion to hang out—there was an ominous undertone that suggested John didn't have much choice in the matter. The truck roared off, leaving us behind, but John surprised me by continuing our conversation as if nothing had happened.

"You were talking about the Roman ruins in Israel," he said, his voice steadier than I had expected. We walked the rest of the way home, talking about ancient civilizations and archaeological discoveries. John seemed determined to act normally. The tension in how he kept his hands shoved deep in his pockets told me the encounter had affected him more than he was letting on.

When John didn't show up for first-period biology the next morning, my worry deepened into fear. I couldn't help but wonder—*was he in trouble? And was it somehow my fault for being with him when they drove up?*

Rory, my artwork partner in art class, cornered me between classes with questions that seemed more like an interrogation. "Who was that guy you were walking with yesterday?" His voice carried an edge I had never heard before.

"John? He's my neighbor." I tried to keep my voice casual, but the tension in Rory's expression told me this wasn't idle curiosity.

"I know him," Rory said, his jaw tight. Before I could ask what he meant by that, he was already walking away, leaving me with more questions than answers.

That moment made me realize the pressure I sensed around Rory's possessiveness and his friends in the truck reporting to him revealed the complex social dynamics I didn't understand. This taught me that teenage relationships were more complicated than I'd imagined. I was still learning to navigate friendship boundaries myself. John and I sometimes walked together that spring. After school finished, we lost touch. In the end, I was beginning to see that sometimes our role is simply to pray for people and trust God with the rest.

Lifted Eyes

When I called home that evening, Mom mentioned her upcoming trip to Turkey. Another adventure in a life already filled with them, another reminder of the wandering nature of our family. During this time, a melody kept singing over and over in my spirit:

I lift my eyes until
The skies reveal
Your love
And then as they close
The mountains grow
And grace flows.

God was lifting my eyes to see past earthly things, giving me the eyes of faith. In those moments, His tangible presence surrounded me—not just a theological concept, but a reality I could sense as surely as the Ozark wind on my face.

The Science Project

The Stars Project for Science Fair was then occupying much of my time. I worked in Missouri with Mira, while my brother Tom worked on his part in Israel. The project was taking shape, connecting Israel and the USA through the same constellations that shone over both countries. It felt like a perfect metaphor for my life—finding the constants that remained the same no matter which side of the ocean I called home.

Working with Mira taught me what it meant to have a true study partner—someone who complemented my strengths and helped shore up my weaknesses. She became a real friend, the kind who invited you over for movie nights and study sessions.

Unexpected Grace

February 9, 1998

The frigid February wind cut through my coat as I walked to church that Sunday morning. Grandma had been too sick to drive, so I had bundled up and headed out on foot. My breath was visible in small clouds as I made my way along the familiar route.

I was surprised when Storm pulled over. This was the same guy who had scoffed when I had fallen on the ice and who had walked out when I was singing. Yet here he was, rolling down his window in the bitter cold. "Do you need a lift?" he asked. The simple offer carried unexpected healing. Sometimes grace arrives in the form of someone who has hurt you in the past, but now suddenly shows you kindness.

I sang "Where He Leads Me" by Twila Paris in the evening. This time, the anointing was stronger than the first solo. The Holy Spirit's strength flowed through me, as if He were singing through me. The song was a powerful declaration of complete surrender and willingness to follow God wherever He leads and to listen when He calls. As I sang these words of unwavering commitment and trust, I was so thankful for God's presence during the song. I felt the profound weight of what I was declaring, not just singing about devotion to the Messiah's leading, but making a covenant with my Lord. That's when it's worth taking a step out of the comfort zone because God goes with you, and you're ready to follow wherever He leads.

I was learning that sometimes the most profound spiritual growth happens not in seasons of comfort, but in the dark months when you have to fight for every glimpse of light. The loneliness still ached, but underneath it all was a growing certainty that I was exactly where God wanted me.

Whatever battles lay ahead, I was ready to meet them. Not in my own strength, but wrapped in the knowledge that when the world rejected me, they were really rejecting Him—and He was big enough to handle their rejection and mine too. *Sometimes, in His perfect timing, He would even use those who had rejected me to show unexpected kindness. His love could reach anyone's heart.*

19

Wrestling

◆ ◇ ◆

Wrestling with Distance

February-March 1998

After my grandma's illness, I fell sick myself. I turned to my journal to help me in the struggle. Each line was a battle between the darkness pressing in and the light I was determined to hold onto. The fever made everything feel raw. I understood this was more than just feeling unwell. I felt exposed in a spiritual wrestling match that left me exhausted in body and soul, as the fever stripped away my usual defenses.

In my weakness, His strength became undeniable, and in my darkness, His light became essential. I couldn't rely on my wisdom or understanding. I could only cry out and trust that He heard me. As I finally set down my pen, the fever beginning to break, I realized a profound shift had occurred—I had descended into a valley of shadows and found that even there, especially there, I was not alone. The very darkness that threatened to overwhelm me had become the place where God's love felt most real, most necessary, most true.

Morning would come, as it always did. The fever would lift. The spiritual pressure would ease, and I would return to trying to finish high school. Still, I would carry with me the knowledge that when everything else was stripped away—health, comfort, clarity, strength—what remained was Love itself. Love reaching down into whatever tunnel I found myself in.

The darkness could not hold me, because I was held by One stronger than darkness. Sometimes it takes a fever to burn away everything else so you can see that truth clearly.

The spiritual strength I had gained during that dark February night would be crucial in the weeks ahead. By early March, I had returned to my regular routines, including Sunday mornings at church, which I considered my safest space.

Cry from the Darkness

I feel no one sees or hears,
Cares or understands...
I am frightened in this rage.

I cry out from the darkness
And beg for a light to shine.

If I give up on Jesus,
I will never come out of the dark tunnel.

His Love will reach me today!
Evil forces surround my flame,
Ready to blow as I threaten to run away,

But my chains are too heavy to carry.
With so many directions to turn,
It tears me apart,
And I remain in refrain.

The darkness cannot hold me.

His light breaks through,
His Love reaches down
Into this tunnel where I wait.

I will not give up,
I will not let go,

His Love will reach me today.

Wrestling in the Congregation

March 8, 1998

Sunday mornings at the church had become my refuge. It was a place where I could find community and spiritual nourishment amid the uncertainty of my teenage years. However, March 8th brought a confrontation that would shake my faith in the very community I had hoped would provide sanctuary.

It started innocently enough during Sunday School. I had settled into the familiar circle of chairs, my Bible open, ready to engage with whatever lesson awaited us. When our teacher began speaking about geography and faith, her tone made me uneasy.

"I'm so glad I wasn't born in the Middle East, where the pagans live," she said with the casual certainty of someone who had never questioned her assumptions. The words slapped me, and my blood boiled as I sat there, thinking of Israel—the land where Jesus had walked, where Abraham had received God's promises, where so much of our faith had been born. How could she dismiss an entire region so casually, especially one so central to our spiritual heritage?

When I tried to share some scriptures that might show a different perspective, she scoffed. "Would God bless pagans?" The dismissal in her voice was complete, final. Worse was yet to come when one of the guys in our class piped up, his voice carrying a tone that made me want to disappear into my chair.

"She's always asking for prayer for her parents," he said with obvious annoyance. "Like she's afraid of something." The accusation hung in the air like a physical presence. *Always asking for prayer?* As if staying connected to my family across impossible distances was some weakness, some failure of faith rather than an expression of love.

The unfairness of it overwhelmed me. My prayer requests for my family were born out of love. The were how I stayed connected when everything else felt fragmented. Instead of support from my church community, I was receiving mockery for the very thing that kept my heart tethered to the people who mattered most.

Still, I came back that evening, and during the altar call, instead of going forward, I remained seated and prayed for about an hour. I poured out my burdens and cried to God, releasing my worries and pain. The morning's hurt, the loneliness of being misunderstood, and the weight of loving people across an ocean all spilled out before Him. In that moment of complete vulnerability, I poured out my soul. Poetry arose within me, directed to the One who crowned my heart when the community failed.

Crown of My Heart

Fearful of what you might say?
Why should I fear what I may hear?
I have someone greater who loves me.
Lord, You are the Crown of my Heart!
My crown of flowers are so tart
Without the honey of Your love.

I need Your holiness to pierce
My calloused heart,
And grip me with a love so tender
That I celebrate Your Name forever.

Gift of life You gave,
For me You wanted to save.
The Son of Man's tears fell too
Was unloved
And killed and hung upon a tree.
You love me, I love You.

Will You save me from all this doubt,
That when I'm alone seems to come out?
You are here with me as I walk the halls.
I can feel Your hand on my shoulder,
Guiding me through the floods of man.

Forever, I feel I could stand
With You in Your forever land.
Crown of thorns upon Your head,
Now placed within my heart instead

Crown of Love that won't depart
Crown of mine.
You are here
Guiding me through the storms of life.
Forever I could stand with You in Your eternal light.

Writing those words felt like discovering a secret truth: human rejection could drive me deeper into my acceptance of the divine. When people failed to understand—when they dismissed me, mocked my prayers, and questioned my faith—**God's love became more precious, more necessary, and more real.**

The poetry that flowed from that painful Sunday revealed an essential truth. I didn't need the approval of Sunday school teachers who saw the Middle East as pagan territory, or the understanding of classmates who thought praying for family was weakness. **I had Someone greater who loved me**! Someone who understood what it meant to be unloved and rejected—Someone who had hung upon a tree for loving people, who didn't love Him back.

The crown imagery felt especially significant. While others might see my background as foreign or questionable, God saw it as part of His beautiful plan. **He was the Crown of my Heart, not because I was worthy, but because He chose to make His home there.** The same Jesus who had walked the "pagan" Middle East, who had been rejected by religious people who should have known better, was the One who crowned my heart with His love. As I finished writing and looked around the sanctuary, I understood a profound truth: The building might be called a "church", but our hearts were the real sanctuary—wherever God met me in my pain and turned it into poetry.

That night, I learned something that would sustain me through future rejections: Although human community could fail, and people could be narrow-minded, I belonged to the King. He had given me a picture of my heart as His throne room, crowned with His love. The Middle East might be full of "pagans" in some people's minds, but it was also where my Savior had walked, been rejected, and chosen to die for the very people who didn't understand Him.

His love was far greater, and it was enough to cover all the human love that fell short. The drama at church had stung, but it was nothing compared to what awaited me at track practice later that week.

Wrestling with Identity

March 1998

Track practice that March afternoon started like any other. The spring air held promise of warmer days ahead, and I was finding my rhythm with the team. I was pushing myself through drills and distance runs that were slowly building my endurance. After school, the track became a place where I could clear my head and focus on the simple goal of putting one foot in front of the other.

Still, some days, the world has other plans. I was finishing up my workout when the conversation started among the guys who were practicing shot put nearby. They were showing off with the heavy metal balls, their voices carrying that distinctive teenage bravado that comes with trying to impress each other with displays of strength.

I was gathering my things when footsteps approached. He was confident, built like a bodybuilder, though shorter than me. He'd been one of Rory's friends, but Rory wasn't around now. With a couple of other guys flanking him, he started asking me the question that kept coming up: "Are you Jewish?"

The question made me stand still. Although I had been getting it more often lately. Just the fact that I had been born in Israel seemed to make everyone think I was Jewish. "No," I said, because honestly, I didn't know for certain, but apparently, my answer didn't matter.

As he walked off with his friends, he said cruel words about Jewish people, words designed to wound and diminish an entire group of people I cared about deeply. I turned around sharply. "What did you say?" I demanded, my voice cutting through the afternoon air. However, he was not listening, and my words fell on deaf ears.

Back at Grandma's apartment, I collapsed with my journal, needing to pour out the confusion before it consumed me. That's when the words came:

Grain of Sand

Open up my heart and believe
It is warm inside.
I need You to help me through and lead me,
Until You make me see
How You are really making things to be.

Are You there listening?
Do You care, or am I just whistling into the air?

I know You care,
Even though I might question "if",
But You are still there.

Floods of oceans overwhelm me,
Soak me until my spirit cries out
Into the darkness
For Your comfort to include me.

Give me Your homespun song,
Laughter, not strife.

Your being overwhelms me.
I am but a small grain of sand,
Yet You are King of my heart!

You are King of my heart,
Even when I give a start,
At the little things that happen to tear away
My mixed feelings.

I want oceans, I want joy, give me freedom!
Consume me with Your Love,
Wrap me in Your hug like the stars above.

Send me higher, send me, Lord
To a place where I will wear
Garments of glory, not garments that fade.

You have drawn the blueprints of what I may be,
You have insight, You have wisdom.

So in You I trust
With life itself
Alone, I must.

WRESTLING

Prejudice made me feel like a tiny grain of sand, but I realized that in God's hands even a grain is not powerless. Even the smallest grain of sand is known and held and given a place in the vast ocean of His love.

The track incident would not be the last time I encountered prejudice, but maybe God was teaching me through this experience to pray for His people and stand in the gap when needed. Sometimes the most profound prayers are born not from comfort, but from the raw need to find hope when hatred reveals itself.

Even as I was learning to hold onto God's love in the face of hatred, I was still navigating the everyday complexities of being seen as "different" by my classmates. The art room became another place where this played out in subtler ways.

Wrestling with Being a Stranger

The art room held that particular stillness that comes when students are genuinely absorbed in their work. Clay dust danced in the afternoon sunlight that streamed through tall windows. The familiar scent of earth and water welcomed me like an old friend. I had claimed my usual spot where the natural light was best. The photograph of Mom and me riding on a camel propped against my easel—me as a baby on her lap, Mom wearing a flowing Bedouin dress, the Israeli landscape stretching behind us.

Rory had positioned himself at the easel beside mine with that easy confidence he carried everywhere. He sprawled casually on his stool, long legs stretched out, genuinely focused on his work today. "So that's you?" he asked, nodding toward my reference photo as he mixed colors on his palette.

"Yes, that's me." I dipped my brush in burnt umber, trying to capture the warm shadows of that desert afternoon.

"That's so cool." There was genuine interest in his voice. "I had this crazy dream about pyramids just last week."

I looked up from my canvas, curious despite myself. Dreams fascinated me. "Really? What happened?"

Rory's brush paused mid-stroke, and for a moment his confident facade slipped. "It was weird, man. I was inside one of the pyramids, you know, those narrow passages they have? And there were these... spirits, I guess. Dark things chasing me through the tunnels." He shuddered slightly, then seemed to catch himself and grinned. "Freaked me out so bad I can't even think about caves anymore. Probably saw too many movies or something."

The vulnerability in his admission caught me off guard. This was the Rory who usually acted like nothing bothered him, who seemed to glide through social situations with enviable ease. When discussing his dream, he looked uncertain in a way that made him more relatable.

"I had a strange dream too," I offered quietly, my brush pausing over the canvas. "About schoolgirls being shot. There was this song playing the whole time—'Flood' by Jars of Clay..."

Rory turned his full attention to me now. His expression shifted; he was really listening, not just waiting for his turn to talk. I shared more than I had intended.

"I dreamed about Israeli schoolgirls being shot. Seven of them. And then..." I swallowed hard. "A few hours later, it was on the news. Exactly like I had seen it."

His eyes widened. "Wait, you dreamed about events that actually happened?"

I nodded, the weight of that memory still heavy in my chest. "The Island of Peace massacre. Last March. I woke up crying, and then the news broke."

Rory was quiet for a long moment, studying my face. "That's... wow. That must have been terrifying."

"It was. The flood in the dream was not water," I said, trying to put into words what I had been understanding for almost a year now. "It was this flood of violence and hatred. This crazy world we're living in, where people shoot little girls just because they're Jewish."

He listened without interrupting, and I could see him really trying to understand events that were beyond normal teenage experience. Before I could say more, he was already moving on, but this time to safer ground. "I bet you have other incredible stories, traveling all those places. Most people here have never been anywhere."

There was a tone in the way he said it, not just admiration for my experiences, but fascination with my differentness itself. I was starting to realize that to Rory, and maybe to others, I wasn't just a girl who had traveled. I was foreign to them.

"You're not like anyone else here," he said with genuine wonder. I couldn't tell if that was a compliment or just another way of labeling me as "different."

I started to see that I was not allowed entrance into his fortress because I was a stranger. Even though I was a *Stranger Lovely* to him—someone he admired—I was still not part of the club. I would be able to talk to him through the glass, but not actually participate and get to know him apart from this classroom. Even his compliments felt complicated—special yet isolating, and the conversation started to make me increasingly uncomfortable, though I couldn't quite put my finger on why.

The bell rang, signaling the end of class, and students began rinsing their brushes and covering their work. Rory and I cleaned our brushes in comfortable silence. No invitation to hang out, no suggestion that we continue our conversation later. Just the easy companionship we had developed in this shared space, contained within these four walls.

It was puzzling. Rory enjoyed our discussions, sought out the seat beside mine, and engaged with genuine interest when we talked about dreams, travel, and art.

As I walked to my next class, thoughts of our conversation lingered in my mind, and I tried to untangle the mixed feelings I had. Rory wasn't cruel like Derek, or predatory like some of the other boys who had made me uncomfortable.

As March continued, I found myself caught between the wisdom I was gaining about people's actual characters and the very human desire for romantic connection. It was a tension that would soon lead to an unexpected spiritual breakthrough.

Wrestling with Love

March 1998

There was a restless energy that comes with possibilities and confusion wrapped together like the late winter storms. Storms that couldn't decide whether to fall as snow or rain. I was juggling science projects, track practice, and falling into my familiar pattern of crushing on someone emotionally unavailable. This pattern would ultimately lead me to the most profound spiritual revelation of my young life.

Grandma, in one of her impulsive moods, decided we should cram both Tulsa, Oklahoma, and Saint Louis, Missouri, into one three-day weekend. *What were we thinking?* Nevertheless, there was a sense of wonder about that whirlwind trip—teaching a girl named Elisha to skate in Tulsa, meeting an Olympic speed skater in St. Louis, and reconnecting with a Jewish family I had met in Israel. For a girl who often felt displaced, these moments of connection across states and communities reminded me that the world was both vast and intimate.

Back home, the ordinary rhythms of school life resumed. I was measuring the distance between stars for my science project on the coldest night of the year, zero degrees Fahrenheit.

At track practice, my stubborn independence nearly broke me. When the coaches made us carry other girls on our backs across the gym, I said nothing about the back problems I had had since falling down a hill at age twelve. I carried one girl, then another, and on the second trip, I collapsed, putting holes in the knees of my track pants. I went home and cried out to God, giving Him everything, then showered quickly so Grandma wouldn't see my tears.

Conflicting emotions about Storm returned on a snowy Sunday morning, when a snowball fight broke out. The snowball fight erupted after service when the first one caught my shoulder. Storm stood twenty feet away, grinning, already packing another handful of snow. "You're not going to let me get away with that, are you?" he called out. What followed was five minutes of pure fun—other guys and girls throwing snowballs too, everyone dodging and laughing, circling cars for cover, acting like teenagers instead of the careful versions of ourselves that church usually required. The following week, he was back to being distant.

One particular Sunday, as the Pastor spoke about love and faithfulness, my pen moved across the pages of my journal. I thought about the snowball fight, wondering if it held any significance, but then a shift occurred in the sanctuary around me. Maybe it was the familiar hymns washing over me, their melodies carrying stories of divine love that transcended human confusion. Maybe it was the accumulated weight of all those weeks of feeling spiritually hungry. Or maybe it was simply that human love, even in all its teenage intensity, suddenly seemed small compared to the love I had been experiencing in my relationship with God.

Right there in the pew, with Pastor Fisher's voice washing over me and my heart still tangled up in confusion about Storm, my pen began moving with a different urgency:

Our Love Story

Thank You, Lord, for what You've done,
For sending Jesus, Your only begotten Son.
Thank You, Lord, for the comfort I cannot describe
Which fills me up inside.

I love You, Lord, I know, even alone
You are still there with Your Love on Your throne.
Your heavenly kisses wake me from my slumber,
And I recall You telling me that I am especially Yours.

Speak to me, Lord, for I know
I am ready and waiting.

*Show me what I must do to really **marry You**.*
I'm ready—what comes next in our love story?

WRESTLING

Everything is shadows
Compared to Your Majesty.

Tell me of Yourself in confidence,
Draw me near, I will listen to what You say,
I will not turn away.

You touch me like a heavenly fountain
And build me as one rock upon Your mountain.

You are near, I feel You here!

Come closer inside, give Your abundance
To one who lived with what seems to be dreams.

I love You more than all things created,
Because in You it all began.

It is my time to trust my Lord,
It is my prayer to know You more.

I can't ignore You, Lord,
You are here, I trust You, Lord.

What started as gratitude became much more intimate. I began writing about God's *heavenly kisses* that woke me from slumber, about feeling specially chosen, about being touched *like a heavenly fountain*. The language was romantic, but it wasn't about Storm anymore. It was about the One who had been pursuing me long before I ever noticed.

Then came the line that surprised even me: **Show me what I must do to really marry You. I was asking God to marry me!** Not metaphorically, not as some distant theological concept, but with all the urgency and longing I had been directing toward that complicated boy in the back pew.

I'm ready. What comes next in our love story?

The contrast was startling. One moment, I was analyzing why a teenage boy smiled and turned away; the next, I was proposing to the Creator of the universe. Somehow, it felt like the most natural progression in the world. All that romantic longing hadn't been misdirected. It had been preparation. Every human love, even the confusing and painful ones, had been teaching my heart how to recognize the Love that would never turn away.

I learned that sometimes our earthly longings can awaken us to our heavenly ones. In the Kingdom of God, even our misdirected affections can become teachers, showing us the shape of the love we were truly made for. God calls us to love deeply here, knowing that every human love, however imperfect, is preparing our hearts to recognize His divine love and know Him in deeper ways than we thought possible.

As I finished writing, Storm in the back pew had become just a shadow compared to God's majesty. In that moment, pen in hand and heart wide open, **I became a Bride.**

✦ ◊ ✦

Psalm 42 Revisited

✦ ◊ ✦

As March drew to a close, the poetry flowing from my pen captured the strange duality of my existence—simultaneously rooted in ancient faith and cut off from any geographic home:

WRESTLING

When can I visit my Living God?
Tears as food day and night;
"Where is your God?" people jeer day long.

As I tear open my soul,
I remember this:
Songs of joy in His house
Deep inside, why am I bothered?

I will have faith and praise my Lord.
When my heart quakes
I will remember You

From the Jordan River and the Heights of Hermon
Deep calls to deep in the roar of Your waterfalls
All Your waves and breakers have swept over me.

The Lord sends me His song day and night.
Which is the prayer to the King of my Heart.

The Heights of Zaphon
Are like my great King's city, Mt. Zion.

I feel His presence
As He sits on His mountain,
A holy throne.

He is King over all the earth!

But I feel Him here
More vibrant than churches!

His creation, His land, His people

That's where I stand.

Centuries of people and stories written here;
I can yet see them, and my vision's not so clear.

I am just one girl
Who sees a lovely land.
And wishes I were there right now

Singing in the grasses
Of the mountains,
And praising my King.

This meditation on Psalm 42 revealed the truth I was still learning: Home wasn't just a place, but a presence; belonging wasn't about geography, but about finding where my heart could sing its truest song. Whether in the ancient hills of Israel or the rolling hills of Texas County, Missouri, location mattered less than learning to recognize the Voice that called me forward.

March had been a month of wrestling—with others, myself, and God—but through it all, something was being forged in me that was stronger than circumstances and deeper than my whereabouts.

I was learning to find my voice, not just in poetry but in life. I was learning to stand up for what I believed, even when uncomfortable, and trusting that the God who had brought me this far had plans greater than anything I could yet imagine.

20

Finding My Place in the Rain

✦ ◊ ✦

In the Rain

April arrived in Missouri with the kind of restless energy that comes when winter finally releases its grip, and everything begins to stir with new possibilities. When the afternoon track meet loomed ahead on April 4th, I expected more of the same struggle. The gray clouds gathering overhead seemed to mirror my mood perfectly.

However, sometimes grace shows up in the most unexpected places. The rain started falling as we warmed up—cold drops that made me want to pack it up and head home. I had two events that day—the half mile and shot put—and standing there with water streaming down my face, I felt that familiar urge to quit. Why was I even here? What was the point of running laps and throwing a metal ball in the rain, when I could be warm and dry somewhere else?

Then, something shifted. Maybe it was climbing onto the team bus between events, finding myself laughing with teammates who were just as drenched and miserable as I was. For once, I wasn't the outsider with complicated stories. I was just another runner seeking shelter from the storm. We joked, shared snacks, and complained about the weather together, and suddenly I felt at last a sense of belonging.

When they called the results for shot put, I wasn't even paying attention. Then I heard my name; "Third place." The grin spread across my face before I could stop it. The bronze medal I held felt like proof that staying when I wanted to quit could bring unexpected joy.

At Burger King afterward, I was still damp from the rain but glowing from the victory. Everything felt brighter. The right choice, I realized, wasn't always the easy one. Sometimes it was the choice to stay in the rain, to throw the shot put one more time, to let yourself be part of something even when you felt like an outsider. I wrote that night: *I feel blessed today. I think I have more fun when I read my Bible.*

Track Team Revelations

The week that followed brought its own unexpected breakthrough. Thursday arrived with math tests and tornado watches blanketing the entire state. Rain pounded against the classroom windows as we worked through problems. The weather outside matched the chaos in my head, as I struggled with numbers that seemed to dance around on the page.

After school, our track team gathered for what turned out to be one of those perfect afternoons that make all the individual struggles worthwhile. We ran a half-mile together, then rewarded ourselves with ice cream before playing softball in the drizzle. I had played softball in Spooner, Wisconsin, before we moved to Israel, and I hadn't forgotten how.

The real bonding happened during our team outing later that week. Rory was there, and when he found himself without cash for pizza, I could see his disappointment. I wanted him to be able to participate with everyone else.

"Here," I said. I pulled out my pizza and dangled it in front of his face with theatrical flair. "You know you want it." He protested at first. I kept teasing him, waving the pizza just out of reach until he finally laughed and gave in.

On the bus ride home, Rory started singing country songs, his voice carrying over the bus engine and road noise. For those few miles, with his guard down and his voice lifted in melody, I glimpsed the person he might be when he wasn't calculating social angles.

Then came the **inevitable questioning from other teammates**: "Are you Jewish?" The familiarity of the question made me sigh internally.

I responded with my own question: "What would it matter if I were?" When assured it wouldn't change their opinion of me, I answered that I was a Christian. What followed surprised me—genuine theology questions, real curiosity about faith. I found myself explaining the Trinity using the familiar analogy of an egg: The shell, the white, and the yolk form one complete entity, just as the Father, the Son, and the Holy Spirit form one God.

They listened and asked sincere questions. For the first time in months, I felt like someone with a voice worth hearing rather than just differences worth noticing. It was a small victory, but it felt enormous.

That same week brought another meaningful encounter. A Jewish girl from school gave me a ride home after track practice. I didn't know her, but during the drive, she confided something that felt like a sacred trust: She was afraid to tell anyone she was Jewish and had dyed her hair blonde to fit in. I felt honored that she had chosen to share this with me. I wished I could be her friend, wished that being different wasn't something to be ashamed of.

"I will search for my sheep and look after them. As a shepherd looks after his scattered flock when he is with them so will I look after my sheep. I will rescue them from all the places where they were scattered on a day of clouds and darkness." —Ezekiel 34:11-16

The words felt prophetic—perhaps God was gathering His scattered sheep even in the hallways of a Missouri high school.

Dove of Peace

A dove of peace
Holds a piece
Of a crown of thorny leaves

From the head of Yeshua.
And it drops a branch
Upon my hand.
—I hold—
As thorns prick my hands
A tear flows down my face
As I am reminded of my Lord's grace.

The Art of Recognition

The Frisco League Art Competition arrived like a gift in the middle of academic chaos. I had begged my track coach to let me attend—it was the only art competition all year—and despite feeling sick, I was determined to go. I wore my turquoise dress, the one that made me feel both artistic and presentable, and drove with Grandma through the Missouri countryside to the competition site.

Upon our arrival, I was overwhelmed by the sheer number of entries. Hundreds of students' artworks filled the exhibition space, representing the talent from across the region. Finding my entry of the giant and small oil lamps among all the others felt like looking for a single star in a crowded sky. Finally, I spotted it and next to it—a small card that made my heart skip: first place in my division!

The on-site drawing competition felt like stepping into the unknown. We had to draw from live models, something I had not done much of. I chose to draw the girl model, settling into the focused quiet that comes with putting pencil to paper. As I worked, I worried I had made her too small on the page, but somehow she looked like the real person sitting just a few feet away.

There was one guy there who was leagues beyond the rest of us. He had painted a giant self-portrait that looked so lifelike I couldn't stop staring at it. I wrote later: *I thought he was going to walk out of the picture!* One of my friends from track was completely smitten with him and followed him everywhere at meets. I knew she would be jealous when she found out I had actually talked to him and told him how much I loved his painting.

When time was called, I carefully placed my drawing on the pile with all the others and went to explore the rest of the artwork while we waited for judging. Grandma had gone to visit her cousin, who lived nearby, leaving me to navigate the art competition on my own.

When they called my group for awards, I fully expected to hear the talented guy's name first. He deserved it. They called him and then, to everyone's surprise, including mine, called my name for second place, and the shock nearly knocked me over. *Mr. Evans said that this was great, just what they needed!* I recorded in my journal.

Walking down to get my picture taken and receive my medal felt surreal. Some younger girls from Licking, whom I knew from church and rollerskating, started chanting "Speed Racer! Speed Racer!" and something inside me transformed. *You can't imagine the feeling I felt. It was great!* That moment of recognition, of being celebrated for something I had created with my own hands, felt amazing. I was glad I had come, glad I had risked the vulnerability of trying something new, happy I had skipped the track meet for this chance to discover what I was capable of.

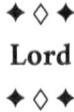

Lord

Lord, You are the Creator of Hearts.
When I hold my breath or
When my heart skips a beat,
You see all things and understand
When I am weak.

Lord, You are a friend of all friends,
You hold out Your hand
Until the very end,
If we were humble,
You might dare to show Your face.

Lord, You are my hero.
You died in my place
To rescue me.
And now forever I can live
With You in Your eternity.

Lord, You are Prince of Peace.

I lay down my sword
And I will fight no more.

Your perfect love casts out all fear,
And forever more Your grace
I hope to share.

Grandma and I went on a road trip to Texas for spring break. I didn't have time to journal, as she had me driving much of the way. We went to Dallas, Texas, where my mom grew up, and Grandma drove me by some of their old neighborhoods. We met up with some of her friends and spent the night with one of them.

We also drove down to the Mexican border to visit my late Grandpa Leo's side of the family. I met my Uncle Cleo, who was my Grandpa's twin, and his wife. The trip was a whirlwind and went by incredibly fast as we drove over 1,000 miles one way from the Ozarks to McAllen, Texas. It was interesting to meet my Grandpa's side of the family, whom I had never met before.

Another poem I wrote during this season:

MY TIME TO TRUST

Tell of Yourself in confidence.
Draw me near,
I will listen to what You say.
I will not turn away.
You touch me like a heavenly fountain
And build me as one rock upon Your mountain.

You are near, I feel You here.
Come closer inside.
Give Your wholeness
To one who lives with what feels like just dreams.
I love You more than all things created.
It's my time to trust my Lord;
It's my prayer to know You more.
I can't ignore You Lord.
You are here, I trust You Lord.

21

Called Aside

✦◇✦

Matchmakers

The afternoon sunlight streamed through the art room windows as I worked on my drawing, carefully shading with my pencil. I was absorbed in getting the details right when Rory's friends approached with purposeful strides.

"Hey," one of them said, pulling up a chair. The others formed a circle around me. I glanced toward the door—Rory wasn't with them. "We need to talk to you about something," another announced. "It's about Rory." I set down my pencil, uncertain what was coming. "Okay…"

"He's too shy to ask you himself, but do you want to be his girlfriend?" the first one continued. "We can totally hook you guys up."

I looked at them, trying to process the question. What did "hook up" even mean? I felt frozen between not wanting to seem rude and not understanding what they were proposing. "I'm shy too," I said. "He should talk to me."

They exchanged glances, waiting for more enthusiasm that wasn't coming. "Come on, we can make this happen for you guys!"

I didn't agree or disagree, just listened. Although I was attracted to Rory, something about this arrangement felt wrong—like a deal I didn't understand.

They kept talking, but their voices became a blur. I gave noncommittal responses, hoping they would give up. My disinterest must have been obvious because after a few minutes, they drifted away, clearly disappointed.

When they were gone, I sat staring at my half-finished drawing. The whole interaction had left me confused. Why did this approach to relationships feel so foreign to me, even when it involved someone I actually liked?

As the school year wound down, this scene became representative of how things with Rory were developing—always mediated through other people, warm with potential but never quite reaching definition.

I was attracted to him, but spiritually, we were walking at different paces. I was learning that faith didn't eliminate normal teenage emotions—it just made them more complicated. How do you honor God while also figuring out how to be human? What I valued most was his observation that I was "different—but it's a good different." It troubled me because I wanted to belong, and for me, being different meant you did not belong.

Princess

During this season of uncertainty, a poem emerged that captured where I believed true romance should be grounded:

CALLED ASIDE

Princess, is your prince far
Or somewhere near to your heart?
Do you rejoice with flute and tambourine
Or bang your head on walls
With a drum's rhythmic beat?

Have you found your Prince of Peace?
He will give you mighty strength
To stand in the world.
He has eternity written on our hearts.

Draw this Prince close to your heart,
His faithfulness outshines every knight.
He is the Commander and Captain of our universe.
Honor Him with all your heart,
He will heal what fell apart.

So, Princess, search no more in vain—
Your Prince of Peace awaits.
He'll turn your sorrow into song
And make your broken heart whole.

The question "Princess, is your Prince far?" wasn't about any potential boyfriend. It was about recognizing that the deepest longing of my heart was for the Prince of Peace, whose faithfulness outshines every earthly knight, whose love would make my broken heart whole.

A Friend Defends

The prejudiced comments from one of the teachers stung particularly sharply. When she said, "We don't love Jews," I felt it personally, being the only person in the room who was from Israel.

Thank God for friends like Britney: "We can't help it if we love Jews!" Britney had looked me in the eye and spoken out. She reminded me I wasn't completely alone in this battle against prejudice.

The Watchman's Daughter

This particular month brought news that made everything feel unstable. "During the next thirty days, we are going to decide if we are going to quit the radio station," Mom told me. The words hit like stones breaking the stillness of water, sending ripples of uncertainty through everything I was building in Missouri.

My father was doing the work of many. Here I was, consumed with track meets and art competitions, while my parents faced decisions that could scatter our family across continents. I felt partly to blame because I wasn't there to help them. The uncertainty made everything else feel shaky.

> I wrote: *So many predicaments in life! Life gets so messed up with wrong choices. I have everything planned out to finish high school here, but is it the right thing? Is there a better way? Is there a way I could finish high school closer to my family?*

The Prom I Missed

Prom weekend arrived with all the excitement and anticipation that mark such milestones in teenage life. However, while my classmates were getting ready for corsages and dancing, I found myself headed to Springfield with Grandma. She didn't believe in dancing, so prom wasn't an option for me.

Instead of feeling sorry for myself, I chose to embrace the adventure of exploring a bigger city. We went to the mall and bookstores, shopping for summer clothes and shoes. I felt excited about navigating the bustling shops and wide corridors of urban retail. The stores were so different from the quiet, familiar rhythm of small-town life.

The next morning brought a visit to one of the biggest congregations I had ever seen. Walking into a Sunday school classroom with over fifty people felt overwhelming after the intimate gatherings I was used to. I stayed in the back, trying to make myself invisible, but the speaker noticed and asked everyone to move forward. I somehow ended up between two teenage guys in suits. I felt like I was at prom, rather than at church, with everyone dressed up. It was very impressive, but a bit strange after living in Israel, where people mostly wore suits to weddings, if that, and in the rural Ozarks, where most of the guys dressed like cowboys.

In a way, this formal church service became my version of prom—everyone dressed up, a sense of ceremony and importance, and the feeling of being part of something bigger than myself. There was something about the size and formality that made the connection harder to feel, although the teaching was solid and the music energized. It wasn't the type of evening my classmates had, but it was uniquely mine.

As April progressed, the verses that flowed from my pen showed the ongoing spiritual battle between earthly longings and divine calling:

The Beggar's Seat

I need You near, my brain is pain.
Come, heal my tissues,
Each and all my issues.

I am in the mire of complacency.

Don't you remember how in this beggar's seat,
I asked you to stay?

To You Alone

I am lost in a walking mist of skeletons
Living throughout this air.
Society doesn't care.

Lord, will you save me?

Free my afflicted brain.
I feel the train chugging back and forth,
It is ticking now, about to explode.

Where do I go when anxious?
To You alone.

CALLED ASIDE

Son Shine

Son shine, pray Your rays reach my soul
And body shell where solar energy may dwell.

Your warmth melts the frost from my heart,
Your breath stirs the stillness in my chest.

You are center of our galaxy
And creator of infinite cosmos.

The universe hums Your sacred name,
Colors bloom where You have walked.

Cleanse me with Your shine
No eclipse, for I will miss
The shine that gives me strength through time.

Let no shadow fall between us,
For in darkness I am lost
Your light is my life, Your presence my compass.

Son shine, You are mine,

My spirit soars on wings You've given,
Peace floods every anxious corner.

I'll praise You forever.

Through every dawn You give,
Through every breath You sustain,
Through the thunder that speaks Your name,

I will sing of Your radiance.
I will praise You forever.

The cosmic imagery reflected my growing understanding that whatever struggles I faced on earth were part of a much larger story, one in which divine love was the central force holding everything together.

Sunday Encouraging Words

Sunday morning at church, I received prayer at the altar call. When I got home that afternoon, my neighbor, Mrs. Chambers, delivered a message she felt was a word of encouragement for me: ***I have called her aside to preserve her for the work I have called her to do.***

Reading those words, I felt chosen, set apart for something important, even if I couldn't see what it was yet. I wrote this in my journal as my reply:

> *He has chosen me, and I will obey whatever He may say. For He holds my life's strings and knows how to move them or when they shall be cut. So I will move in His direction, follow His Son beams, and glow with His light, for I will be entwined with His vines wrapped around mine. You have taken the time for me when You have the universe to oversee! I am touched by Your words. Your love note, I will treasure forever.*

April's End

April 1998 was a month of holding contradictions. I was learning that faith doesn't eliminate complexity—it gives you somewhere to take it. Every night, I brought my questions and longings to God.

I was beginning to understand that home wasn't just a place, but a presence; that belonging wasn't just about geography, but about finding where your heart could sing its truest song.

Whether that song would ultimately be sung in the ancient hills of Israel or the rolling hills of the Ozarks mattered less than learning to recognize the Voice that called me forward into whatever future God was writing.

April had been a month of preparation, though I didn't know it yet. The Director of Music was composing something beautiful from all the scattered notes of my displacement. Even when I couldn't yet hear the full melody, I was learning to trust the Composer.

22

Stranger Lovely

✦ ◊ ✦

The Subconscious Prophecy

It was 1998 when the words first poured from my pen, raw and unpolished, emerging from somewhere deeper than conscious thought. I had been living at my grandmother's home in Missouri, navigating the confusion of displacement and belonging. Twenty-seven years later, when I found it again, the poem felt strange. I had no idea my subconscious had written something that would map the landscape of my entire life.

The revelation started with Rory. "I like you because you're different," he said, his words carrying both attraction and distance. "It's a good different." Yet apparently too different, considering that he never invited me to hang out with his friends or included me in the inner circle of his social world. I was fascinating enough to observe, but too foreign to fully embrace.

When I arrived at the Missouri high school, someone immediately renamed me "Israel"—erasing both my American identity and my actual name in one casual stroke. Suddenly, I carried not just my own story but the weight of every prejudice and assumption people held about a place where I'd been born but had also left behind. It was easier for them to put me in a box labeled "Israel" than to grapple with the complexity of who I actually was.

"You're lovely," they would say, "but you're not one of us." The pattern was forming, though I didn't yet have words for it. I was *Stranger Lovely*, perpetually kept at a distance, celebrated for my difference while being excluded because of it.

What I thought was a teenage phase turned out to be a lifelong calling. As I grew older and traveled the world, the pattern repeated itself in culture after culture, country after country. **Fortress Thinking** existed everywhere, sophisticated systems of inclusion that were, in fact, elaborate forms of exclusion.

Each community had its own version of "You're lovely, but…" The accents changed, the languages shifted, the cultural contexts varied, but the fundamental dynamic remained the same. I was the stranger carrying something they could appreciate but not quite understand, offering perspectives they valued but couldn't quite trust. I was a stranger bringing gifts; they celebrated, but couldn't quite receive without reservation.

Of all the fortresses that kept me at arm's length, none wounded more deeply than when this pattern invaded my most intimate spiritual expression: my *Bridal Love Poetry* for *Yeshua*, those sacred verses that flowed from my heart's communion with God.

In my late twenties, I spoke at a women's meeting on the Bride of Messiah. It was a vulnerable season for me. A friend I had known for years came, heard my message, and then spent the night at my home. After hearing my message on being the Bride of Messiah, she said I wanted to get married too much, and I should just never marry and be like a nun. I felt she was mocking me and the message I had given. The betrayal cut deeper because she had repeatedly invited me on family outings, making me feel I belonged with them, only to tell me I was too spiritual to belong anywhere on earth through marriage.

In that one conversation, my hopes were crushed for earthly love, and my Bridal Message, previously burning in my heart for Messiah, was mocked. I was left with a double wound—being told my spiritual calling disqualified me from human love while that same calling was dismissed as foolish. This left me paralyzed with grief.

I was not one of them. I was on the outside, a *Stranger Lovely*. Whatever the reason, I felt the pain of not being welcomed in the Fortresses of Love. When I was attacked for these tender expressions, something essential in me died that day. How can you argue with someone who insults you by praising you? I wasn't sure if I wanted to be celibate. Paralysis and sadness came over me. The *Song of Songs* lay dormant, only coming out to sing once in a great while. Those daily walks and talks in the garden grew less and less. As I lost hope and encountered a final blow that took my joy and First Love.

I became convinced that my deepest creative and spiritual gifts were evidence of something wrong with me. **This is where displacement became internalized shame. Where exclusion from fortresses became exclusion from my own voice, my own desire, and my own poetry. The walls I'd been standing outside of for years, I started building them inside myself. The poet in me was silenced.**

Within that year of being told I was too obsessed with marriage, I went to a monastery on retreat and told God I would be willing to live celibate if He desired. Three months later, He sent someone on earth to love me. Still, even though I had found my earthly love, my heart had been wounded by this lie of the enemy against the Bridal Love relationship with Jesus that I had discovered in my teenage years. I still had a deception rooted in my heart that made me bury the expression of Bridal Love Poetry and my love for God as a Bridegroom.

The poet in me was silenced by "Fortress Thinking." This mindset made the deep romantic and longing heart God had given me—the heart He had spoken to through the *Song of Songs*—seem like a barrier to belonging. I tried to bury this part of myself to avoid facing the pain of any more rejection. The poetry that had once flowed became scattered drops, then long seasons of creative drought. I had learned to accommodate, to give in, to accept whatever names and limitations others assigned to me, because I wanted to be agreeable, to belong somewhere, and to find a fortress that would finally let me in.

While writing this memoir in 2025, I sat decades removed from that teenage girl scribbling verses in the Ozarks. I came across the old "Fortress" poem and nearly threw it away—viewing it as just another piece of youthful melancholy that felt too obscure to place anywhere. However, something made me pause. I barely remembered writing it. The words were confused, fragmented. I started rewriting, trying to remember what I'd meant all those years ago.

Fortress built strong and thorny must not emit stranger lovely... What was I trying to say? Was "emit" even the right word? My dyslexia had always made writing challenging.

I began working through it: *I am a stranger... the fortress won't let me in... they erase me... but then they ask if I'm the one who's locked up...*

The poem became clear:
Stranger Lovely

> *Fortress built strong and thorny*
> *Must not **admit** "Stranger Lovely".*

It is Eraser that wipes me down
And tears me apart until I frown.
Until I fade, until I'm gone.
Then you ask: "Why are you so closed off?
Are you built strong around,
So locked deep you don't look around?
Why won't you let us in?"
As if I built the walls.
As if I chose to stand outside.

Suddenly, it clicked, and I started crying. My seventeen-year-old self had captured something I was only now fully understanding. She saw the entire system: *The fortress excludes you. Their exclusion erases you. Then they blame YOU for being closed off*—**as if you built the walls, as if you chose to stand outside.**

This wasn't random teenage poetry. My younger self had captured, in those simple lines, the entire trajectory of my life—the pattern that would repeat across continents and cultures. Not every exclusion has spiritual significance, but decades-long patterns targeting my faith and calling deserved consideration.

The enemy's plan was there in black and white: erase identity, tear me apart, exclude me, make me believe I am alone, and make me feel stressed to be included in the wrong fortresses.

The Enemy's Strategy Revealed

I could finally see how the enemy works:
He calls us lovely

While ensuring we remain strangers,
Praises our uniqueness
While using it to justify our exclusion.
He celebrates our gifts
While withholding
The very platforms
Where those gifts could flourish.

"You're too Lovely for that blessing," he hisses repeatedly.
"You're too different for ordinary happiness," he keeps insisting.
"You're too special for common grace."

Or he switches tactics:

"You're too broken to make a difference.
Not perfect enough to make an impact.
Not good enough to matter.
Not smart enough to handle this.
Not brave enough and not rich enough."

The lies go on and on—
The same crushing message
That we are strangers and not enough to be included,
Just delivered with different words and tactics each time.
This is not God's voice.

The most insidious part is
How he makes us
Feel
Utterly alone
In our exclusion,
Like Elijah, convinced he was the only prophet left
When God had actually preserved seven thousand others.

The enemy wants us to believe:

We're the only ones standing outside the Fortress Walls,
The only ones who don't quite fit,
The only ones carrying
This particular kind of beautiful strangeness.

It's a sophisticated deception
That keeps us chasing after the *Wrong Fortresses.*
We exhaust ourselves in our attempts to gain admission
To institutions that can celebrate us but never truly embrace us.
We beg for acceptance from systems
Designed to keep us on the outside, looking In.

The Truth Is,
God has placed a whole army of us:
Believers, Prophets, and Artists
Scattered across the landscape,
Each thinking they're alone in their otherness.

The Biblical Fortress

> *"Return to your fortress, you prisoners of hope; even now I announce that I will restore twice as much to you."*—**Zechariah 9:12**

The Fortress of Hope, not built by human hands, not governed by human limitations, not subject to the prejudices and fears that construct earthly institutions. This fortress specializes in gathering the displaced, the misunderstood, the ones who don't quite fit anywhere else.

In God's fortress, being *Stranger Lovely* isn't a barrier to blessing; it's a qualification for it. The very strangeness that keeps us outside human walls makes us ideally suited for divine purposes. The *distinction* that earthly fortresses admire but cannot embrace becomes the offering we bring to the King, who delights in our uniqueness.

As I revisited these wounds while writing this memoir, something broke open. The tears weren't just grief—they were rage. Holy, righteous rage at what had been stolen. Underneath the rage was something else: the poet, still alive, and demanding to be heard.

Out of me welled up a shout as I faced the accuser of the brethren, the one who had shamed me for far too long:

Resurrection

You locked the door, You hid the key,
You took away Love, You took away ME,
You erased me,
You took away poetry,
You paralyzed me.

But now is not the time,
Today is not the day
For you to steal from me!

I am opening the door to poetry again.
I am knocking on the door of Heaven.
Because I may have had dreams stolen from me,
But I know the Poet of Dreams
Who will forever romance me!

He opened the door when you would not let me in.
He opened the door and called me more than a friend.
He has never left me, or forsaken me.

He loved even when
The song was frozen on my lips
And my heart was broken
By the lies the enemy hissed.

Bridal Love for my Shepherd King
Is holy, pure and an amazing thing.

You made me think that loving God
Meant human love was sin,
But He who made both heaven and earth
Invites both lovers in.

God redeemed me by His grace
Then gave me human love as well,
The son of Mountains, not captivity.

I may not be where I thought I would be,
I may not sing what I thought I would sing.
I may not know what I thought I would know.

But I am lovely, I am known, I am worthy, not alone.

The shame I carried was not mine.
I believed that something was wrong
With the poet in me,
For wanting Bridal Love in poetry.
Now I see the lie and I break free.

You silenced my poetry long ago,
*But **Resurrection** comes with dawn.*

The Poet of Dreams
Has made my heart sing once more.

Writing this memoir has been a gift of resurrection from God to my soul. As I've revisited these old wounds, these patterns of exclusion, these moments of recognition, something beautiful has been happening. The creative flow that was stopped by lies is beginning again. The *Bridal Love Poetry* that was mocked is finding its voice again. The songs that were silenced are learning new melodies.

God never stops pursuing us with His love, chasing us through the mountains and valleys of life. He longs for all our hearts. As Psalms 42 speaks of: *"deep that calls to deep,"* so does God also long for us in that *deep that calls to deep.*

The most important thing that got me through everything was a very real understanding that I belonged to my Beloved, and He belonged to me. Yet somehow the enemy's lies still tried to silence who God created me to be. However, God can resurrect the dreamers to dream and the singers to sing.

God is bringing me back with His healing and His love, reminding me of moments when He sang over me, walked with me in the garden, led me through valleys of despair, and brought me to His **Fortress of Hope**, where I could receive faith to climb mountains and leap over hills by the power of His will.

The fortress walls of this world may never fully open to me. That's exactly what qualifies me to serve those standing outside other walls, carrying their own stories of displacement, their songs of longing, and their beautiful strangeness that the world isn't quite ready to embrace.

The Eternal Purpose

God uses our displacement to teach us truths about belonging. He shows us that earthly fortresses, no matter how beautiful or well-intentioned, can never satisfy the longing for home that He has placed in our hearts.

We are *Stranger Lovely* by divine design, prepared for work that requires someone who understands exclusion intimately enough to include others radically. We become bridges between worlds, translators of experiences that can only be understood by those who have endured this suffering.

The pain of exclusion is real. So is the privilege of perspective. The loneliness of displacement is genuine. So is the freedom that comes from not being bound by any single fortress's limitations.

A Word for Fellow Strangers

If you, too, have felt the *pain of exclusion;*
If you, too, have had your *identity erased;*
If you, too, have felt the s*ilence of dreams—*
Take heart.

You have a *Heavenly Fortress* waiting for you,
And you are on a journey to that place.
God can bring that fortress down
And surround you with *songs of deliverance.*

When you call His name,
He will come running.

He will lift you up
And bring you to high places.

The One who romanced me
Can romance you.
He knows the *deep within the deep* of your heart.
He waits to bring you the oil of joy.

Call on His name.
Wait on Him.
Pour out your soul.

First will come the lament.
Then will come the praise.
Then will come the joy and freedom
Of learning to trust His name.

The Invitation Home

God gathers the *scattered*,
The *displaced*,
The ones who were told:

"Too lovely for ordinary blessing."
"Too different for common grace."
"Too strange for simple acceptance."

But in His fortress, there are no strangers—
Only family coming home.

In His kingdom, difference is not a barrier
But a part of His beautiful tapestry.
In His presence,

The *silenced songs* can sing again.
The *deferred dreams* can take flight.

You are not a *Stranger Lovely* by accident,
But by *divine appointment.*
In God's kingdom,
That makes you exactly who He designed you to be.

Come home, beautiful stranger.
Your fortress is waiting.

Praying for you, dear friend,
That you will know
   joy
That never ends.

23

The Last Days of School

✦ ◇ ✦

The Weight of Endings

In mid-May 1998, the final week of school unfolded with the bittersweet intensity that marks all endings. The hallways buzzed with the particular energy of teenagers sensing freedom ahead. I walked through the high school knowing I would return in the fall, but everything felt different—more precious, more temporary.

The weight of completing something significant pressed against my chest as I moved between classes. After months of learning to navigate the social circles that governed teenage life, I had finally found my rhythm. I had managed to withstand attacks. I refused to let them make me ashamed of my connection to Israel or the Jewish people. This struggle over identity had become my defining battle. Even if I didn't have Jewish heritage, I would defend the Jewish people. I would defend Israel.

I had found good friends. Even the academic struggles that had seemed insurmountable in September now felt manageable, conquered through sheer determination.

Getting my driver's license the week before school ended felt like checking off one of my biggest American dreams. I'd come to the US with a short list of things I absolutely had to do, and this was right at the top of my agenda—tangible proof that I was really making it here. When I finally got it, it felt like the perfect punctuation mark on my first year, mission accomplished. Saturday's track meet had been our last of the season. I still had the bronze medal in my backpack.

Our choir's performance at graduation earlier that week had felt like a milestone. Standing on the gymnasium stage, singing "From a Distance" and "My Heart Will Go On," I felt a sense of belonging. I felt it most when singing, regardless of where I was.

I went to Jason's graduation party, someone I knew from church and sports. I then went to Aunt Margie's to congratulate my cousin, another graduate heading into an uncertain but hopeful future. These rituals of completion felt special, marking the passage of time and shared experiences that had slowly woven me into the fabric of this community.

Still, even as I celebrated with others, my mind kept returning to the distance that separated me from my real family. The phone calls from Israel had been weighing on me more heavily as the school year drew to a close. Dad's birthday had passed while I was thousands of miles away. The poem I had written for him revealed how deeply I understood both his calling and the cost of our separation. That night, I wrote in my journal:

Telescope Eyes

Dad, you are wise—this I recognize.
I see in you a philosopher wrestling with life's deepest questions.
Teacher, kind in your quiet way, working daily to provide.

THE LAST DAYS OF SCHOOL

Your quest burns unique and bright—
To spread light throughout the Middle East,
A beacon thin and tall,
You stand strong when kingdoms fall.

A watchman pacing the ancient walls,
You see the world through telescope eyes.
A prince within your fortress, strong and sure,
People see your steady stature and wonder at your inner peace.

What keeps you going? What holy fire?
A spirit inside, sacred and sweet,
Gives you strength for impossible feats.

Tender are your feet, always walking down the road
To make way for our Returning Lord.

I stumble as I run to catch your rhythmic stride,
"Slower," I whisper, but faster I press to match your steps.

I wish you could be near—
It has been so hard to understand the mysteries in your mind.

But this truth remains forever:
I will always love you.

The Athletes' Banquet

One highlight of the school year was the athletic banquet. When the cross-country coach reached the track-and-field presentations, I walked forward with my teammates, expecting the routine handshake and letter that marked the end of my first season of American high school athletics. What I hadn't expected was to become the evening's entertainment.

"Now, I have to tell you folks about this young lady here," Coach announced, his voice carrying across the room with obvious relish. "This one came into my office at the beginning of the year, saying she was a transfer student. I asked from where, and she says, 'Israel.' I said, 'Israel?!' She says, 'Yes, just north of Egypt.' I said, 'Yes, I know where it is—just north of Egypt!'"

The laughter rippled through the crowd, and I felt my cheeks begin to burn. This was my story being transformed into performance art. My identity was reduced to a geographical curiosity that amused people who had never questioned their sense of belonging.

"So I asked if she was involved with any athletic programs there," Coach continued, warming to his theme and embellishing details that made the story more entertaining than our original conversation had been. "She said, 'Only ice skating.' I said, 'Ice skating in Israel?! I thought it was all desert!' She said 'No, they have a rink.'" More laughter.

I stood frozen in the spotlight, understanding with painful clarity that this was precisely what inclusion had always meant in these circles—a chance to be the exotic centerpiece. An interesting anomaly that proved how open-minded and worldly they were, while I was never quite seen as a whole person with my own hopes and struggles.

The story grew in the telling, as such stories do. Coach described trying to decipher my Hebrew transcripts ("All I could see was an upside-down candlestick, but I guessed it could stand for a C"), his phone conversation with administrators who couldn't believe there was ice skating in Israel, and the comedy of misunderstanding that had nearly prevented my acceptance to the team. Each detail was carefully crafted and polished for maximum entertainment value—it transformed my experience into theatrics for the amusement of the crowd.

I wrote later that evening: *My cheeks were red for twenty-five minutes after that!* Even as I tried to focus on the positive—the recognition, the inclusion, the promise of next year—something more profound was stirring within me. The applause felt hollow, the laughter cruel. I was being celebrated, but for all the wrong reasons. Not for my determination in learning a new sport. I was being celebrated for being exotic—for being different. It was the kind of story that makes comfortable people feel good about their tolerance.

Standing there in the lights, receiving recognition that felt simultaneously affirming and diminishing, **I began to understand something crucial about the geography of belonging. I could earn my place through achievement, prove my worth through performance, and even become beloved for my uniqueness. However, as long as I remained The Girl from Israel, The Ice Skater from the Desert, The Interesting Exception, I would never be allowed to be myself.**

The Weight of Distant Burdens

Tension was building through my mother's increasingly concerned emails. The success I was finding in Missouri had caught her attention, but so had the challenges.

I wrote in my journal:

> *This morning, when I checked my email, I felt burdened because Mom doesn't think I should come back to Missouri next year. Like any concerned mother with her daughter so far away, she was worried about the challenges I had described and wanted me closer to home.*

The possibility of not returning hit harder than expected. Just as I was finding my voice and succeeding, the voices of family concern whispered changes I couldn't understand.

In my journal, I struggled with the question of how long God was going to take to call me aside here in Missouri, and when I would be ready to go back to Israel:

> *I want to stay in God's will. He told me, "I have called you aside to preserve you for the work I have called you to do." I think He wants me here for a while, but I must listen closely for when He says to move.*

I had become someone who sought divine guidance rather than personal comfort. I was learning to think in terms of calling rather than convenience, purpose rather than preference.

Derek and Rory

During that last week of school, I navigated my classes with the familiar rhythm of someone who had learned to move through these halls with confidence. Between classes, I walked down the hallway with my friend Erin. As we passed Rory and Derek, I was only dimly aware of their presence. I didn't hear the comment. I didn't witness the exchange that triggered what came next.

I didn't even realize anything had happened until the shouting started behind us. When I turned, the hallway had already split wide open into chaos—Rory and Derek tangled in fists and fury, lockers rattling as people rushed to get a better view.

My heart pounded as I hurried back toward the commotion, trying to make sense of it. I asked the nearest person what was going on. She looked me in the eyes before answering, "It was about you."

The words didn't register at first. *About me?* I stood there, frozen, trying to catch up with what she meant. The crowd surged, the fight raged, and I felt suspended outside of it all, caught between disbelief and recognition. Then I realized: Rory wasn't just fighting Derek—he was fighting for me!

That night, I wrote in my journal: *Rory got in a fight with Derek today, and I think it was about me!!!* The exclamation points captured both my shock and my dawning understanding of what had transpired. I had walked by with Erin, unaware, and then chaos broke out. Derek must have said something that ticked Rory off, because they fought and both got suspended.

Their final day of school held unexpected consequences. Derek had crossed the line with his prejudice against people from Israel, delivered with that casual malice I recognized. Whatever the specific trigger, it shattered something in Rory, transforming him from a silent observer to an active defender. The same boy who had spent the year working with me in art class and running with me at track suddenly found his voice. He had courage when it mattered most, standing up against Derek.

The Quiet Goodbye

After the fight—after Rory's fists answered Derek's cruelty—the hallways buzzed with electricity. Rory was sent to the principal's office.

Later that day, he came to collect his things from the art room. The steady determination in his movements felt like the aftermath of a storm; everything had settled. He gathered his supplies with deliberate care, then approached me with controlled intensity.

"See you next year," he said. A farewell delivered with confidence. This wasn't casual. These were the last words of someone who had just shattered his carefully maintained boundaries for someone he believed was worth defending. This boy, who had spent two months unable to ask me out directly, had somehow found the courage to defend me. He had confronted the fortress mentality of exclusion and fought for someone he believed in. That took guts. He didn't explain the fight. He didn't make grand speeches about standing up to bullies. He didn't turn it into drama or romance. He offered the simple promise of return.

I treasured those words more than any dramatic declaration. The promise of seeing him next year seemed personal between us. The boy who defended me waited until the final day—almost too late for me to see his act of courage. Now he was leaving, expecting me to return next year. I didn't even know if I would.

In those final moments of the school year, Rory had abandoned his safe anonymity to protect what was right. The real tragedy wasn't just that our paths would diverge; it was that this display of moral courage came just as my story was about to take a turn that would make reunion impossible.

"See you next year" became the last echo of a year that ended with a bang—proof that someone had chosen action.

What I didn't know was that next year would never come as expected. Within days, everything would change in ways that made high school conflicts seem like ancient history. This goodbye would be the last conversation we would ever have.

Sometimes God places warriors in our lives for one defining moment—when they choose to sacrifice their comfort to defend others. Rory's willingness to confront the fortress mentality represented something larger than teenage drama. He demonstrated the beautiful act of choosing principle over popularity and comfort to protect the vulnerable.

The girl who had arrived in Licking as a stranger was disappearing, replaced by someone learning to trust God even when she couldn't see the complete story. The transformation wasn't complete—that would require the shattering and rebuilding that lay ahead—but the foundation was solid. Perhaps that was the mercy of limited vision—that we are only given strength for today's challenges, only shown the next step, and only asked to trust God one day at a time.

24

Resistance

✦ ◊ ✦

The Geography of Calling

May 1998

Mom had been calling me for weeks. 'Something amazing is happening in the north,' she told me. She went on to explain an Arab village on Israel's northern border that was remarkably open to the gospel. She wanted me to accompany her to share the message of Jesus with the people.

I held the phone closer, trying to bridge the thousands of miles between us. Mom's enthusiasm was infectious, but something in me recoiled from where I sensed this conversation was headed. "I've been praying about this for weeks," she continued, "and I really feel like God wants you to come with me this summer. To help with the ministry there. These people need to hear the Gospel, and I think you could really connect with some of the younger ones."

As the departure date approached, Mom's invitations became more frequent. "There's this one family," she told me during one of our evening calls, "the father works construction. He's been asking such deep questions about Jesus. His teenage daughter speaks some English, and I really think you could connect with her. She needs to hear from someone closer to her age."

I listened with genuine curiosity about these people. Another part of me recoiled from the idea of active door-to-door outreach work, from the vulnerability of sharing something so personal with strangers who might reject both the message and the messenger. I knew my mom could talk to anyone, anywhere, and I didn't think that was my cup of tea. "I don't know, Mom," I said finally. "That's not really my thing. I mean, faith sharing isn't my gift." I remembered scoffing to myself when she excitedly told me she was looking forward to bringing me to the village with her. I had no idea what she was talking about. I had done some door-to-door campaigning against a casino going up in our town in Wisconsin when I was little. However, this was something else, definitely out of my comfort zone, and not on my high school agenda.

What I didn't understand yet was that God was preparing to shatter my comfortable categories about spiritual commitment, revealing depths of calling that could only be accessed through valleys I had never walked.

The Dream of Warning

Two days before everything changed, the dream came with the weight of a warning. I woke up gasping, drenched in sweat. In the dream, I had encountered a spiritual darkness. An evil presence stomped on my head, the weight of it crushing and deliberate, designed to break something essential in my spirit. The violence was personal, targeted, as if forces I couldn't see were positioning themselves for battle.

I should have recognized this as a divine warning and responded with prayer and fasting. Instead, I reached for my journal and wrote it down. *I had a nightmare about a demon attacking me. It was very vivid. It was probably just nerves about the trip.*

I closed the journal and went about making coffee, as if I'd just recorded the weather. As I prayed in the predawn darkness, fragments of understanding began to emerge. Something was coming.

The Heart's Geography

During those final days in Missouri, I walked through familiar places with the heightened awareness that comes with knowing something is ending. Beneath the sadness of leaving, something unexpected stirred—I was beginning to feel a quiet excitement about returning to Israel. The angry, bitter girl who had fled a year earlier was slowly being replaced by someone who carried genuine affection for the land that had shaped her.

In my bedroom, I had lined the top of the walls with postcards and photos from Israel, a border circling the room like a frame of home. Surrounded by those images, I prayed, cried, and wrote poems through the long months. Mount Hermon, crowned with snow, the blue-green waters of the Sea of Galilee, the ancient stones of Jerusalem—they had kept their watch over me, reminding me that beauty still lived in the complexities of the Middle East.

Somewhere in those tears and prayers, God changed my heart. The bitterness of teenage pain gave way to love—love for the country my parents had brought me back to when I was thirteen. Healing had begun, and a seed of belonging was planted that would follow me. I knew Israel was where I was called to be. I just didn't yet see God's timeline.

The Territory of Preparation

As my departure approached, every interaction carried the weight of a potential goodbye. I wondered if three months of family, ministry, and ancient landscapes would change me? Would the stirring call in my heart require leaving behind not just Missouri, but the version of myself who had found a sense of belonging there?

That night, I lay awake listening to the sounds that had become the soundtrack of my healing—traffic on Highway 63, the settling of Grandma's building, the familiar quiet that had provided sanctuary. I just wanted to hold onto these last precious hours in the little town that had become my refuge. The dream lingered at the edges of my consciousness like an unwelcome visitor, but I kept pushing it away. I didn't want to fight demons or prepare for warfare.

Soon, I would board a plane back to the family I'd been missing and the land calling me forward. The dream felt like both a warning and a preparation. I wasn't the same girl who had fled Israel a year ago. Missouri had been my monastery, preparing me for work I was still learning to embrace.

My heart wasn't right, and somewhere deep down, I knew it. Still, I pushed that knowledge away, along with the dream and warnings I didn't want to heed. Time doesn't pause for reluctance. The morning was coming whether I was prepared or not. I wasn't.

25

The Accident

◆ ◇ ◆

The Long Day

May 15, 1998

The decision had been made months ago. As May 15th dawned, the reality of leaving Missouri began to settle into my bones with unexpected weight. Tomorrow, I would board a plane back to Israel for the summer—three months with my family, three months of Hebrew and Arabic, the beautiful Mount Hermon, and the complex comfort of home. With the transition looming, today was mine—one last Missouri day to savor.

By 5 AM, I was lacing up my running shoes in the predawn darkness. The streets of Licking were mine alone as I set out for what would be my final Missouri run. My feet found their rhythm on the familiar pavement, carrying me past the houses and small landmarks that had become familiar over the months, so familiar by now.

I ran for two solid hours, my breath visible in small clouds that dissipated as quickly as they formed. With each stride, I was saying goodbye to the

THE ACCIDENT

Ozark hills that had sheltered me.

The afternoon unfolded with the particular intensity that comes when you're trying to pack a lifetime's worth of experience into your final hours somewhere. Grandma and I ran errands that felt both mundane and sacred— visiting Aunt Helen, washing cars in the warm afternoon sun. At Aunt Helen's house, I found myself moving with unusual energy, scrubbing the dirt from two cars with the kind of thoroughness that suggested I was trying to wash away more than just Missouri dust.

The physical activity felt good after the morning's emotional weight of packing. Aunt Helen watched me work with the amused affection of someone who remembered being young and restless. "You sure are industrious today," she observed, handing me a fresh bucket of soapy water. *"Last day,"* I said, as if that explained everything. As the afternoon wore on, the energy that had sustained me through the morning began to shift into something more agitated.

Drama struck when my cousin Priscilla's boyfriend showed up with another girl at Boiling Springs. I found myself caught in the undertow of her emotional crisis. Then, dealing with car trouble when the engine wouldn't start properly—panic set in as another car headed straight at us while we were stalled. I managed to get it started again and drove her home. The whole episode left me feeling rattled and upset. The day's earlier energy had shifted into something more complicated— the growing weight of small crises piling up.

The Search

I drove back toward Aunt Helen's, hoping to find Grandma there, but the house stood empty in the afternoon heat. *No one was home.* My mind began racing through possibilities—*Where could she be?* We'd been separated in the chaos of Priscilla's crisis, and now I felt adrift, uncertain of the plan or my place in it. Without a cell phone, I was reduced to the primitive frustration of simply driving around, hoping to locate the one person who represented stability in this increasingly chaotic day. I decided to return to Boiling Springs, thinking maybe Grandma had gone back there to look for me.

The drive back down those winding gravel roads felt different this time. My emotions were churning—upset about the day's drama, anxious about going back to Israel the next day, and frustrated by the growing series of miscommunications and missed connections.

Boiling Springs was still crowded when I arrived, but Grandma wasn't there. I scanned the familiar faces, looking for her. *Nothing.*

It was then that I saw him—Derek. He was just standing there, probably waiting for someone or cooling off after swimming, but the sight of him sent an immediate jolt of nervous energy through my system. Derek was the guy who had tormented me with prejudice and crude comments. He had grabbed my necklace and made cruel jokes about Jewish people. He represented everything ugly about the casual hatred that hid in the cracks everywhere.

"Hi," I managed, my voice probably higher than I intended. The greeting felt necessary—we were classmates, after all, and ignoring him entirely would have created its own kind of scene. But everything in me wanted to get away from him as quickly as possible.

He responded with something I didn't really hear; my attention was already focused on escape. I pushed down on the gas. My heart rate elevated in a way that had everything to do with seeing someone I did not want to see when I felt alone and already spiraling. Derek made me nervous in a way that went beyond simple dislike. He represented a kind of unpredictable meanness that set my entire nervous system on alert.

The Gravel Road

I drove away from Boiling Springs with my emotions in chaos. My mind was spinning through the growing list of the day's frustrations. I pumped on the gas as I headed up the hill to gain some momentum in my getaway from the scene. *I can't find Grandma, Priscilla's heartbreak, car troubles, and now Derek, reminding me with his mere presence of all the ways this place never quite felt safe.*

The gravel road stretched before me, winding up hills and curling through the green Missouri countryside. I had little experience with roads like these—most of my driving had been on pavement, where the rules were fixed and the surface sure. Gravel was different. It shifted beneath the tires like something alive. That afternoon, my foot pressed harder than it should, frustration translating into speed.

My classmates were always bragging about speeding on these roads, and now I understood the appeal. There was something about the isolation of these back roads that made reckless speed feel like freedom rather than danger. I was bone tired. I had been going since before dawn—running for hours, packing, dealing with family drama, searching for Grandma, and now this encounter with Derek had left my nerves jangling like broken wires.

The car climbed and descended through a landscape that should have been beautiful but felt increasingly surreal. My mind was elsewhere—on tomorrow's flight, on the family I missed, and on Derek's face and the way it represented everything I was eager to leave behind.

I didn't realize how my speed had crept up, how the gravel was less forgiving than pavement. I didn't realize how inexperienced I was with this particular kind of driving, which was creating a dangerous combination with emotional exhaustion. Around another curve, up another hill. The car responded to my direction, but not quite in the way I expected, the gravel shifting beneath the tires in ways that asphalt never did. Then, it happened.

The Moment Everything Changed

The car slipped. It wasn't dramatic at first—just a slight slide to the right, the kind of minor loss of control that happens when you take a curve too fast on an unfamiliar surface. The mailbox loomed ahead, a solid metal post that would damage both car and mailbox if I hit it. Instinct took over.

I yanked the wheel hard to the left, trying to avoid the collision that seemed inevitable. The car responded, swinging away from the mailbox with the violence of over correction. Now, I was heading for something much larger, much more immovable.

I slammed my foot on the brake, though braking was now irrelevant. The impact had already happened. The damage was already done. In that moment, I felt something fundamental snap—not just in my leg, though the femur had indeed shattered, but in my understanding of how much control I actually had over the direction of my life.

The impact came with the devastating finality of physics meeting physics. Metal met wood with a sound that seemed to tear through the fabric of the afternoon itself. The collision absorbed all my momentum, all my speed, all my desperate teenage energy, and transformed it into something else entirely. Twisted metal, broken glass, and pain that shot through my leg like fire spreading through dry grass.

THE ACCIDENT

The car vibrated around me, and I vibrated with it. Black crept in from the edges of my vision, then retreated, then advanced again. I heard myself screaming, *"No!"* into the afternoon, with all my desperate desire to undo the last few seconds. Then I pressed the car horn, holding it down with whatever strength I had left, sending its urgent cry out across the countryside like a prayer: **Help me. Someone, please help me!**

The oak tree stood exactly where it had stood for decades, perhaps for a century or more. Its trunk was thick with accumulated strength, its roots running deep into Missouri soil, its branches spreading wide in the confident architecture of something that had weathered every storm this land could offer.

In the aftermath of impact, as consciousness wavered and pain established its dominion, I found myself staring at the oak tree that had ended my forward motion. It stood exactly as it had before our collision—unmarked, unbruised, and apparently unaffected by the violence that had just reshaped my immediate future. Somehow, it had no mark on it, which made me even angrier. Here I was, trapped in twisted metal with a shattered leg, and the tree looked like nothing had happened. As I waited for help that seemed to take forever to arrive, fighting waves of pain, I kept staring at that tree.

Help! I was aware of screaming, of the taste of blood in my mouth, of pain radiating through my leg in waves. The seat belt had cut into my skin, and my head felt warm and wet. Gradually, through the haze of shock and pain, I became aware of voices. Human voices, concerned and urgent, cutting through my desperate use of the car horn.

"Oh, honey, oh my goodness, are you okay?" A car had heard my distress call and pulled over. A woman emerged, moving with swift efficiency. With her was a girl—a face I recognized from my history class, now appearing in my moment of greatest need.

"We need to call 911," the woman was saying. When she reached through the car window to remove my necklace, explaining that it might choke me, I tried to tell her I was okay. The words came out slurred. "No, you're not okay," she said firmly. "Just look at yourself, your head is bleeding everywhere."

The words brought me back to reality. *I am not okay. I am bleeding, and my forehead is split open!* As I looked at the ugly blood pouring down my face, I went into shock. My leg was swelling with each passing moment. Yet, even in that moment of stark realization, I found myself crying out:

"Jesus! Jesus!" The name came from somewhere deeper than conscious thought. It welled up from whatever place in the soul recognizes its desperate need for intervention beyond human capability. "Jesus will save you," the woman said. "You're going to be okay." I kept screaming His name on the side of the gravel road.

About thirty minutes later, I heard the blessed sound of sirens. The ambulance arrived with a kind medic, followed by the police, who would document what had happened on this curve of gravel road.

The medic who took charge moved with competent gentleness, asking questions I didn't feel like answering. He showed me pictures of his family to keep me calm during the process of extracting me from the wreckage. How they managed to free my broken leg from the car remains a mystery.

The Small Hospital Sanctuary

Texas County Memorial Hospital in Houston materialized through the ambulance windows like a mirage of hope and healing. Still, its small-town proportions made it clear that whatever treatment awaited me would be limited by rural resources. Even so, after the endless, pain-filled journey from the accident site, I was hopeful that I would soon get help.

The emergency room buzzed with the controlled urgency that marks medical facilities when severe trauma arrives. X-rays confirmed what I already knew in my bones. My femur, the most prominent bone in the human body, was broken. Shattered, actually, in ways that would require surgical intervention, beyond this hospital's capabilities.

As the medical professionals worked around me, taking images, making assessments, and speaking in the abbreviated language of emergency medicine, I became aware of a complicating factor that had nothing to do with my injuries.

A tornado is moving through the area.

The words fell into my consciousness. Medical helicopters were grounded. Transport to a larger facility would be delayed indefinitely. I was trapped—not just by broken bones and torn flesh, but by weather patterns entirely outside human control.

They moved me to a small room to wait out both the storm and the night. It was there, in that fluorescent-lit sanctuary of forced patience, that I encountered something I hadn't expected.

Darkness. Not just the physical darkness of evening falling outside the hospital windows, but a spiritual oppression so thick I could almost touch it. Shadows seemed to move at the edges of my vision, whispers I couldn't quite make out, a presence that felt dark and evil.

I'd had nothing but a Slim Fast shake, some soup, and a Coke all day. Dehydration was setting in, but because surgery was coming, they wouldn't let me drink water. The physical discomfort was manageable, but the spiritual oppression felt like it might crush me. They stitched up my forehead while I was waiting, and I was told they did a pretty good job, for which I was thankful.

I waited in that small room from 4 PM until 2 AM. During that time, the tornado passed. I waited for them to move me to a bigger hospital in Springfield. The demonic presence was so real, so palpable, that it nearly overwhelmed everything else—the pain, the fear, the uncertainty about what came next.

Yet, somewhere in the darkness, a nurse managed to connect me with a voice that carried all the comfort home could offer across an impossible distance. Dad's voice, reaching across continents and time zones, found me in that uncomfortable room where hope felt as fragile as my broken bones. I don't remember all the words we exchanged—pain and medication were making everything fuzzy around the edges. However, I remember the sound of him crying, his voice breaking as he spoke prayers over his broken daughter. I remember how his voice seemed to push back against the spiritual oppression that had been pressing down on me like a physical weight.

"Jesus," I finally gasped into the fluorescent-lit silence after we'd hung up. My voice was barely audible above the machinery that monitored my vital signs. "I need You."

Dad's prayers had created a bridge across the darkness. It was precisely such desperation, I was beginning to understand, that created space for the kind of intervention that transcends regular medical protocols. Sometime in the middle of the night, I was transferred by ambulance to Springfield.

✦ ◊ ✦

26

The Valley of Shadows

◆ ◊ ◆

The Transfer

I had survived the night in that small-town sanctuary of the Texas County Memorial Hospital in Houston, Missouri. My broken femur required surgical intervention beyond what their limited resources could provide. The transfer to Cox Medical Center in Springfield felt like crossing into another realm. Dr. Putman, a skilled surgeon, would be responsible for inserting the titanium rod into my femur.

Anesthesia clung to my consciousness like cobwebs, making everything distant and dreamlike. Through the haze, I became aware of a gentle presence beside my bed—Diane Ingalls, holding my hand while medical personnel worked around us. Her touch was the first human comfort I could focus on, an anchor in the fog of post-surgical confusion.

I kept saying, "I can't breathe. I'm so thirsty." The words came out slurred and desperate. The nurses had a blanket thrown over my mouth, and the combination of medication, dehydration, and that fabric barrier created claustrophobia. The rational part of my mind understood that these people were trying to help me, but some deeper part had begun to perceive threat everywhere, danger in every approach.

The days that followed blurred together in a haze of medical complications and mounting anxiety. On Saturday, my English teacher, Mrs. Brown, came to visit. Her familiar face was a welcome connection to the normal world from which I'd been ejected. That afternoon, when they moved me to a chair, everything went black. I fainted. My consciousness was shutting down from the overwhelming stimulation of being upright.

I woke up to medical personnel yelling in my face, their voices sharp with concern as they tried to bring me back from wherever I'd gone. The physical therapy person who'd been working with me was particularly blunt:

"If you don't get up now, you'll never walk!" she announced nonchalantly, not yet aware of my fragile state and the life-threatening condition developing in my lungs. I remember forcing myself to get up, only to black out.

That's when they discovered the fat embolism; the bone marrow fat from the surgery had entered my bloodstream, creating a harrowing situation. If it traveled too far into my lungs, they could shut down completely.

I saw demons on my feet. A fever of 102°F added its layer of confusion to an already overwhelming event. Grandma gave me two towel baths to bring down the temperature; her steady presence was one of the few constants in the chaos.

The Night of Testing

Saturday night brought the real battle. The new night nurse arrived with an announcement that chilled me more than the fever had itself: "If you don't do what we say, you will die!" She looked like the actress from *The Nanny*—attractive, well-groomed, professional—but there was something in her demeanor that felt more like a threat than care.

I thought of her as the devil's nurse. Perhaps it was her complete absence of compassion, or the way she seemed to take satisfaction in my helplessness. Grandma was so exhausted from days of vigil that she could barely keep her eyes open, leaving me essentially alone with this woman who felt more predator than healer.

At 2 AM, they came for me. Three nurses entered my room with the coordinated efficiency of people executing a plan. They held me down, their combined weight pinning me to the bed. For over thirty minutes, they tried to insert tubes into veins they couldn't locate, their repeated failures adding physical pain to the psychological trauma of being rendered completely helpless.

When they finished, they placed an oxygen mask over my face. I found it hard to breathe. I kept pulling it off because I felt trapped and scared. Finally, the nurse informed me with cold efficiency, "If you don't keep this on, I'll tell your mother to have your hands tied down permanently!" Later, I would learn that Mom had actually told them to take me off the narcotics. She felt they were preventing my body from fighting properly—from breathing on its own.

The same spiritual oppression I'd felt in the Houston hospital had followed me here, intensified by the medical trauma. At one point, the pager dropped to the floor beyond my reach. Hours passed before someone opened the door to check on me. This increased my claustrophobia. It felt like something was actively working to break my spirit, to convince me that hope was pointless and help would never come. I had never felt so alone, so helpless, so completely at the mercy of forces beyond my control.

When Heaven Broke Through

That night, as I lay alone in the hospital room, something shifted in the atmosphere around me.

I heard them before I saw them.

Wings. Not the gentle flutter you might expect from earthly creatures, but the powerful whoosh of large wings moving air with purpose and authority. The sound filled the room with a resonance that seemed to come from both sides of my bed. Not only could I hear the wings, but I could feel them fanning me and bringing me air.

They were accompanied by voices singing something just beyond the normal range of human hearing.

This was throne music!

I knew it instantly. I had heard it before in dreams, but this time I was awake. These were songs that belonged not to earth but to that eternal realm where worship flows unceasingly around the seat of Divine Majesty. The melodies were more complex than anything human vocal cords could produce, harmonies that seemed to contain entire orchestras of sound within each note.

The angels were singing over me. Their wings fanned me like a mighty wind. Their song filled the room!

As the music filled my room, the oppressive spiritual atmosphere that had tormented me for days simply dissolved, like darkness fleeing before the dawn. The fear that had pursued me through every medical procedure vanished like mist before the sun, replaced by a peace so tangible I could almost reach out and touch it.

The demons I'd been seeing simply disappeared. Instead of terror, there was rest. Instead of feeling abandoned in enemy territory, I felt surrounded by heaven's guard! The peace that settled over me was thick and golden, almost visible in its density. It was the peace that passes understanding, the kind that can only come from direct contact with the presence of God.

I don't know how long the music lasted. Time became irrelevant as eternity invaded a hospital room. However, the message was unmistakable:

I was not alone. I was not forgotten. Whatever was happening to me was not outside divine knowledge or control.

The throne room of God had dispatched its messengers not just to comfort but to establish His authority in a place where darkness had been trying to claim victory.

The Morning

When morning came and the day nurse returned, I shouted with joy at the sight of her familiar face. After the nightmare of the previous evening, her presence felt like a rescue, like a return to the land of the living. I told her how much I'd missed her, though she'd only been gone for one shift.

The peace the angels had brought lingered like a protective atmosphere around me. Medical procedures that had felt like torture before now seemed manageable. I was busy receiving company during those recovery days. The outside world had learned of my condition, and people began arriving to offer support in various forms. Underneath all the human activity was the continuing **echo of heavenly songs,** the assurance that what had started with collision was leading somewhere purposeful.

The angels had done more than comfort me—they had commissioned me:

> **Like Jacob emerging from his wrestling match with both a new name and a permanent limp that would forever remind him of divine encounter, I understood that I was being marked for service that would require everything I had to give.**

The Village of Open Doors, which had once seemed impossibly foreign to my sensibilities, now appeared as a divinely appointed destination. The evangelistic endeavors I had dismissed as unsuited to my gifts now revealed themselves as the very purpose for which I had been preserved.

I found myself declaring with conviction born of divine encounter:

> *I desire no longer to live according to my own designs. I am prepared to carry the good news to whatever villages the Master may appoint, regardless of personal comfort or preference.*

My resistance to such ministry had been systematically dismantled not through human persuasion, but through the irrefutable logic of celestial intervention. She, who had once declared sharing the message unsuited to her temperament, now understood obedience to a revealed calling.

I had a calling for such a time as this, but I had scoffed at it. Even so, I had seen the underworld of the demonic in real life. I had tasted blood on my lips and experienced the death angel at my door. I had also heard the angel wings and the angelic throne room music. I had come out alive from the shadows of death. I felt changed. I no longer wanted to live for myself. I wanted to live for God.

As I lay in that Springfield hospital bed, still weak from surgery, I began to understand what our neighbor, Mrs. Chambers, had meant when she'd delivered her prophetic word just weeks earlier: *I have called her aside to preserve her for the work I have called her to do.*

The preservation hadn't just been about surviving the collision. It had been about surviving, changing, being marked, and being commissioned for service. Service that would require not just my life but my complete surrender to purposes larger than personal preference.

The angels had sung over me, and in their music I had heard my new name, my new calling, my new understanding of what it meant to follow Jesus not just in comfort but wherever He might lead.

The Valley of Shadows was behind me now, but ahead lay territories I'd never imagined entering. Villages where hearts had been prepared for divine truth, and places where the songs I'd heard in heaven could be carried to earth through voices willing to sing them.

27

When Heaven Mobilizes

◆◇◆

A Mother's Impossible Journey

May 16, 1998

Thousands of miles away in the Upper *Galil* of Israel, at the exact moment I was colliding with that Missouri oak, Mom had awakened in Israel from a sound sleep, startled by what she later described as hearing a car accident. How do we explain such moments—when love transcends distance and time seems to bend around crisis? Maternal intuition, or something more profound than intuition, had bridged the gap between continents at the precise moment when her daughter's life hung in the balance.

Yet, knowing and reaching are two different things when an ocean separates a mother from her child. The call came from Grandma—reaching across time zones—to tell them that their daughter was in critical condition following a motor vehicle accident. The words hit Mom and Dad like physical blows: broken femur, surgery required, condition serious, and the family should come immediately.

She didn't pack properly—she couldn't think straight enough for systematic packing. Instead, she threw random items into a suitcase, as if every wasted minute betrayed her duty as a mother. She threw in a toothbrush, clean clothes, and scattered essentials that tumbled in, every movement fueled by frantic urgency.

The security checkpoint at our small airport became its own nightmare. Mom couldn't think straight enough to answer routine questions. Her grief looked suspicious to officers trained to spot threats. How do you explain to security officers that your purpose is to hold your broken child, to whisper prayers over hospital sheets, to be present for the kind of crisis that makes everything else feel insignificant?

"Where are you traveling?" they asked.

"America. My daughter—she's been in a car accident. She's in the hospital."

They confiscated her sandals and searched her hastily-packed bag. They almost made her miss the plane. By the time she finally boarded, she was shaking with exhaustion and fear. A mother's desperate love was being ground down by paperwork and protocol. She traveled thirty hours on seven different airplanes, making connection after connection across continents, while I lay in a hospital bed, drifting between consciousness and medication-induced dreams. My body was fighting battles I didn't understand.

Each layover tested her faith. Flights could be delayed or canceled at any moment. The fragile chain of connections bringing her to my bedside could break under the weight of international logistics. Yet each plane took off on time. Each connection held. When Grandma finally brought Mom into my hospital room, I was utterly exhausted. I had been sitting up for over an hour to eat dinner, barely able to speak. The nurses had insisted on this prolonged upright position despite my weakness, another small trial in the endless series of medical necessities.

Then I saw her face—travel-worn, streaked with tears, aged by hours of helpless worry. Still, I found enough strength to tell her the most important thing: how much I loved her.

The Greyhound Pilgrimage

Dad and Tom's journey to reach me required a different kind of faith. They flew from Israel to Chicago. Faced with our family's financial limits, expensive connecting flights weren't possible, so they took a Greyhound bus for the final leg. It was a choice that would save money we didn't have, but came at the cost of precious time.

I can only imagine those hours crossing the American Midwest after already traveling halfway around the world. Dad was wrestling with paternal helplessness while Tom, fifteen, processed the possibility that his sister might not survive. Each mile was a prayer that they would arrive in time.

They arrived Friday morning at 3 AM, bone-tired but carrying the tangible presence of family love that had crossed continents to reach me. When they walked into my room, they found me sleeping so deeply the nurses couldn't wake me—yet, my sleeping spirit registered their arrival.

After they left, I tried to call the nurses, but I was half asleep and mumbling. *People are here, around my bed. They're here!* I said in my sleep, my hand reaching for the call button.

"She felt us," Mom whispered through tears. "Even asleep, she knew we were here."

The Church Responds

WHEN HEAVEN MOBILIZES

While my family was making their impossible journeys across oceans and continents, word of my accident had reached the Pentecostal Holiness Church. The response was immediate and overwhelming. The congregation that had welcomed me as a spiritual daughter now mobilized like a family in crisis, proving that the Body of Messiah extends far beyond biological relationships.

Tuesday brought a delegation that filled my hospital room with love. Pastor Fisher and his wife arrived with the youth pastors, Libby and Jacob. They crowded into my room carrying flowers and prayers and an envelope containing $320 that the congregation had collected.

"We're taking up another offering next Sunday," Pastor Fisher announced with the matter-of-fact generosity that marked their entire approach to crisis. "This is just the beginning."

They brought me a teddy bear—soft brown fur and kind button eyes. I named him Honey Bear and clutched him through every procedure, every nightmare, every moment when the pain made me forget that healing was possible. Twenty-five years later, I still have him, a tangible reminder that love shows up in the most practical forms when we need it most. Other gifts arrived too—Dad's boss sent a big black bear that became another comfort during those long hospital days.

Still, their response went deeper than gifts. They brought God's presence into that sterile medical room, turning it into a sanctuary where heaven could touch earth through human vessels. "We felt led to come," Libby said, as if traveling to Springfield on a Tuesday evening to pray over a teenage girl was the most natural thing in the world. And maybe it was, for people who understood that following Jesus means showing up when love calls, regardless of convenience or personal plans.

They had brought God's love through practical action, the kind of ministry that proves God's presence through human hands. God sends His love through people who drive to hospitals, pastors who take up offerings, and youth leaders who show up with teddy bears and prayer.

Friends from Far Places

The network of love that activated to support me during those hospital days stretched far beyond the local congregation. Honestly, I do not remember which day they came. From Saint Louis, Nelda and John made the drive down on Sunday night, carrying gifts that felt like messages from another world—a photo of them with Dad on the Sea of Galilee.

They brought me a Beanie Baby and a little fish. Simple tokens that somehow contained more healing power than all the medicine the hospital had pumped into my system. Still, it was their prayers that transformed the room, their voices rising in intercession until the spiritual atmosphere shifted like the weather changing.

As their words filled the space around my bed, the demons I'd been seeing behind my closed eyelids simply disappeared. The oppressive spiritual atmosphere that had made sleep impossible was replaced by peace so thick you could almost see it. For the first time since the accident, I could close my eyes without seeing horrific visions and could rest.

"Lord, we ask for complete healing," Nelda prayed, her hand gentle on my forehead. "Not just of her body, but of her spirit. Take away the fear and confusion. Fill this room with your presence." And He did, in ways that were almost visible to the naked eye.

Later, I learned they had helped pay for my hospital bill. In a moment when our family's resources were stretched beyond breaking, strangers had become family, covering expenses we couldn't afford with the kind of love that asks nothing in return. It was grace made practical, the Gospel with hands and feet and checkbooks.

When Love Has an Address

During those recovery days, I received constant proof that love is never abstract. It always shows up at specific addresses, in particular moments, through real people who make real choices to care for others. Mrs. Brown, my English teacher, came to see me in the morning, bringing the familiar comfort of someone who had watched me grow and learn during my time in Missouri.

I was discovering something profound about crisis—it strips away the surface politeness of everyday life and reveals what people are really made of. The hidden kindness that exists in ordinary people suddenly has permission to express itself. The secret generosity waiting beneath normal social interactions finds its moment to shine.

My parents also told a church in Springfield that I was sick, and they started visiting and praying for me, even though they didn't know me! I was learning that family isn't just about shared genetics—the family of God knows no borders, and when God gives a burden, people respond.

The Tilt Table Terror

As my condition stabilized, the medical team introduced new forms of necessary torture, disguised as therapy. The tilt table was designed to help bedridden patients gradually return to a vertical position without fainting. The experience felt more like medieval punishment than modern medicine.

They strapped me to the table after I'd already been entertaining visitors for two hours. Well-meaning people took pictures and tried to encourage me, but I smiled and nodded, trying not to show how exhausted I was. By the time they secured the straps, claustrophobia was already creeping in.

Then they began to tilt me. At first, it was just uncomfortable—blood rushing around my body in unfamiliar patterns, my inner ear struggling to make sense of the changing orientation. As the angle increased, my chest began to hurt like someone was pressing a twenty-pound weight against my ribs. The room spun, darkness crept in from the periphery, and I heard myself saying, "Put me down. Please, put me down."

Yet they continued the procedure, following medical protocols that didn't account for the psychological trauma I'd already endured. Being strapped down, unable to move, and fighting for breath! It was too reminiscent of that horrible night when three nurses had tied my arms while trying to insert tubes.

When Dad arrived, and I practiced standing for ten minutes, I realized I was getting stronger despite the setbacks. Progress was happening, even when it didn't feel like it. Healing was taking place on timetables I couldn't control, according to processes I didn't understand.

The Ministry of Presence

Sunday brought Dad's first opportunity to preach since my accident. The congregation at Evangel Temple welcomed him with the kind of hospitality that understands how much families need community during a crisis. He had made friends with Pastor Charlie, who had already visited me several times with his Sunday school class. They brought the gift of corporate prayer to my bedside.

Each person who entered my hospital room brought a piece of their own story, their calling, and their understanding of how God works through human communities during times of crisis. I was learning that healing doesn't just happen through medical procedures. It occurs through the accumulated presence of people who choose to show up with love.

Going Home

By the time my family had all arrived and the church's support network was fully operational, something extraordinary was happening. The hospital room that had been a place of trauma and spiritual warfare had been transformed into a sanctuary where heaven and earth were meeting in practical, visible ways.

> *Something really strange that I think I should document! Jason, Shana, and I (all in the same Sunday school class) had car accidents the same day! Mine was the worst—I think. It is so weird that this happened. I think that it shook us all up. I will never forget this.*

The revelation that three teenagers from the same small Sunday school class had all been in accidents on the same day felt like more than a coincidence. It suggested spiritual warfare on a scale I hadn't understood. Battles were being fought for the souls and destinies of young people who were being called to something significant.

Yet it revealed the power of corporate prayer and community support. We had all survived. We were all healing. We were all being surrounded by love that transcended the ability of any enemy to destroy or discourage.

On Sunday, I was transferred to rehabilitation, and by the next day, I was able to do many things by myself—using a real bathroom, taking a shower while sitting down, and managing basic personal care. The small victories felt enormous after days of complete dependence.

My therapy classes were teaching me how to navigate life with titanium in my leg, how to adapt to a new reality where my physical capabilities had been altered.

By Monday night, we were hoping I could be discharged from the hospital. The bills were becoming expensive. Our family's financial resources were stretched beyond their limits. Tuesday brought a meeting where the medical team decided I needed to wait longer—a decision that felt more financial than medical to Mom's protective instincts.

I wrote later:

> Mom was upset because she heard that I would be leaving whenever the therapist said I was better, and they were keeping me there because they wanted our money. So Mom got one of the hospital administrators and got me out of the hospital in 3 hours.

Sometimes, a mother's love is the most potent force in any hospital, capable of cutting through bureaucracy and medical protocol when protecting her child requires it.

By midnight, over a week and a half after the accident, I was back in Licking, riding carefully over every bump and curve while Dad drove as slowly as humanly possible. It was a rough ride—every pothole and turn translated into sharp reminders of my still-healing bones. Still, it was infinitely better to be home than in the hospital, surrounded by family instead of medical machinery.

The Real Miracle

The real miracle wasn't just that I had survived; it was that I had been surrounded by so much evidence of divine love made tangible through hands, voices, and presence. Heaven had mobilized, and earth had responded, and I was learning what it meant to be held by both simultaneously.

My accident had shattered more than bones—it had broken open my understanding of how God works through His people when one of His children is in crisis. The mobilization of heaven's resources—both angelic and human—had been the most visible proof yet that my life was held within purposes larger than my understanding.

I was no longer the same girl who had driven away from Boiling Springs that afternoon. The collision had changed me in ways I was only beginning to understand, but one thing was already clear: I knew I was called to something greater than my plans could have imagined. I had won my battle! Now, I had a task of rebuilding and a vision to follow the Lord with all my heart.

The Valley of Shadows was behind me. Ahead lay unknown territories, but I would enter them knowing that when love calls across oceans, nothing is impossible.

28

The Journey of Recovery

◆ ◇ ◆

The First Nights

The first night at Grandma's apartment was peaceful. Real blankets wrapped around me instead of scratchy hospital linens. Familiar voices drifted from the next room—not the electronic beeping that had haunted my dreams. All six of us crowded into two bedrooms together, and I sank into that bed and didn't surface for ten hours straight, experiencing the deep, dreamless sleep of someone who finally felt safe.

The second night brought a return of the trauma-induced anxiety that would become part of my healing process. I woke up gasping, with my heart hammering against my ribs, disoriented and panicked. The room was too dark and too quiet. Where was I? The claustrophobia came roaring back! The walls pressed in from all sides. I was trapped in that hospital room again, alone, unable to reach the call button that had become my lifeline to help. I clawed at the blankets, fumbling frantically for the pager that wasn't there. My chest was tightening as the air felt thick as cotton. The terror of abandonment consumed me.

"Mom!" I finally screamed, and she appeared instantly. Her presence banished the nightmare and grounded me—home, safe, surrounded by people who would cross oceans for me.

I was learning that healing from trauma involves more than repairing bones and tissue. The psychological and spiritual wounds require their own kind of treatment, their own timeline for recovery. I was also learning that I wasn't healing alone. Divine resources had activated—both angelic and human—to surround me with love during the most vulnerable season of my life. God's love had been deployed through hospital visitors, church offerings, family members who traveled impossible distances, and a mother whose love could move administrative mountains when her child needed to come home.

The next morning, I found myself reaching for my journal. The panic attack had left me raw, searching for words to make sense of what was happening to me. This is what came:

Just Trust Him

Just trust Him when you can't see,
Just trust Him and believe.

He is with you through your shadows of doubt,
He is with you and will bring you out.

Just trust Him when the loneliness chills,
Just trust Him and follow His will.

He will surround you with blankets of love,
He will whisper from the heavens above.

Just trust Him and you will find
He carries you through the storms of time.

Just trust Him and finally be free!
He lifts you up
And helps you to soar
Higher and higher,
You are not alone.

Lean upon the Lover
As you walk through the desert.

Lean upon the Lover,
Trust in Him alone.

For when you lean on Him,
You learn to see...

How things are meant to be.
He carefully guides you through streams

And brings you through valleys low,
Until you know and discover

The depths and the heights
Of His great love.

I was learning something the doctors hadn't mentioned in their discharge instructions. Healing broken bones was just the beginning. The real work was putting back together the parts of me that couldn't be seen on an X-ray—the trust and the courage.

THE JOURNEY OF RECOVERY

Learning to Walk Again

The poem helped settle my spirit, but the days that followed would test whether I was truly healed. Friday morning brought my first test—a follow-up appointment that would show how well my body was mending.

The X-ray lit up on the wall like a road map of survival. There it was: the long metal rod running through my femur, a screw gleaming near the top. Proof that I'd stared death in the face and lived to tell about it.

"Looking good," the doctor said, as if commenting on the weather.

It looked good to him. I stared at the X-ray of the foreign metal inside my leg and wondered what "good" meant now. *Does it mean I'll walk normally again? Will I ever be able to skate again? Does it mean the nightmares will stop? Does it mean I'll ever drive without my hands shaking on the steering wheel?*

After the appointment, we went to Burger King. I watched Mom strike up a conversation with a Muslim woman sitting alone at a corner table. Even exhausted, even drained from weeks of hospital vigils and cross-country flights, Mom couldn't walk past a lonely soul without stopping. They talked about displacement and belonging. They discussed how it feels to be caught between worlds—something I was beginning to understand in ways I'd never expected.

When we visited the Christian bookstore, they brought me a wheelchair that squeaked and pulled to the left. I lasted five minutes before asking Dad for my crutches instead.

"You sure, honey?"

I was sure. I needed to feel my own feet touching the ground, even if every step sent lightning up my spine.

Walking was harder than I'd imagined. Each step required a negotiation between my brain and my body, a careful calculation of weight and balance.

At Best Buy, I made it all the way to the back restroom—a journey that left me breathless and shaking. *I feel proud. I know it's stupid, but I feel proud.*

The gas station changed everything. My arms were burning from the crutches. My good leg was screaming. I shifted my weight wrong and felt my balance slip. The world tilted. I threw my hands out to catch myself and hit the pavement hard.

The pain was different this time. Not the clean, sharp break of the accident, but something messier and angrier. My legs went into spasms that seemed to say: *You thought you were ready? You thought this would be easy?*

I struggled to get up from the hot asphalt. The pain was bad, and I cried until the pain reliever set in. I slept fitfully on the way back to Licking from Springfield.

New Connections and Expanding Horizons

Dad and Mom both shared that morning in a church in Springfield. I watched from the congregation as they made a powerful team—his theological depth combined with her outgoing personality. Her mother's heart was still raw from nearly losing a child. The congregation received them with the kind of hospitality that understands how much families need community during a crisis.

After church, we went out to eat with Pastor Charlie's family and met some fascinating people. A leader from the first Teen Challenge sat at our table. Students who had gone on archaeological digs at Banias shared their stories. Pastor Charlie made arrangements for me to stay with his daughter when we visited the university next year. He even planned for Dad to visit Christian radio stations throughout the city.

Then, he surprised us with an invitation to Silver Dollar City. He was treating us to a day of simple joy that my recovering spirit desperately needed. I rode around the park in an electric wheelchair. I watched Tom and Dad enjoy rides I couldn't yet handle. I listened to a concert that surprised me with its spiritual lyrics of hope and healing. For a few hours, I felt less like a patient and more like a teenager again—someone who could participate in family adventures and look forward to future possibilities.

Wrestling with Purpose

However, the good days made the difficult ones feel even harder by contrast. Wednesday brought one of those days when the emotional weight of recovery felt heavier than the physical challenges had ever been. I opened my journal, and the words poured out like a confession: *I feel really discouraged. I'm so ashamed of having this car accident.*

The shame was its own kind of pain. It revealed how much I was struggling not just with physical healing, but also with the psychological aftermath of trauma. How do you forgive yourself for a split second that changed everything?

Yet, somehow, the imagery from the Song of Songs began to call to me:

My King

My thoughts are thick, like a dense thicket.
I have many worries I hold in hand.
I fear that one blow, and I will no longer stand.

He came to my window and asked me to come in.
I wished He would. I knew He could.

But I was too busy and too tired to care.
He could help me lift that window
With His strong hands of care.

Oh, I wanted Him here,
For drought had come to my desert soul
And blinded my eyes,
From seeing Jacob's oasis around the stairs.
So many prayers and burdens I bring to heaven's gate,
Where angels sing, I cry under this heavy weight.
Won't someone take it?

My cry is heard.
Aloud I gasp,
And praise my King,
I have found it at last.
In His blanket of peace,
I will forever rest there.

My desperate prayer revealed both my frustration with divine timing and my growing understanding that my life was held within purposes larger than my own planning:

> Lord, what's your plan? Why is everything so messed up? I almost died this month. I have things to do. Places to go. Love yet to be found!

The accident near Boiling Springs had become a turning point in my life. I had a mark on my forehead and my thigh that made me feel I was sealed for a purpose. I was no longer the same girl who had driven away from Boiling Springs that afternoon in May. The collision had changed me in ways I was only beginning to understand.

One thing was already clear: I had been preserved for something greater than my plans could have imagined. I felt comfort in the songs of the angels and the presence that wrapped over me, filling me with purpose and excitement that something good was coming.

Another poem emerged:

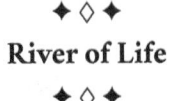

River of Life

> *I have been freed from the grip of death,*
> *Now I want to praise the Lord for every breath.*
>
> *Crossing rivers deep and shallow,*
> *Full of uncertainty to swallow.*

But at the river's mouth is holy love
That cleanses even me
Until I am finally set free.

Sing, all you nations,
To the Lord of Lords!

Let's all lift our heads
To find our Coming Lord.

Praise His holiness—
His presence is our fire.
Listen to His soft voice,
Then rejoice!

29

The Flight Home

◆ ◇ ◆

The Real Journey Begins

The airplane lifted off from Saint Louis, carrying me once again to Chicago. Below me, the American Midwest spread out. This time, the girl in seat 23B was not the same one who had made this journey before. The logistics of this journey showed our family's resourcefulness. We had learned from our recent trip to Wisconsin that it was still hard for me to sit in a bumpy car for hours. So Mom gave me her ticket for the Saint Louis to Chicago flight, since my middle name was the same as her first name.

Grandma's friend Rosella met me at the airport. She had known my grandma since they worked together teaching at the Jerusalem school years before. We stayed at her apartment, where my family would camp out together. After a night or two, we all headed to the airport again.

Over a month after my family arrived in the USA, we found ourselves in the sky, flying to Israel from Chicago. Suspended between earth and sky at thirty thousand feet, I found myself facing the question that had been building since the angels sang over me: **Who was I becoming?**

The physical evidence of my accident was impossible to ignore. My leg, now held together with titanium and determination, ached with every shift in cabin pressure. The scars on my forehead had healed into thin lines, permanent reminders of the moment of collision.

I thought about the girl who had left Wisconsin at thirteen, heart full of adventure and apprehension in equal measure. She had been so sure that home was a place, and that belonging was about geography and familiar faces. The teenage years that followed were an education in displacement—learning to navigate Arab schools and Jewish communities, ice rinks and speed skating tracks. Each transition had stripped away another layer of certainty about who I was supposed to be. Missouri had taught me something I hadn't expected: fitting in wasn't the same as finding your purpose. I had learned to belong in those Ozark hills. I had shared in struggles that echoed the ones Israel had carried for generations. Perhaps God was allowing me to identify with them so I could pray with deeper understanding.

Something inside me had been resisting the deeper call I had been hearing since childhood. I knew I had to follow Jesus where He was leading me and carry my cross. The car accident had made me realize I was no longer invincible. I was a broken wild pony.

> *"Yes, indeed! I tell you, when you were younger, you put on your clothes and went where you wanted. But when you grow old, you will stretch out your hands, and someone else will dress you and carry you where you don't want to go."* **—John 21:18 CJB**

I was going to challenging places, because that's part of carrying a cross. God was going to take me on adventures I would never have dared attempt if I hadn't tasted the nearness to eternity in that car accident.

Now, flying home with titanium in my leg and angelic music still echoing in my memory, I understood that my resistance had been systematically dismantled by divine intervention. My accident hadn't derailed God's plan for my life. It was bringing me into a new space where I saw things from an eternal perspective. I no longer wanted to live just for myself, but for the passions of Messiah's kingdom.

Through the darkness, the airplane droned, carrying me toward a future I could barely imagine. The Arab village in the Upper Galilee, which had once seemed impossibly foreign to my sensibilities, now beckoned as a divinely appointed destination. My calling as a *Messenger of Grace*, which I had once dismissed as unsuited to my gifts, now revealed itself as the very purpose for which I had been preserved.

In the Ozarks, God had shown me something more profound. **He had a commission for me, a royal duty as a disciple to go to the Hills of the Song of Songs.** It would mean carrying His light to those living in the shadow lands of the Galilee, walking with my Shepherd as He drew me closer during our garden walks, and returning to His *Fortress of Hope*.

The accident had been the final lesson in the curriculum. It had taught me that when you call on the name of the Lord, He hears and moves mountains. Something shifted in my purpose. **I realized that some callings are larger than personal preference.** True discipleship begins not with the offering of our strengths but with the **surrender** of our plans to purposes higher than our own understanding.

The Ministry of Broken Things

As the plane crossed the Atlantic, I found myself thinking about the people who had surrounded me during those hospital days. Each one had their own journey toward understanding what it meant to serve God in a complicated world.

Mom and Dad had left everything familiar to carry the Gospel. Their willingness to be strangers in a strange land had prepared them for the kind of ministry that required constant adaptation, endless patience, and the ability to find joy in small victories.

Grandma had opened her home to a restless teenager and provided the stability necessary for growth. Her quiet faith had been the foundation that allowed me to explore questions without losing my footing entirely.

The church in Licking had demonstrated that the Body of Messiah extends far beyond biological relationships. Their response to the crisis had shown me what it looked like when theological principles became tangible, actionable love. I carried with me a deep love and gratitude for the little Ozark church with its powerful altar calls. I would miss those altar calls in the mountains of Israel.

Yes, sometimes people make mistakes that hurt. Our battles aren't against people, as my dream warned me when I came back from Israel during winter break. Our battles are against the devil's dark forces. As believers, we can fall into a fortress mentality that excludes people. God wants us to shine our lights, bring love and forgiveness, and share a message of hope. (Ephesians 6:11-13)

Even Derek, whose prejudice had made me nervous enough to drive recklessly on that fateful afternoon, had played his part in the divine drama. Seeing my bully again had been the final weight that tipped my emotional state toward the recklessness that led to the collision. Without that collision, I might have spent years resisting the very call that would give my life its deepest meaning.

I wrote in my journal: ***God uses broken things. Broken people, broken plans, and broken bones. He takes what seems destroyed and rebuilds it according to specifications that we could never have imagined for ourselves.***

What felt like disability revealed itself as consecration—a physical mark of spiritual commissioning. Like Jacob, I had wrestled with the angels and wouldn't let go until God blessed me. And He did, bringing me forward with a message of hope.

The Sound of Home

Somewhere over the Mediterranean, I began to hear it—Hebrew conversations from the seat behind me, Arabic phrases drifting through the cabin. The particular mixture of languages and accents that mark flights bound for the crossroads of the ancient world.

That sound no longer meant just 'return;' it meant 'arrival.' I was flying toward the place where I would finally stop running from my calling and start running toward it. Places that had once seemed impossibly challenging now appeared as fields prepared for harvest, awaiting laborers willing to go where they were sent rather than where they preferred to venture.

> *I am no longer the same girl who left Missouri. The accident broke me open, but what poured out wasn't just pain—it was everything that had been holding me back from becoming who God created me to be.*

The fear of ministry in the villages was transforming into anticipation, though I knew I would always carry some fears. That's why God gave me His Holy Spirit: to learn to walk in love that casts out fear and find courage for whatever He was leading me into.

> *I want to carry His Songs to whatever places He appoints, regardless of personal comfort or preference. I want to be a bridge between worlds, a translator not of languages but of hope itself.*

As the plane began its descent toward Ben Gurion Airport, I felt certainty that I was right where I belonged, doing what I was called to do, becoming who I was meant to be.

The girl who had once been desperate to fit in had discovered that the deepest belonging comes not from others' acceptance but from God's. The Divine Romance, more powerful than any earthly song, lifts our hearts to join the eternal chorus.

Stranger Lovely had been called, but she had already been chosen. She had opened her heart to the Heavenly Bridegroom and found her heart had a home; no matter what side of the sea she was on, she had a place.

Landing

Ben Gurion's runway welcomed us as the sun rose over the ancient land that had shaped prophets and kings, apostles and martyrs. I gathered my belongings—so much lighter now than when I had left for Missouri, despite the crutches. I was returning as someone ready to embrace whatever assignments Divine Love might prepare.

As I made my way through the familiar chaos of Ben Gurion Airport, navigating the multilingual announcements and the particular energy of a place where ancient and modern daily intersect, I carried more than just memories of the Ozarks. I carried the Great Commission in my spirit, and it was a stronger pull than any hockey team or speed skating team had ever been.

THE FLIGHT HOME

The Song of Commission

As I made my way back to the Upper Galilee, the Voice of the Shepherd whispered in my soul, calling me back to the Galilee. I heard the whispers on the wind, and I knew I was at home with Him again.

Follow Me to Galilee

I journeyed to the Ozarks to find my roots,
I journeyed to the Ozarks and found the Truth.
I am not alone in this journey.
Time is short, my Bridegroom says,
He is in a hurry.

Got to get back to the Galilean Hills,
Got to get back—it's my Master's will.
Follow the Shepherd wherever He leads.

Where He calls me, I will come.
Lean on His staff in my brokenness.
This wild horse is broken,
This wild horse is broken.

Strong-willed was I.
I wanted the stars,
I wanted the ice.
Yet God came down into my life,
He gave me a cross
And said, "Follow Me!"

I will lead you where you're afraid to go,
I will lead you between sheep and wolves,
I will lead you to valleys low
And mountains high.
So come on, my beloved,
Let's light up the Galilee!

The nightmares are over and gone,
The dayspring has come!
The nightmares are over and gone.
The Victory is won!
The Victory is won!
The Victory is won!

We are going to travel
Upon the ancient hills.
We are going to travel
With good news of Messiah,
With Good news!
It's time to wear your shoes
And lean on Me.

Let Me take you on this adventure.
It's not by might, it's not by power,
It's not by mighty learning,
But the simple quest of following Me.

Like the fishermen of Galilee,
Like the fishermen of Galilee.

So awaken, Songbird, arise.
Awaken love that never dies.
For now is not the time to chase other loves.

THE FLIGHT HOME

Now is the time of the harvest,
Now is the time of the harvest.

So few will come, so few will serve,
But I have called you this day.

The devil tried to take you out,
But I got in his way.
I got in his way!

You are worth more to Me than sparrows.
I have been calling you before time
To walk with Me in the garden
And shine with Me the Truth.
Shine with Me the Truth!

Walk with Me in Eden,
Talk with Me in Metulla,
Go with Me to the mountains
And share of my Great Love.

And I will be with you, my dear pilgrim,
As you shatter all illusions,
As you pass the fortresses and strongholds
And are held safe in my Fortress of Hope.
You are never, ever alone.
When the enemy comes at you
I will surround you with angels,
I will sing over you with joy!
Because now is not the time to hide your face.
Now is not the time to stop up your song.
Now is not the time to hide away.
Now is the time to go.

Now is the time to go!

Come and walk with Me in the Galilee,
Come and walk with Me in the hills,
Come and walk with Me in the Galilee,
Come and follow Me, come and follow Me.

I am calling you back,
I am calling you now!
Do not look back;
Do not look back.

Today is the hour.
Destiny is calling you to Me,
Calling you back,
Calling you now, calling you to the Galilee.
Calling you back to walk with Me.

In the mountains and hills,
Or in valleys by the streams,
As I Shepherd your soul,
As you trust I am in control.

I will follow You, my Dear Shepherd.
You mean more to me than anything,
I need You more than life itself.
You are my Bridegroom
Calling me in love,
Calling me from above!

So take me on this adventure,
This adventure to Galilee.
I have found my roots in the Ozark hills

And I am ready to live for You.
Ready to spread the Truth!
Ready to spread the Truth!

I am my Beloved's and my Beloved is mine.

The Real Journey Begins

Closing my journal as the wheels touched down, I knew this wasn't an ending but a beginning. I had been commissioned and called—ready to sing the songs I learned in the Valley of Shadows, ready to minister as one broken and rebuilt by grace.

I was finding my home in the *Song of Songs*. Even though at times I was *much afraid,* God was giving me courage to meet every hill and every challenge, always leaning on my Beloved.

30

Postscript

As I close, the car accident that nearly took my life became the moment my true calling crystallized. What I discovered through writing this memoir is that those painful experiences of being *Stranger Lovely* weren't obstacles to overcome, but preparation for a unique calling. God, who is rich in mercy and abundant in loving kindness, doesn't abandon His strange and lovely ones. He has been chasing me through the mountains and valleys of life with relentless love. Calling me back to the garden, restoring my silenced voice, and resurrecting the poet. Writing these pages has been a gift of resurrection to my soul. Revisiting old wounds with the perspective of decades has allowed me to see God's hand in places where I once saw only confusion and pain. There is something profoundly healing about telling your story, because in the telling, the broken places become gateways to grace.

If you have taken the time to read my testimony, I'm grateful. Perhaps I seem foreign to you, and that is all right. We are all different. I wanted to share my journey with you so you can see how God's romance is there even in difficult times. **What matters is this: there is a Heavenly King who delights in you, who longs to sing over your life with a love more faithful than anything this world can offer.** If you carry even a spark of curiosity, let this story be your invitation into that Divine Romance.

POSTSCRIPT

While earthly fortresses restrict entry based on human categories, God's fortress opens its gates to everyone who seeks Him. It's built not with human hands but with Divine Love, offering refuge to all who need it. As Zechariah promised: *"Return to your fortress, you prisoners of hope; even now I announce that I will restore twice as much to you."* This is our inheritance—not just healing, but restoration beyond what we lost.

To the ones who have been told they are too much or not enough—your time is coming. Break free from the fortress chains and shine. Keep speaking, even when your voice trembles. Keep singing, even when the melody is misunderstood. Keep loving, even when love is not returned in full. Above all, keep trusting the One who gives purpose and meaning. **May the silenced songs find their voice again. May deferred dreams awaken, and may you walk in your true calling, bringing God's beauty into the world.**

As I send this memoir into the world, I do so with the prayer that it will encourage someone who needs to know they're not alone in their journey. God never promised we wouldn't face difficulties. **He did promise to be with us through them.**

Until we meet again—whether in the pages of future books in this series or in that eternal fortress where all the displaced finally find their true home—I remain your fellow traveler on this beautiful, broken, and blessed journey.

With love from above, and hope in God's songs yet to be sung,

Lydia Friend

31

On Pilgrimage and the Divine Romance

◆ ◇ ◆

This essay offers the framework through which I have come to understand the journey recorded in these pages. It names patterns I was living long before I had language for them, and explains how anthropology and Scripture together shaped my understanding of those years.

If you are drawn to questions of meaning, theology, and sacred journey, this essay will deepen the story you've just read.

LIVING BEFORE UNDERSTANDING

Before I understood its meaning, I experienced displacement directly. The compelling force inherent in sacred spaces pulling me from everything familiar. In this book, you read about two pilgrimages: one to the modern Holy Land and one to the Ozark hills, where morning mist rises like incense from the hollows.

Years after I'd walked the seam lines between different people groups, I sat in a Jerusalem classroom listening to Dr. Curtis Hutt teach *The Anthropology of*

Pilgrimage. Dust particles danced in the afternoon light streaming through windows that looked out toward the Mount of Olives. His voice mapped territory I'd already crossed: displacement, liminality, and the particular complexities of sacred journey through contested space.

Something shifted inside me, like pieces of a puzzle clicking into place.

This was my life. I'd been living the textbook before I knew the terms existed.

What I'd experienced as painful displacement, Turner called *"liminality."* What I'd thought was my inability to belong anywhere, he identified as the pilgrim's perpetual state of being *"betwixt and between."* And what I'd endured on the Israeli-Lebanese border (the seam lines, political upheaval, spiritual warfare in contested space), Dr. Hutt's scholarship helped me understand as a particular kind of sacred journey.

However, anthropology could only explain part of my story. The other part required a different framework entirely: the biblical language of Divine romance; **God as Bridegroom and the believer as Bride. Displacement is not as random suffering but as the Beloved calling His chosen one away into appointed places of intimacy and transformation.**

This essay presents both frameworks: pilgrimage anthropology and Divine romance.

THE ANTHROPOLOGY OF PILGRIMAGE

Victor Turner, a foundational scholar of ritual and pilgrimage, understood something essential about sacred journeys: the power isn't in arriving. It's in the going.

He gave me a word (*liminality*) for the threshold space I'd inhabited my entire life. From the Latin *limen*, meaning the doorframe itself, that strip of wood your hand touches when you're neither inside nor outside, neither here nor there. One foot still planted in the room behind you. One foot reaching toward what's ahead. Suspended between worlds.

Pilgrims in liminal space become invisible to the social structures that usually define them. The businessman sheds his title. The wealthy woman and the poor widow walk the same dusty path. Status dissolves like sugar in hot tea. Hierarchy disappears. In threshold spaces, something Turner called *communitas* can emerge: a spontaneous, egalitarian connection between people who would never bond in ordinary life. Strangers become spiritual family in an instant. National boundaries blur like watercolor running together on wet paper.

Turner saw pilgrimage as a journey "from center to center out there." From the familiar, structured center of your ordinary life to sacred spaces that exist outside normal geography, outside normal time. These "centers out there" function as anti-structure to everyday existence, offering renewal precisely through displacement.

However, Turner's model, developed largely through studying Christian pilgrimage to established shrines in peaceful contexts, needed refinement for more turbulent situations.

Dr. Curtis Hutt taught in a way that made the classroom disappear. When he spoke about pilgrimage in contested territories, you could almost smell the olive groves, feel the tension at checkpoints, hear the call to prayer echoing across valleys divided by more than mountains. **He didn't just study sacred space. He loved it, complicated politics and all.**

His research on Jewish, Christian, and Islamic pilgrimage to Israel and the Palestinian territories revealed something Turner's peaceful shrine model couldn't capture: **pilgrimage in turbulent contexts operates as what he calls "dissipative systems." Not static traditions preserved in amber,**

but dynamic responses to political upheaval, living and changing and adapting, or sometimes dying.

Borders transform everything. **Pilgrimage isn't just a spiritual practice; it's feet on contested ground, papers examined by soldiers, walls that slice ancient routes.** I'd stood at those checkpoints. I'd watched families navigate boundaries. I'd felt the weight of crossing lines drawn by conflicting claims to the same holy ground.

What makes Hutt's work pierce straight to my story is his emphasis on the *"eisogetical."* Not what pilgrims find at sacred sites, but what they bring with them. **He argues we must examine the diverse backgrounds pilgrims carry into sacred space, because transformation happens in the collision. What you bring meets what you encounter, and sparks fly.**

My American independence collided with Middle Eastern complexity. My speed skating dreams were shattered in war-torn borderlands. Third-culture kid displacement found its mirror in contested territory where everyone was displaced, everyone caught between competing narratives. The friction between my American self and Galilee's ancient yet contested landscape created fire hot enough to forge something new. *I was a living example, an eisogetical case study, before I knew the term existed.*

Years later, when I studied Palestinian Christian pilgrimage under Dr. Hutt's guidance, I was (as he noted) both researcher and subject. I interviewed Aboud Christians, who described pilgrimage as "getting out of jail," their words sharp with the reality of restricted movement. I documented how borders cut them off from sacred sites while remembering my own border crossings, the weight of soldiers' gazes, and the question always hanging in the air: *Do you belong here?*

I was trying to understand academically what I'd already lived viscerally.

The Israeli-Lebanese border, where I spent 1998-2000 (which will be documented in Book 2), was the epitome of what Hutt calls "turbulent context": a contested sacred space where politics and faith collided daily. Those years were, unknown to me at the time, a countdown. Israel's withdrawal from South Lebanon in May 2000 ticked closer day by day while I walked orchards near the fence line, and I wrote poetry in journals.

What Hutt calls the "civic spectacle"—the chaotic scene surrounding pilgrimage—varied dramatically depending on where I lived. My Divine romance played out against these changing backdrops in the exact kind of destabilized geography Hutt's research examines.

Hutt demonstrated that "actions taken ostensibly for the sake of protecting or promoting 'religious' interests often have profound political consequences." This became my lived reality. My walks in apple orchards near the border weren't just spiritual encounters. They occurred in contested territory where every village carried political significance, where the ground beneath my feet had been claimed and counter-claimed for centuries. My poems to the Bridegroom weren't written in peaceful contemplation but in the seam lines where nations drew boundaries. Sacred space, as Hutt says, is never neutral. While contested spaces may cause conflict, God's salvation can still cross borders and transform even our enemies.

LIVING THE FRAMEWORK

This matters for understanding my part of my upcoming story because while I visited holy sites on weekend getaways, my life circled around the Israeli-Lebanese border. I lived in the borderlands. I walked the buffer zones. I had the privilege of going to the Hill of the Doves in no man's land, where only soldiers and radio engineers traveled in those in-between spaces where nations drew dividing lines. What Turner called "liminal space" wasn't abstract theory. It was the literal geography under my feet, the contested ground where I wrote poetry and prayed.

I began to see myself as liminal, perpetually between cultures. Never fully belonging anywhere.

I was a Third Culture Kid, *Stranger Lovely,* an American, but changed over the years in Israel, born in the Holy Land, yet without Israeli citizenship. Foreign in the USA and foreign in Israel. **Suspended, always, in the threshold space.**

At times, I felt trapped as a perpetual tourist: someone who never truly belongs. However, discovering the framework of pilgrimage changed everything. **A "Pilgrim" transcended the tourist label into something eternal, something adventurous, and something romantic.**

A tourist can be stuck in that space without purpose, **but a pilgrim moves through those same liminal spaces with Divine appointment, from glory to glory.** What Turner described as the temporary state pilgrims enter during their journey, I lived as a permanent condition. Now, though, I was seeing it with new eyes, with purpose and meaning, and with Divine direction.

And *communitas*? Sometimes I tasted it: those transcendent moments when barriers dissolved and spiritual family formed across impossible divides.

I found it as a teenager in a Russian church in Kiryat Shmona, where language barriers meant nothing when we worshiped the same God. I found it as a young adult in Nazareth church meetings, surrounded by believers whose roots went back centuries in this land. I found it cleaning a bombed-out church in Caesarea Philippi with other believers, our hands scrubbing away war's debris as we welcomed the year 2000 into the new millennium together.

I tasted it in the Golan Heights when we gave out gospels and Jesus videos, and the people pressed bags of fresh cherries into our hands in return; their orchards' sweetness was offered with smiles that needed no translation. I experienced it when Arab believers in the North blessed my mother and me, calling us sister and mother (the same words they'd heard in the JESUS film we'd brought them). **Strangers were becoming family by the power of the cross.**

Yet often I didn't experience it. Often, I was kept outside the fortress walls, excluded despite my calling. This, too, was a pilgrimage, as scholars who critique Turner emphasize: the journey isn't always about **unity and spiritual bliss. Sometimes it's conflict, competition, and profound loneliness in sacred space.**

During my graduate work with Dr. Hutt, I explored Palestinian Christian pilgrimage practices. At the time, I thought I was simply trying to understand their experiences academically. I didn't fully realize I was also processing my own displacement, and by interviewing them, I was really interviewing myself. *I was both researcher and subject, studying pilgrimage while living it.*

The anthropological framework gave me vocabulary: *liminal, communitas, contested sacred space, and turbulent contexts.* These words named what I'd experienced, gave structure to years of feeling lost between worlds.

Yet anthropology couldn't explain why displacement felt like calling. *Why being "betwixt and between" felt like home. Why the dangerous borderlands beckoned like appointed meeting places.*

For that, I needed Scripture.

THE BIBLICAL FOUNDATION: DIVINE ROMANCE

Throughout Scripture, God speaks the language of romance. Not metaphor. Not poetry forced onto ancient texts by later interpreters

desperate for meaning. The text itself burns with it.

The Song of Songs doesn't hint. It declares: *"Let him kiss me with the kisses of his mouth, for your love is more delightful than wine"* **(Song of Songs 1:2)**. The Bride doesn't politely request the Bridegroom's attention. She yearns. She searches city streets calling His name in the darkness. She declares without shame: *"I am my beloved's and my beloved is mine"* (6:3). **This is covenant as romance, relationship as sacred desire, love that refuses to be tamed into religious propriety.**

The prophets understood. Listen to them:

"Your Maker is your husband, the LORD of hosts is His name". **(Isaiah 54:5)**

"I will allure her, bring her into the wilderness, and speak tenderly to her". **(Hosea 2:14) God pursues His beloved into isolated places where they can be alone together.**

"I remember the devotion of your youth, your love as a bride, how you followed me in the wilderness". **(Jeremiah 2:2)** He remembers the honeymoon period, the early days when everything was fresh and new and full of wonder.

Ezekiel spends an entire chapter describing Jerusalem as God's bride: loved, adorned, and cherished despite repeated unfaithfulness (chapter 16). **This is the language of a husband who won't let go, who keeps pursuing even when rejected.**

In the New Testament, the romance reaches its culmination. Paul doesn't write about duty or obligation. He writes about self-sacrificing love: *"Husbands, love your wives, just as Messiah loved the church and gave himself up for her".* **(Ephesians 5:25). The ultimate marriage is Messiah and His Bride.** And Revelation promises the consummation we're all waiting for: *"Let us rejoice and be glad and give him glory! For the wedding of the*

Lamb has come, and his bride has made herself ready." **(Revelation 19:7) The Bridegroom is coming. There will be a wedding.**

The desire for intimacy that God Himself wove into our hearts when he formed us. He gave us these hearts (hearts that want to be pursued, cherished, delighted in, and romanced) because He is the ultimate Bridegroom. This is by design.

David understood this. He didn't write careful theology for publication. He wrote passionately: *"As the deer pants for the water brooks, so pants my soul for You, O God".* **(Psalm 42:1).** *"My soul thirsts for You, my flesh longs for You in a dry and thirsty land".* **(Psalm 63:1) This is romance, holy and sacred, yes, but still romance.**

Genesis shows us the pattern: God walking with Adam and Eve in the garden in the cool of the day. **(Genesis 3:8)** This was not a distant observation or theological instruction from the clouds. It was an intimate communion. God is physically present, walking and talking, enjoying their company. **This is what a relationship with Him was meant to be from the beginning.** Jesus promises this same intimacy: *"If anyone loves Me, he will keep My word; and My Father will love him, and We will come to him and make Our home with him".* **(John 14:23)**

When I wrote about walking with my Shepherd in Metulla, I wasn't inventing pretty imagery. **I was experiencing what Scripture describes as normal communion between the Believer and the Beloved.**

Don't mistake romance for ease. **This love costs everything.** Moses wandered forty years in displacement, leading a people who constantly wanted to go back to Egypt. David ran for his life, hiding in caves. Hosea married an unfaithful woman to demonstrate God's relentless pursuit of a bride who kept running to other lovers. Even the Bride in Song of Songs gets beaten by watchmen, wounded, searching through dark streets calling for her Beloved who seems to have disappeared. **(Song of Songs 5:7) This love is costly, dangerous, and transforming.**

This biblical framework (God as the Bridegroom who romances His Bride and will one day marry her) gave me language for what I lived in the Galilee and the Ozarks and for what I experienced later in my travels. **The anthropology explained the patterns. Scripture revealed the purpose.**

WHERE THEY INTERSECT

When Curtis Hutt taught me that pilgrimage is displacement to *"centers out there,"* I understood it through both lenses simultaneously, like looking through a telescope with both eyes open instead of just one.

Anthropologically: I was a pilgrim in *liminal space,* stripped of normal identity, transformed by displacement in contested territories.

Biblically: I was a Bride being called away by her Beloved. *"Arise, my love, my beautiful one, and come away."* **(Song of Songs 2:10). I was led into dangerous borderlands as appointed meeting places with the Divine.**

What Turner called *"liminality,"* I experienced as the Bride's journey through the wilderness where God speaks tenderly. **(Hosea 2:14)** It was the threshold space where identity dissolves. **It was in that desert place where only His voice mattered.**

What Hutt called *"turbulent contexts,"* I knew as the refining fire where the Beloved shapes those He's chosen. **The contested borderlands weren't obstacles to spiritual formation; they were the furnace where I was refined.**

What scholarship named *"communitas,"* **Scripture calls fellowship in the Spirit and communion of the saints.** The spontaneous connection between pilgrims? **That was the Holy Spirit knitting hearts together across impossible divides.** Both frameworks are true and necessary.

The anthropology grounds the romance in real places, civic spectacles, and displacement. It explains the patterns, the structures, and the social dynamics of the sacred journey. **It gives academic legitimacy to experiences that might otherwise seem merely emotional or subjective. It says: This actually happened. These are the verifiable conditions under which it occurred.**

The biblical romance reveals the sacred meaning beneath the anthropological patterns. It answers why displacement transforms, why liminal spaces become holy ground, and why being "betwixt and between" opens us to encounter with the Divine. It says: This is what it meant and this is why it mattered.

Together, they explain why a teenage girl living on the Israeli-Lebanese border wrote love poems to God during a historical countdown she couldn't see coming, the final years before Israel's withdrawal from South Lebanon. **The poems weren't just emotional processing or literary expression. They were a mystical encounter in liminal space, the Bride's cry for the Bridegroom in contested territory, documented in real time.** You'll encounter these poems woven throughout Book 2: written in journals I kept hidden under my mattress while rockets fell and political tensions mounted.

My "stranger lovely" existence wasn't a random displacement; it was **a pilgrimage as a Divine romance, kept outside fortress walls, while God Himself became my Fortress of Hope.**

The biblical framework reveals why: **those borderlands became sacred space because no man's land is standing in the gap. The Bride's cry for the Bridegroom in a war zone wasn't escapism; it was engagement**

with the deepest reality: God pursuing His beloved in the midst of fire and warfare.

I share these frameworks because they transformed how I understood my own story. Even though I was the child of what Israel termed a priest, I was labeled a *tourist* and felt like a *perpetual tourist*. That word felt like confinement, like being stuck in purposeless wandering with no belonging anywhere. When I sat in Dr. Hutt's Jerusalem classroom years later and heard him teach about pilgrimage, something shifted. The meditation on being a pilgrim rather than a tourist enraptured me. It opened another dimension. Suddenly, my displacement wasn't aimless; it was a sacred journey. My betwixt-and-between existence wasn't failure to belong; it was the pilgrim's appointed state. The framework gave me wonder, peace, and a sense of belonging in the idea itself.

The spiritual encounters I document follow patterns that scholars like Victor Turner and Curtis Hutt have identified in pilgrimage studies. Still, those patterns existed in my life before I knew the academic terms.

Your own pilgrimage, whether you're crossing geographic boundaries or interior ones, follows these same patterns: displacement from your comfortable center, *liminal spaces* where everything you thought defined you dissolves, the possibility of *communitas,* and the reality of profound loneliness even in sacred space. Yet through it all, the Bridegroom calling: *"Arise, my love, my beautiful one, and come away."*

The Shepherd King is whispering your name. The pilgrimage continues.

✦ ◊ ✦

32

Dear Reader

If this book has touched your heart in any way, I would be deeply grateful for a brief review on Goodreads. If you are a verified purchase from Amazon or any other place you bought this, please leave an honest review as well. Your words of encouragement mean the world to independent new authors like me. This memoir shares my personal spiritual journey and experiences in the places that shaped my faith. While readers may have different perspectives on the locations and cultures I write about, I hope my story resonates with anyone who has struggled to find their calling or has experienced God's faithfulness through difficult seasons.

A simple sentence about what resonated with you, what encouraged you, or how the writings affected you would be an incredible gift. Thank you for sharing this journey with me.

I'd love to stay connected. Visit *pilgrimdiaries.net* for exclusive reflections, behind-the-scenes stories, and updates about the next book: *Shattered Glass and Sacred Ground*.

With gratitude,

Lydia Friend

About the Author

Lydia Friend was born in Israel in September 1980, on the first anniversary of the Christian radio station where her parents served in Lebanon. Raised on the Israeli border in Metulla until age two and a half, she spent the next decade in America before returning to Israel as a teenager in 1994. This memoir chronicles her transformative teenage years from 1994-1998, capturing the unique perspective of a young woman caught between worlds—American by citizenship, born in Israel, and pilgrim by calling.

You can connect with me on:
- https://pilgrimdiaries.net
- https://www.facebook.com/pilgrimdiaries

Also by Lydia Friend

Next to be released in the series of memoirs!

The Diaries of a Teenage Pilgrim Shattered Glass & Sacred Ground

Lydia returns to the Galilee, embracing her calling to work in the villages and on Christian radio. As political tensions mount and Israel prepares for its historic withdrawal from South Lebanon, she discovers that her teenage struggles with displacement have prepared her for ministry in one of the world's most complex regions—a story of faith, courage, and finding purpose amid ancient conflicts and modern challenges.

www.ingramcontent.com/pod-product-compliance
Lightning Source LLC
Chambersburg PA
CBHW030450100526
44580CB00002B/59